Gender and Sexual Fluidity in 20th Century Women Writers

This book analyses twentieth-century writers who traffic in queer, non-normative, and/or fluid gender and sexual identities and subversive practices, revealing how gender and sexually variant women create, revise, redefine, and play with language, desires, roles, the body, and identity.

Through the model of the "switch"—someone who shifts between roles, desires, or ways of being in the realms of gender or sexual identity—*Gender and Sexual Fluidity in 20th Century Women Writers: Switching Desire and Identity* examines the intersecting locations of gender and sexual identity switching that six prolific, experimental authors and their narratives play with: Gertrude Stein, Jeanette Winterson, Kathy Acker, Eileen Myles, Anne Carson, and Anne Carson's translations of Sappho. The theory and identities revealed create and give space to—by their playful, exploratory, and destabilizing nature—diverse openings and possibilities for a great expansion and freedom in gender, sexuality, desires, roles, practices, and identity.

This is a provocative and innovative intervention in gender and sexuality in modern literature and gives us a new vocabulary and conversation by which to expand women's and gender studies, LGBTQ and sexuality studies, identity studies, literature, feminist theory, and queer theory.

Lesley C. Graydon, Ph.D., is an educator, writer, and therapist. She has taught at City College, Hunter College, Bronx Community College, and New York City College of Technology. She also leads workshops, groups, and has a private practice. She has the honour of being awarded the first Ph.D. interdisciplinary concentration in LGBTQ/Sexuality Studies in the United States. Her alumnis include Simon Fraser University, City College, and The Graduate School and University Center of The City University of New York.

Interdisciplinary Research in Gender

www.routledge.com/Interdisciplinary-Research-in-Gender/book-series/IRG

Gender and Sexual Fluidity in 20th Century Women Writers

Switching Desire and Identity

Lesley C. Graydon

Routledge
Taylor & Francis Group

LONDON AND NEW YORK

First published 2021
by Routledge
2 Park Square, Milton Park, Abingdon, Oxon OX14 4RN

and by Routledge
52 Vanderbilt Avenue, New York, NY 10017

Routledge is an imprint of the Taylor & Francis Group, an informa business

British Library Cataloguing-in-Publication Data
A catalogue record for this book is available from the British Library

Library of Congress Cataloging-in-Publication Data
Names: Graydon, Lesley, C., 1969– author.
Title: Gender and sexual fluidity in 20th century women writers:
Switching desire and identity / Lesley C. Graydon.
Other titles: Gender and sexual fluidity in twentieth century women writers
Description: Abingdon, Oxon; New York: Routledge, 2020. |
Series: Interdisciplinary research in gender |
Includes bibliographical references and index.
Identifiers: LCCN 2019056605 (print) | LCCN 2019056606 (ebook) |
Subjects: LCSH: American literature–Women authors–History and criticism. |
Gender identity in literature. | American literature–20th century–
History and criticism | Women and literature–United States–
History–20th century. | Queer theory.
Classification: LCC PS151.G785 2020 (print) |
LCC PS151 (ebook) | DDC 810.9/353–dc23
LC record available at https://lccn.loc.gov/2019056605
LC ebook record available at https://lccn.loc.gov/2019056606

ISBN: 978-0-367-43915-6 hbk)
ISBN: 978-1-003-00673-2 (ebk)

Typeset in Sabon
by Newgen Publishing UK

MIX
Paper from
responsible sources
FSC
www.fsc.org   FSC™ C013985

Printed in the United Kingdom
by Henry Ling Limited

This book is dedicated to all the switches
and to Sebastian.
The world is so much more beautiful with you in it!

Contents

Acknowledgements

I wish to express my deep gratitude for the encouragement, excitement, and support that my colleagues, teachers, students, clients, family members, and friends have so freely given to me. This book and theory have been in existence many years and a great many people have supported my work.

Lyn Di Iorio, Wayne Koestenbaum, the late Eve Kosofsky Sedgwick, and Paul Matthew St. Pierre have been a few of the very generous readers of my experimental writing and ideas and I am in gratitude to all of you. I also wish to sincerely thank the scholars who generously provided feedback for various chapters in the Routledge review process, my incredibly supportive and skilled editors at Routledge, and all my writers and contributors who gave me permission to use and reprint their work.

Elysia Brunet, Scott Humphries, Wilbur Turner, and, most especially, Sebastian Graydon Flynn: you have been unwavering in supporting my vision, and I could not have done this without you. I am blessed to have a team of wonderful friends who have welcomed my ideas and work, offered encouragement, attended my lectures and workshops, and stood for me to release my work. From New York to San Francisco, Vancouver to London, you have held my hand and vision in sacred circles, kept the lodge fires burning, sent a loving card at the perfect time, celebrated victories and challenges large and small, and shared in both research and play. Thank you!

I want to acknowledge and thank all the courageous folks who are committed to creating and supporting inclusive feminist and LGBTQ practice and praxis: locations where we get to experience affinity, growth, and freedom. I am so grateful to all the bold writers and artists, activists and feminists, doers and creators, who continue to inspire me (and the world) with sharing your creativity.

And finally, I give thanks to my ancestors, guides, and the Creator of it all. My head is bowed in gratitude. Thank you.

Copyright acknowledgements

1 "Thinking sex"

Presentation, representation, and manifestation; an unveiling

The broad aim of this book is to expand the horizon and discourse of variant gender and sexual identities and practices through introducing the theoretical model, practice, and typology of *the switch* and *switching*; radical new readings, knowledge, understanding, acceptance, and a new sexuality and gender studies, queer, feminist, and identity theory emerge. This emergence has the added impact of immediately and powerfully validating reader's lives and experiences; by extension, the possibility is established for all people—regardless of gender or sexuality—to live with greater freedom, self-expression, and authenticity in exploring and playing with identity, desires, roles, and practices. My focus is on contemporary and twentieth-century women and/or lesbian writers who dwell in queer, variant identities and subversive sexual practices.

This chapter will map out my focus, present the premises and vocabulary necessary, introduce my key theoretical concepts, subjects, and method, position my work in relation to specifically relevant historical and contemporary conversations, and invite an openness with which to delve into my topics. I bring some attention to the policing of sexual and gender self-expression; however, the main intention of this book is to engage in possibility-based conversations and dialogue (rather than criticism or past-based ones) that demonstrate my theory of switching.

Focus and terminology

My specific focus is to look at, deconstruct, and celebrate variant gender and sexual identities. My specific aim is to reveal where and how gender and sexual variants create, revise, redefine, and play with language, roles, desires, bodies, public and private sex practices, and identity in the action known as "switching." To *switch*, and the process of engaging in the action of *switching*, can most broadly be described as dwelling in, and having the intention of, honouring, exploring, and sharing different, switchable aspects of a state of being, idea or concept, person, persona, or character. These different aspects can be, and very often *are*, seen or constructed as opposites, or as incongruous, so by its very nature the switch is riddled with complexities and uncertainties that can be both individualistic and change-able; hence the switch is not easily classifiable or conducive to generaliza-tion. Identifying and honouring different, switchable aspects and ways of being as *equally authentic* and valuable is, at heart, one of the important intentions of my theory and this book.

More specifically, a *switch* is someone who shifts between roles, desires, identities, or ways of being in the realms of gender and/or sexuality. Switching has almost exclusively been referred to in a BDSM (bondage, dominance, sadism, and masochism) context within the loci of subversive sexual desires, roles, and play. My theory proposes a new definition wherein switching reaches far beyond BDSM and the sexual: it is an action *and* an identity, which may or may not be a pleasure-centred action that moves into the broadness of an identity. A switch incorporates and moves *between and betwixt* gender and/or sexual identities. This book asserts that switching along a continuum of gender and/or sexual identities is a profound and powerful route by which to re-examine the notion of stable identities and dwell in fluid, destabilized ones. In both the action and the experience of switching, a whole new realm of possibility and freedom arises.

In the area of gender, switching can be located in shifts of experimenting and playing with gender preference and identity, feminine and masculine clothing, appearance, presentation, naming and/or playing with the per-formative aspects of expected versus unexpected gender expression(s). Physical features, such as switching between masculine and feminine physical features, traits, behaviours, manifestations, and/or body parts, and gender-bending to and from differing gender locations are all gender-switching moments. Any gender, male, female, or non-binary, including genderqueer, two-spirited, bi-gendered, or trans-identified, can switch and move betwixt and between the varied ranges of feminine and masculine facets, roles, and/or identities.

In the area of sexuality, switch moments are marked by shifts in the language of desire, sex, and orgasm—language occurring as a key turn to switch—in moving between gentle or loving sex and rough or animalistic-like sex, when moving between vulnerability and strength, submission and dominance, pleasing and being pleased, pleasure making and pleasuring giving, in the locations of sexual taboos, playfulness, and games and, of course, in switching between roles: between top and bottom, receiver and giver, dominant and submissive within an erotic or BDSM context. As with gender switching, there are no constraints to sexual switching: one's sexual preference is irrelevant.[1]

In the overlap that intersects both and/or either sexual and gender switching, shifts in roles, fantasy, desire, time, spirituality, language use, various concepts of identity (such as human and animal), spirituality, point of view, age, playfulness, and a s/witchy magical realism are locations of switching intersection. The locations of certainty and uncertainty, time shifts that accompany gender and sexual shifting, and adhering to, versus overturning, acceptable social conventions are also switch moments that can be sexed or gendered.

My primary focus is thus specific: I am looking at the intersecting practices of non-normative/variant gender, sexual, and identity switching that all of my experimental authors and their characters play with. Gertrude Stein, Jeanette Winterson, Kathy Acker, Eileen Myles, Anne Carson, and Carson's translation of Sappho all demonstrate and play with the language of desire and switching; also, all of their narratives can be described within a sexually variant and gender-variant reading. While my book is specifically centred in gender and sexually variant writing and reading, I want to stress that this project resists all "strategic essentialism" of gender and sexual variancy (Butler, 146). The identities I deconstruct create and give space to by their playful and exploratory nature, a great deal of gender, sexual, and identity play and masquerade (whether they are stable or in flux); they elicit openings, possibilities, and ambiguities in writing, reading, deconstructing, and recreating gender identifications, sexual identities, sex and gender roles, and subversive and perverse practices, as well as subcultural and personal practices.

This book is concerned with *variant, fluid,* and *non-normative* gender and sexual identities, performance, and exploration. I use these terms to illustrate mutable locations, instances, preferences, and choices that are different from or outside the standardized ideologies and points of view that govern socially conventional sex and gender norms. Variant, fluid, and/or non-normative gender imply locating the subject's gender identification, playfulness, choices, and/or performance outside of the mainstream, male/female, masculine/feminine fixed gender-norm binary; variant, non-normative sex and sexualities imply locating the subjects sexual preferences, desires, and/or practices outside of the mainstream, heterosexual/heteronormative, reproductively based, acceptable societal norm. Simply put, the gender and/or sexual variant is outside mainstream societal structures in their gender and/or sexual preferences, choices, and practices.

The term *gender* is used to refer to one's own sense of gendered self, regardless of genitalia.[2] This implies that gender can be constructed, that we have choice, and that gender is mutable. The term *women* may feel exclusive to some people who do not identify as female. When I use the words *women* and *woman*, it is the broadest sense possible and with all the vastness that can be implied and conjured; thus, *women* includes both assigned female at birth (cisgendered or non-trans) women, transgendered women, and anyone who identifies as a woman and female—however that looks, has been, and is for her. I use "*she*" and "*her*" throughout this book, while occasionally using s/he or they.

While some gender variants may resist and/or dislike the term *woman* or *women* and opt to use other words, spellings, and/or gender neutral pronouns, in part because of the words historically, culturally, and socially constructed constraints and assumptions (which is *one* effective strategy for ushering in a rethinking of gender and identity categories), I find great value in choosing to challenge the assumptions that are evoked by the term *woman* precisely by using it within a progressive, expansive, and feminist framework and context. Many of the issues that affect women, across race, class, and economics are informed by sexism and gender discrimination. No girl or woman escapes growing up and/or living in patriarchy without being deeply affected—the effects are far-reaching and insidious. It takes tremendous and consistent effort to dismantle the social and cultural conditionings of what it is to be a woman, to survive in a hostile climate, and to *thrive*.

Using the words *people* or *folk*, or changing the spelling of "woman" to "womyn" or "womxn," is not inclusive or descriptive enough for the purposes of my book's intention and, while these terms most certainly allow for greater inclusion and openings in gender variancy and possibilities, using them could lessen the importance of *this book's* particular focus and intention, which is to apply my theory to looking at a decades-long marginalized, invisible, and understudied segment in the literary, intellectual, academic, social, and political conversation: the writing of *gender and sexually variant women who switch*.[3]

By *sexually variant* I am referring to those who choose to dwell outside of the socially proscribed and sanctioned "normal" heterosexual roles, desires, identities, duties, performances, presentations, and practices generally regarded as acceptable in North American culture and society. This would include looking at those who desire and/or engage in non-mainstream, non-reproductively based sex.

By *gender variant* or *fluid* I mean anyone who chooses to live outside of the mainstream socially proscribed, sanctioned gender roles, duties, performances, presentations, and identities in North American culture and society. Some gender variants identify as fluid, androgynous, LGBTQ, or non-binary. While written somewhat obtusely, I find that Judith Roof's explanation and placement of fluidity amongst binaries, which she says "points towards a polymorphousness," are helpful. She writes that

> the figure of the fluid occupies an eccentric position in relation to the insistent taxonomies of binary gender systems. On the one hand, it would seem to represent a completely alternative economy. On another hand it already frames the binary as its other. On a third hand ... it depends on binary categories for its sense—even paradoxically—in order to exceed, outstrip, reform, reorganize, resituate, redeploy, redefine, or reinvent them. The fluid is curiously a "re-": redemptive perhaps, but also a reiteration, a reflection and a repetition.
>
> (*What Gender Is, What Gender Does*, 175)

Gender variancy and gender switching constitute a location of reinvention, one which is still bookmarked by notions of gender that are based on binaries our society is quite entrenched with. While we have made great strides in LGBTQ theory and activism, I hope to demonstrate that switching is a powerful term and concept to add to the redefining and reinvention, reforming and reorganizing, of gender and sexual identities and categories. Another popular term used to describe gender and sexual variants is *queer*, *genderqueer*, *fluid*, or *non-conforming*.

I use the term *genderqueer* as an umbrella term for a gender identity that is outside the heteronormative, patriarchal, gender binary system. It is a term used to situate an internal, self-identified, and self-constructed sense of gender and gender identity. Depending on the circumstances, some genderqueer and gender fluid folks may choose to alter or "switch" their preferred use of pronouns or descriptors depending on their current preference and/or circumstances. Some genderqueers may use one or multiple pronouns such as *she, he, s/he, her* or *him* while others prefer *they, ze*, and/or *hir*. Still others may prefer to use only their given or chosen names for all self-references, thus circumnavigating the issue of gender assumptions and designations altogether.[4]

A gender variant may stay in their born female or male body or choose to morph, alter, or transition their gender in some way to better reflect their gender identity. A gender-fluid person may consistently, or mercurially, appear to exhibit androgynous, masculine, and/or butch traits, behaviours, presentations, preferences, identities, and so forth and may shift along a spectrum. The gender and/or sexually variant woman or person may identify as a lesbian, dyke, queer, androgynous, genderqueer, trans, trans-identified, transgendered, intergendered, ambigendered, nongendered, non-binary, two-spirit, bisexual, pansexual, gay, a fag or however else she or they may want to refer to themselves. Choice, self-agency, and the ability to revise one's identity association(s) and description(s) are deeply valued, respected, and expected. Further, the language of sexual and gender variancy is one that morphs and changes, sometimes quite quickly, with new terms and words added by each new wave of LGBTQ activism, theory, youth culture emergence, sociopolitical climate, and/or pop or subculture wave.[5]

Certainly, while some genderqueers may identify with some of the identities and subcultural communities noted above (such as woman, trans, trans-identified, androgynous, non-binary, lesbian, and queer), genderqueers may also embrace and/or reject a wide range of feminine and masculine sensibilities or traits, ebb and flow on a gender continuum, and/or create, seek to live within, and be sustained by a third, fourth, or fifth gender identity. While for some there may be a degree of fluidity and movement on the gender spectrum, other genderqueers choose androgyny or trans as a location. Genderqueers use the term to blur one, some, and/or all lines of gender associations and, additionally, those of sexuality.

The fragility of society

To consider and be comfortable with authentic displays of variant genders and sexualities seems such a basic, healthy, productive, powerful, potentially opening and enlivening premise; yet, sometimes, when switching presentations or ways of being occur, conflict, questioning, confusion, doubt, judgement, invisibility, and shame arise—both within the text/narrative or personal, interior life *and* in the external reading or outside within the external group, community and/or society.

One question to ask is, why dwell/consider variancy? But much more empowering is to ask, why not? In his groundbreaking two-volume *The History of Sexuality*, Michel Foucault asks readers to begin to look at their individual and societal beliefs and values and to be open and willing to reconsider their positions and points of view regarding sexuality.[6] He encourages us to consider the following: "There are times in life when the question of knowing if one can think differently than one thinks, and perceive differently than one sees, is absolutely necessary if one is going to go on looking and reflecting at all." I invite us to deliberate and examine what Foucault is asking us to do in regard to sexuality and gender: consider giving up the ways we perceive, and *think we know as the truth*; choose to be willing, to consider thinking and perceiving, gender, sexuality, and identity differently than we do. In the areas of sex and gender, which are two areas of our life and society that are heavily culturally and emotionally laden with "truths" and knowing, this is a fundamental step in opening up what is possible for both individuals and larger society.

An important first step is to reflect on the conscious and unconscious moral rightness that is deeply embedded and accepted in our culture vis à vis heteronormativity. Western society is infused with an ethics-constructed (made up) history of proper sexual and gender conduct. Sexual and gender conduct is regulated by ideologies that have found their way into our laws, administrative, governmental, legal, social and family codes, procedures, and foundations; and these avenues of socialization, religion, education, and institutions of mainstream ideology, expression, and thought are powerfully influential, heavily guarded, and maintained. Our society does not view the revisionary creating of sexual and moral norms as very valuable; rather, variant and experimental creative contributions are often highly suspect and sometimes shunned.

It is thus exceedingly important that those of us committed to supporting full expressions of gender and sexuality expose and pay attention to the false and constricting stereotypes that form and influence our gender and sexual expressions. Both intentionally and unintentionally, North American society, our smaller communities, and even our subcultures keep nontraditional identities and desires (and arguably, desire in general) closeted. Controls around desire, sexuality, and identity are maintained both overtly and covertly.

The invention of sexual norms and conduct—and its wicked sister sexual perversion—was a gradual process that took form over the course of the nineteenth and early twentieth centuries. Sexologist and psychiatrist Richard von Krafft-Ebbing was an influential voice as nineteenth-century psychiatry accepted his theories, which still permeate modern thinking. He wrote, "[E]very expression of [sexual instinct] that does not correspond with the purpose of nature—i.e.: propagation—must be regarded as perverse" (*Psychopathia Sexualis, with Especial Reference to the Antipathic Sexual Instinct,* 52–53, as cited in *Sexuality,* Ed. Robert A. Nye, 149). For some, this may seem a very limited, and outdated, view of sexual pleasure or instinct. However, propagation/reproduction still informs the strong societal foundations of what is regarded as the purpose behind sexual instinct; the heteronormative, mainstream currents of gender and sexual purpose that run beneath most cultures and religions can be seen in how language defines us: a woman's vagina is as a sheath for a sword (*Oxford Dictionary*).

Krafft-Ebbing's theory specified that

> *perversion* of the sexual instinct … is not to be confounded with *perversity* in the sexual act … in order to differentiate between disease (*perversion,* seen as involuntary) and vice (*perversity,* seen as willful), one must investigate the perverse act. Therein will be found the key to the diagnosis.
>
> (*Sexuality,* 147)

The involuntary wilful distinction still informs, most obviously, psychiatry, law, and religions. It could be asserted that the rigor and zeal with which some twentieth-century psychologists (such as Freud) and sexologists (such as Krafft-Ebbing) had for investigating perversity were acts of perversity themselves, outweighing any of their subjects' acts: wilful or involuntary.

Arnold I. Davidson's *Closing up the Corpses: Diseases of Sexuality and the Emergence of the Psychiatric Style of Reasoning.* Davidson takes Krafft-Ebbing's defining one step further. He writes,

> in order to be able to determine precisely what phenomena are functional disturbances or diseases of the sexual instinct, one must also … specify what the normal or natural function of this instinct exists in. Without knowing what the normal function of the instinct is, *everything and nothing* could be counted as a functional disturbance. There would be no principled criterion to include or exclude any behavior from the disease category of perversion. So one must first *believe* that there is a natural function of the sexual instinct and then believe that this function is quite determinate (italics mine).
>
> (148–149)

Krafft-Ebbing and Davidson's concept of the heterosexual reproductive function of sexual instinct form a belief and criteria system of sexual normalities and perversions. *Functional deviations* was another term used to describe unnatural sexual instinct. These interpretations became natural and, without doubt, "had anyone denied either that the sexual instinct has a natural function or that this function is procreation, diseases of perversion, as we understand them, would not have entered psychiatric" study and psychology (149). Homosexuality, as well as S/M and fetishism, all became perversions. Leopold von Sacher-Masoch's 1870 novel *Venus in Furs* gave birth to the term *masochism* via the writings of Krafft-Ebbing, while the Marquis de Sade ushered forth the term *sadism* in his exploratory novels.

By the turn of the twentieth century, the spectrum of social variability and individuality had contributed to the notion that any perversity might become a potential perversion, a perverse individual, and a pervert. Perversion began to have autonomous meaning when compared to the unexamined norm of reproductive sex (*Sexuality*, 143). In *Consuming Desire : Sexual Science and the Emergence of a Culture of Abundance, 1871–1914*, Lawrence Birken writes that, in the context of celebrating the cultural right to self-expression,

> we must perceive a moral basis for the universally experienced but radically idiosyncratic desire that fuels the sexual revolution. The most varied sexual repertoire, the most abandoned promiscuity[,] takes on a positive moral significance, however loath we are to admit it, in a culture in which the desire of the masses is as important as their labor.
> (12)

The term *perverse* is currently defined as "showing a deliberate and obstinate desire to behave in a way that is unreasonable or unacceptable, often in spite of the consequences; contrary to the accepted or expected standard or practice" (*Oxford English Dictionary*). The first part of this definition certainly may be seen to apply to non-consensual, heinous acts, such as rape or molestation. However, as many pro-sex advocates have asserted and relentlessly sought to explain[7] the context of consent and pleasure is most often absent when the word *pervert*, or *perverted* is used in the mainstream, which is governed by a heterosexual standard; this absence of context and subcultural standards has a profound effect on how we view sexual activities and proclivities. If we value, and hold the belief, that we as individuals have the power to choose which actions we consent to, and if they are empowering or not, how can *any sexual act we choose* be regarded as perverted, "unreasonable, or unacceptable"? To pervert is to "alter (something) from its original course, meaning, or state to a distortion or corruption of what was first intended" or to lead (someone) "away from what is considered right, natural, or acceptable." A "pervert," even if one considers them at the source of choosing what is acceptable and consensual, thus becomes someone "whose sexual behavior is regarded as abnormal and unacceptable."

The majority of Krafft-Ebbing's reproductive, propagation, and heterosexually based perspectives and judgements continue to form our sexual belief and practice systems. They can be seen in our language use and word meanings. For example adjectives of the word *perverted* as found in the *Oxford English Dictionary* support the negative, unhealthy inference and run along the lines of "unnatural, deviant, warped, corrupt, twisted, abnormal, unhealthy, depraved, perverse, aberrant, immoral, debauched, debased, degenerate, evil, wicked, vile, amoral, wrong, bad, ... sick, sicko, kinky, and pervy." What is pertinent here is the base assumption of abnormal and unnatural, the unacceptability of difference or *different* from that which is normal and/or standard; different *becomes* and is seen as a negative, wrong, and evil—and so to be avoided and/or thwarted. Charting this point of view on sex and sexuality, which has such an implicit and damning moral judgement within it, allows us to distinguish that a moral compass that is more inclusive and less damning could be used. Considering the word *pervert* or *perverted* allows us space to reconsider our language use with what is gendered and sexual and, further, what *is* normal, healthy, and acceptable.

Havelock Ellis was one of the most influential, forward thinking sexologists of the twentieth century. Unlike many sexologists and psychologists who offered a plethora of interpretation, Ellis, with research-based methodological consistency, detailed hundreds of cases without coming from a reproductively based point of view or perspective to distort them. His two-volume *Studies in the Psychology of Sex* is still indispensable as a resource for case studies of sexual study and variancy. In his preface to Volume I, Ellis writes, "[I]n this particular field [of sexology] the evil of ignorance is magnified by our efforts to suppress that which never can be suppressed, though in the effort of suppression it may become perverted" (*SPS, Vol. I: The Evolution of Modesty: The Phenomena of Sexual Periodicity, Auto-Eroticism*, 1919, iii–v. First published in *Sexual Inversion*, 1897). It was Ellis who brazenly led the way for future sexologists and philosophers like Kinsey and Foucault, to examine sexuality and perversion without interpretation and without the moral judgement or belief system of "wrong." Ellis wisely asserted that "when the rigid secrecy is once swept away a sane and natural reticence becomes for the first time possible" (*Vol. I*, iii–v).

Bringing further awareness to the construction of sexuality, this time from a woman's perspective, Margaret Sanger advocated for birth control and thus the visibility of women's sexual emancipation. Theodor van de Velde and Marie Stopes asserted that oral pleasure was important, and Alfred Kinsey extensively studied varying sexual practices over a forty-year career. Kinsey's commitment to honouring sexualities which had been previously deemed "unnatural" had him document twenty thousand interviews. In an effort to position what was perceived as "abnormal," Kinsey's research demonstrated that "abnormal" sexualities were, really, quite normal. In 1948 he would assert that the "heterosexuality or homosexuality of many individuals is not an all-or-none proposition[;] ... it is a fundamental of taxonomy that nature rarely deals with discrete categories. Only the human mind invents categories and tries to force facts into separated pigeon-holes" (*Sexual Behavior in the Human Male*, 638–639).

One can scarcely fathom that this 1948 concept has not taken to shaping our society's proclivity to put others and ourselves in simply constructed and easily identifiable familiar boxes. Kinsey worked tirelessly in his effort to expand gender and sexual norms and paved the way, much as Ellis did, for all those who would take on the study of sex and sexuality. Decades of progressive sexual politics and gender theories could be seen to be based on a few lines of Kinsey: "[T]he living world is a continuum in each and every one of its aspects. The sooner we learn this concerning human sexual behavior the sooner we shall reach a sound understanding of the realities of sex" (63). Certainly, we could take out the words "sexual behaviour" and "sex" and put in *any* descriptor that equates to full self-expression and living a life of aliveness: the sooner we move towards a theory that the living world and human beings exist on a multidimensional continuum, ever changing and fluid, the sooner we can reach a new reality that radically accepts gender and sexual diversity (as well as all other forms of diversity, difference, and change).

Concurrent with some of the movements in sex studies noted above, emancipation led the discussion of the responsibility of both participants (sex happened in couples) to take place. In his chapter on "New Male Responsibilities," in *Ideal Marriage: Its Physiology and Techniques*, published in 1930, T. H. Van de Velde wrote, "monotony can only be relieved by variation" (338). A radical concept for those who choose monogamous and/ or reproductively based sex! Van de Velde would still equate sex with love and within marriage, however. He asserted, "[A]s a rule women are frigid and cold," yet made this leap: "until taught by her husband, after which, if successful, her desire efficiently will be at least equal to his endurance, if not surpass it" (271). I raise this notion from 1930 to make the point that while both a heterosexist, reproductively based sex was considered the "norm," other currents of sexual liberation, even if housed within a sexist framework, have long been operative.

Libertine obstacles

For the most part, heteronormativity, bourgeois hegemony, sex-role stereotypes, and a culture of surveillance continue to govern and dictate the display of North American gender and sexual identities. Asking, "Where is heterosexuality privileged?" and "Where it heterosexuality not privileged?" "Where are scripted gender binaries limiting my or another's life?" and "Where and how might I be contributing to policing gender and sexual norms?" could be useful questions when checking in with how pervasive heteronormative and patriarchal standards govern our societies. Without really choosing for ourselves, we can hold fast to a centre of unconscious and subtle societal values, which are constructed as "normal." These values are primarily based on reproduction and are seen as consistent, unquestioning truths to be lived and carried out without much deviation. These values influence how we were raised and how we child-rear; how we are educated and how we educate; how we vote and how we align our moral compass; how and what we read and write; how and what we consider literature and theory and academic scholarship and contribution; how we consider ourselves, our lives, our group conscious, our communities, and our world. It is these values, social contexts, and gender and sex socialization that provide us with "the institutional and cultural arena in which we create our sexualities" (Kimmel and Plante, 73).

In a thoroughly evocative study that asks, "How Libertine is the Netherlands?" Gert Hekma cites five obstacles to sexual freedom, five frameworks that create our sexual arenas that have prevailed in Western thought and thinking despite our experiencing various gender, sexual, and identity revolutions: *The first obstacle is "the sexual–gender division"* (212, italics mine), which asserts that sex exists within the male sphere or domain. The reality is that women's spaces, engagement, and sex practices are barely visible and/or demonized compared to men's. Consider two glaring examples that demonstrate this dramatic inequality based on gender: the first is that women's sexual visibility most predominantly exists in prostitution and the selling of something via their bodies: women's bodies are often used against them. The second is the "Just say no" campaigns, which are most often related to girls, rarely to boys. Our culture promotes sexual gender divisions with the foundational (and often passionate) belief and dichotomy that sexually engaged girls are "easy," "loose," or "sluts," while boys are "experienced." And, while many women are liberated in their sexuality and body, especially lesbian and queer women, it could also be argued that "no one in this culture has a sexuality that is completely unfettered from these moral and ethical pronouncements" (Kimmel and Plante, 73).

"The second is the view that sex and sexuality belong to nature" (Hekma, 212). This belief can readily be seen in the fact that "masturbation is not considered something you have to learn; supposedly, it comes naturally." For some, even more pronounced than the radical notion that sex and/or masturbation would be something that our teens may need to learn is the notion that it is healthy. For girls, especially, masturbation and touching oneself is, often, harshly discouraged. While masturbation is seen to come naturally, it is also linked to unhygienic, inappropriate, and promiscuous actions; similarly with boys, touching oneself is often associated with having adverse affects later in life (desensitization is still a common angle of approach to discourage masturbation while past approaches within the medical and psychiatric fields included homosexuality and penile dysfunction). So, while we live in a culture that screams sexuality via images, media, advertising, jokes, representations, and conversations, sex education is generally approached as teaching our youth the biological functions of the sexual organs and "the prevention of disaster, not about the producing of pleasure" (214). Sex is

seen as a natural drive, instinctual: "although most contemporary social theorists believe that sex is culturally constructed, very few people outside this discipline or academia share that view point" (214).

The third obstacle is "that sex and love should be combined" (212). For many in the industrial world, sex is often associated with love, commitment, and/or potential love or marriage: marriage is the future expectation. Interestingly, faithful, monogamous sex is a recent twentieth-century invention. For the most part, gay, queer, closeted, and/or straight men, sex trade workers, and a few liberated others are the only ones that separate love and sex. Sex consumed for pleasure (which includes the need to relieve stress and tension as well as the need and quest for intimacy) is, for the most part, removed from society's conversations of/on healthy, normative sex. Kimmel and Plante make the added claim that "sexual identity itself is the basis for inequality as gay men, lesbians, bisexuals, transgendered people … and those who practise marginalized sexual activities are marginalized, labelled deviant, and the subject of scorn … and discrimination. To desire the 'wrong' person and enjoy the 'wrong' behavior, may be risking your life" (73).

The fourth obstacle is "that sex is a private affair" (Hekma, 212). As Gayle Rubin, Pat Califia, and many others have documented, "the idea of sexual privacy is deeply ingrained in western cultures and makes all signs of sexuality in public highly problematic, from sex acts to sex education to erotic imagery on the streets and in the media" (217).[8] Consider that the public sides of sex and sex education mostly consist of laws, policing and enforcement, scandals (usually in the realm of politics), social ostracization, and social, institutional norms. Those who engage in public displays of affection witness the chagrin and finger-wagging of those around them, often accompanied by the advice to "get a room."[9] To add, while our "sexual culture shrouds sexuality in secrecy and shame—it's dirty and shameful—"it also exists as delightful and ecstatic within the "proper" spheres (Kimmel and Plante). Hekma makes the keen, and often unconnected, assertion that the "rejection of claims to space by Gays and Lesbians and others with alternative sexual interests makes public space into a heterosexual, respectable sphere that confirms the heterosexism of … society" (217).

The fifth obstacle is the notion that "*sex should be non violent*" (Hekma, 212). While some may have resistance to looking at intersections of roughness and sex, because we equate sex with love—and thus loving, tender acts—Hekma raises the point that "sexual pleasures can be stimulated by various contrasts, such as gender, bodily aesthetics, power, age, class, color and so forth … difference, like disgust, is a frequent companion to desire" (219).

In coexisting within these obstacles to sexual freedom noted above it is not surprising that very real aspects of sexual practices and sexual diversity are understated, silenced, controlled, repressed, and/or admonished. While we witness and experience waves of gender and sexual emancipation and freedom, waves of stagnation and repression also crash upon our shores.

Healthy, safe, honest, integrous, and fully self-expressed variations of desire, especially for women, are rarely seen and witnessed in mainstream culture. As discussed further on, while subcultures exist to support freedom of sexual expression, the repression and denial in and around variant sexuality can lead to underground and/or distorted expressions and manifestations.

Carefully examining our individual and group beliefs and truth systems—which may be operating as obstacles—provides a framework to unpack and reflect where we, as keen thinkers, cultural makers and informers, may sit in our beliefs, fears, and discomfort with sex and gender norms and variances. This important step could be shied away from, yet acknowledging our points of view, judgements, beliefs, and/or biases, as well as where and how they are formed and what conversations and contexts they are based on, can greatly inform our practice and work. We could consider: Where do we allow ourselves room to reconsider, rethink, and move beyond what we know to be "true"? How can we allow for complicated views and experiences with gender *and* sexual variancy to both respectfully coexist and inform each other? How can we include cross-coalitional issues of racial and ethnic variancy? Economics and class? Especially when moral codes, beliefs, and value systems are operative? These reflections are advantageous for teachers, students, professionals, and activists.

Transgressive shifts and building bridges

In the still profound manifesto, "Thinking Sex," Rubin discusses the history and concepts surrounding the visibility and inclusion of transgressive sexual and identity practices. She challenges sexual essentialism and hierarchies and introduces a very useful tool, "the wheel of sex hierarchy,"[10] to begin to question where we stand in accepting or damning gender and sex practices and preferences. This wheel juxtaposes "the charmed circle" of "good, normal, natural, blessed sexuality" with "the outer limits" of "bad, abnormal, unnatural, damned sexuality" (Rubin, 13). Rubin's wheel illustrates key ideological beliefs and values that are relational and operative (consciously or not) in the conversations of normative/variant gender and sexuality. The inner circle comprises heterosexual, married, monogamous, procreative, non-commercial/free, coupled, in relationship, same generation, private/at home, bodies only, and vanilla sex practices and preferences. The damned outer circle comprises homosexuality, unmarried/in sin, promiscuous, non-procreative, commercial/for money, alone or in groups, casual, cross-generational, public/outside the home, pornography, manufactured objects, and sadomasochistic sex practices and preferences. As with any binary there exist gradations between what is considered normal and unnatural, dangerous and safe, good and bad.

While we have many decades of education, advocacy and theory that have bridged protective/sex panic arguments with freedom/pro-sex activisms, the field of study is still marginalized, under-researched, and contested. Thus, when in a conversation on gender and sexual variancy it may be useful to revisit some of the historical conversations. The "sex wars" of the 1970s and 1980s followed from the anti-abuse and anti-porn crusades of the 1960s. The religious right and the second wave feminism of anti-violence and rape-crisis activists, most notably voiced in the work of Andrea Dworkin and Catherine MacKinnon, became strange bedfellows. For some, heterosexual sex and pornography was wrong and a defamation of character and personhood. For the anti-pornography feminists, sex was positioned as abuse, and women as victims, with vaginal sex/thrusting seen as a "persistent invasion" (Dworkin, 122); while, for the religious right and purists, sex was equated to love within the marriage system. [11]

We have witnessed the notion, belief, and construction of "bad sexual citizens" move through the state-sanctioned harassment and persecution of the 1950s, through the liberationism of the 1970s and into various assimilations since. Waves of legal reform and activism have balanced tolerance versus equality in a "don't ask, don't tell" society in which—depending on the town, state, or country—people exchange marriage vows and desires in closets seeking to be free from public scrutiny and policing. The "national ideal of the heterosexual citizen" is considered normal by many globally, the vows and legalities of a marriage commitment defended as reserved for those that are "citizen enough." It could easily be argued that liberationism lives "primarily as a cultural sensibility" (Seidman, 227). As the recent fifty-year anniversary of Stonewall was celebrated, early community movements and activist groups such as The Gay Liberation Front, The Mattachine Society, The Daughters of Bilitis, Act Up!, NOW, The Lesbian Avengers, Sex Panic!, Radical Faeries and Furies, and Radicallesbians who worked, lobbied, sustained, and celebrated huge efforts towards equality and celebrating differences, were remembered—and yet, the well-cemented foundation of heteronormativity still controls and governs our society and sensibilities.

What requires transparency is the dichotomous norms of gender, sexuality, ethnicity, class, and difference: these dichotomies lie behind government controls, laws, policing, and a repression and fear of the "other" or what is different. Might we continue to engage in some probing questions to spark our scholarship and activism: where do we witness and/or support equality between "normal" and "abnormal" sexualities and sex practices? Where do we continue to witness and/or condone inequalities between "normal" and "abnormal" genders and gender identities? Where and how can gendered, racially and/or class-privileged people support those that are disenfranchised and discriminated against? Marginalized communities are expected to participate as equals, yet what structures, embedded in our psyche, culture, and society, are obstacles? If we seek to value, celebrate, and welcome our differences, and embrace ever-expanding continuums of gender expression and sexual preference, might our privileges—which manifest through social controls and enforcement that divide us into "good" and "normal" or "bad" and "abnormal" citizens—need to be addressed and challenged? The reluctance to interrogate our beliefs and fears, our behaviours and actions, is very real; great courage, tenacity, and idealism is required at all levels of our educational systems for sexism, racism, homophobia, classism, and elitism to be challenged. Plainly put, our contemporary, progressive scholarship needs to continue to be rigorous in advocating that we continue to provide inclusive spaces and avenues, via the classroom and scholarship, for us to think and discuss these complex topics and issues.

It has been mostly local, grassroot, educators, activists, and organizations who, in times of rampant LGBTQ bigotry, demonstrated a demand for alternative, variant personal and lifestyle choices to be accepted: they sought to move LGBTQ folks from the margins of unwelcome, unnatural, outsiders to the centre as acceptable citizens. Whereas it used to be that "the fight for gender justice was viewed as inseparable from struggles to transform gender roles, the institution of marriage and family, and the political economy of capitalism and imperialism," Seidman and others assert that assimilatory politics and practice did not challenge "the broader spectrum of sexual-intimate norms that govern behavior, such as the norm of marriage, monogamy, or gender norms of sexuality" (226–227). The question of marginal or central lives and acceptance continues to be a relevant question: can one absorb, resemble, and integrate without losing that which makes one distinct and unconventional?

While some LGBTQ folk seek a more traditional or conservative lifestyle, others want the freedom to celebrate variancy and difference without fear and risk. Conversely, we could consider the radical notion that sex differences and queer desires are not personal; thus, they cannot be owned, claimed, or worn as badges. How might this idea serve one's individual freedom? Might accepting that people simply *are* double as a way to resist all strategic essentialism and mean a greater collective freedom? Would a depth of acceptance and authenticity that has never been known be possible?

The construction and sensibility of both insider *and* outsider, which serve to keep binaries and polarities in place, if arrested in all structures and thinking within our society (and not just within sexual or gender constructions), would possibly allow for equality in every segment of society to have the wide latitude and effect that many of us seek. In *Virtual Equality : The Mainstreaming of Gay and Lesbian Liberation*, Urvashi Vaid writes that

> civil rights strategies do not challenge the moral and antisexual underpinnings of homophobia because homophobia does not originate in our lack of full civil equality. Rather, homophobia arises from the nature and construction of the political, legal, economic, sexual, racial, and family systems within which we live. As long as the rights-oriented movement refuses to address these social institutions and cultural forces we cannot eradicate homophobic prejudice.
>
> (183)

Building bridges among movements for equality by engaging in cross-coalitional and intersectional educational and social justice work and activism is something that feminist women writers and scholars, many of them lesbian, queer, and/or women of colour, began in the 1970s and 1980s. I am indebted to many decades of feminist literary theory, feminist lesbian criticism, and queer theory which challenged the myriad forms that systemic systems of phallocentrism, heterosexism, racism, classism, and exclusion exists, often in the face of harsh judgement from the literary and academic establishment. Rooted in a feminist equality movement that intersected gender, sex, race, ethnicity, economics, class, and our environment, the teachings and writings of Audre Lorde, Cherrie Moraga, Gloria Anzaldúa, bell hooks, Elizabeth Meese, Annette Kolodny, Elaine Showalter, Kate Millet, Luce Irigaray, Julia Kristeva, Hélène Cixous, Gloria Steinem, Bonnie Zimmerman, Catherine Stimpson, Jane Marcus, Joan Nestle, Karla Jay, Monique Wittig, Riki Wilchins (to name just a few, and along with many of the cited authors in this Introduction and book) laboured in their feminist efforts to challenge hegemonic assumptions and, further, to create, nurture, and include a diversity of feminist women's voices, experiences, and writing.

Decades of groundbreaking activism and early writing, anthologies, lectures, community gatherings, and organizational work paved the way for the rich intersections between feminist theory and intersectional activism, the personal and the political, that we continue to be so fortunate as to be influenced by. Added to these voices, we have a solid canon of intersectional, feminist, queer theory, and sexuality studies scholarship that has ushered in new theories and arguments both inside and outside of academia. It would be impossible to list the hundreds of LGBTQ writers and thinkers who bridged revolutionary feminist writing, ideas, and scholarship with gender, sexuality, sex, desire, identity, and roles as they occur in destabilized locations. A very short list would include Adrienne Rich, Leslie Fienberg, Eve Kosofsky Sedgwick, Judith Butler, Carole Vance, Teresa de Lauretis, Judith (Jack) Halberstam, Anne Fausto-Sterling, Pat Califia, Rachel Blau DuPlessis, Danae Clark, Elizabeth Grosz, Gayle Rubin, along with *many others*.

Gender and sexual fluidity and variancy have been given the space to be constructed and deconstructed in these theories and activist landscapes. A great number of intellectuals and philosophers have provided a much-needed and formidable scholarship that has greatly influenced the inclusion of gender and sexuality into the readings and studies in our classrooms and universities. Further, these inclusive, interdisciplinary theories have rippled into our society, as both feminists and queer folk work collaboratively and in conversation with other writers, intellectuals, artists, educators, activists, and professionals in their educational and activism aims.

Just as LGBTQ grassroots organizations had varying ideas concerning the mainstreaming of LGBTQ liberation and lives, both feminist theory and queer theory are complexly layered and contested, as ideas and theories constantly move through states of evolution. I will discuss a few of those axes of debate, and, what is binding to all of them is that these conversations continue to challenge our social, cultural, and institutional systems in fostering both equality and visibility. As a result of the continued exploration of feminist and queer writing, teaching, and activism many educators and theorists have taken up the necessary work to bridge cross-coalitional social and political movements that were previously isolated or marginalized. As a result, locations and discussions of both privilege and disenfranchisement, while not always easy, have become areas of study, scholarship, and activism. Linking human rights with gender and sexual rights has become a mainstay of gender and sexuality studies.[12] That said, many of us would agree that our feminist and LGBTQ scholarship on gender and sexual variancy is ever evolving and that we must continue to create *new paradigms and new conversations* in gender, sex, race, class, and economic equality *at every social and cultural level* for equality in all of these areas to be fully experienced.

In the informative book *Sex in Crisis : The New Sexual Revolution and the Future of American Politics*, Dagmar Herzog supports a key aspect of my book's premise: inclusivity of diversity is of paramount importance in scholarship and movements that advocate for a world of equal rights and equality. She writes that what remains missing is

> [a] defense of sexual rights that does not privilege those who match the norm over those who do not, that does not lie about the complexities of human desire, that does not need to pretend that sex is perfect every time (if only you follow the rules and/or buy this product), and that does not root sexual rights only in the negative imperative to reject sexual victimization but also affirms humans' rights to sexual expression, sexual pleasure, and the freely chosen formation of intimate relationships. What's missing is the basic idea that sexual rights are human rights—for adolescents, sexual minorities, and for individuals both within and outside the institution of marriage.
>
> (182)

While this might seem basic to many, the anti-pornography sentiment in academia and feminism can question how pornography or BDSM could be regarded as a sexual and human right worthy of scholarship. For those who dwell in queer theory and sexual rights, the conversation might devolve when "adolescents" or "sexual minorities" become the agents or narrative voice for such rights. For such advocates, the notion that such acts and preferences could be consensual is regarded as a false pretense. Many of the arguments assert that pornography and BDSM are misogynistic and replicate oppressive hierarchies and relationships which, ironically, is a line of thinking similar to the notion that butch/femme relationships mirror the heterosexual model. While a great deal of mainstream, heterosexual pornography *is* sexist, homophobic, and racist: made *by men for men*, lesbian and queer women's pornography driven and made by lesbian/LGBTQ women for LGBTQ women is very different than lesbian pornography made by heterosexual men or women and driven by and for heterosexual men's consumption. What is often missing in a conversation of pornography and BDSM is how the context informs the participation, product, experience, and impact.

Sexual orientation and gender profoundly alter and change sexual practices. The effects of pornographic writing and material on heterosexual women in comparison to lesbian women is entirely different due to our subject positions. Heterosexual use of pornography causes women to experience high degrees of comparison and body dysmorphia as well as lowered self-esteem and confidence. While not immune to the tentacles of patriarchy's reach and distortions, lesbian, queer, and trans women's subject point of view, which is often infused by a feminist awareness, tend to experience more curiosity, body acceptance, visibility, and relatedness with LGBTQ made pornography. The majority of LGBTQ people operate outside of heteronormative privileges and society. So, for example woman-centric pornography, which is made *by women for women* (or men), is not riddled with the same misogynistic, racist, ableist, or transphobic gaze that informs male made heterosexual pornography, which is made by men for men. A host of women in the 1980s and 1990s paved the way for women and LGBTQ folks to reclaim sexual expression and pornography in new ways that were empowering, and their work was both underground and subcultural. LGBTQ art, performance, and music, such as drag and burlesque performance, are longstanding and current, good examples of where LGBTQ women and folks create new contexts for reading gender *and* sexuality.

Queer sex has its own *queerly informed* context, which is *very* different from heteronormative standards, thinking, and practices. For example in women's LGBTQ sex practices and culture, sexual consent is a foundational, expected practice, and considered "sexy," especially with those who practise BDSM. Using a heterosexual lens to access LGBTQ sex practices and desires is a long-running error and a very damaging mistake.[13] Straight, white, and able-bodied centred sex is most often not considered within a social, political, or intersectional context; LGBTQ sex (most often) *is*.

Surely one can see the fractured logic in thinking that heterosexual norms would be adopted and/or superimposed by queer folk? At the same time, acknowledging that heterosexual and misogynist norms and conditioning are subtle in their systemic manifestations and manipulations is also important. Those of us who have been in the conversations of gender, sex, and race equality and freedom for some time may or may not be surprised to discover that, just as it has been for decades, the subject of sex, pornography and BDSM continues to hotly debated and ideologically fracturing in young, millennial, and feminist conversations, organizations, and circles. A recent *London Review of Books* article by Lorna Finlayson asks the legitimate question: can the law be feminist? Finlayson reviews

Catharine MacKinnon's latest book, *Butterfly Politics*, in her article "They Would Come to Me" (January 25, 2018), which very eloquently details and examines the same fierce debates and discussions we have been tirelessly having for decades in the name of "women's rights," "sexual liberation," and "LGBTQ rights and freedom." When MacKinnon's latest sex panic arguments receive a very balanced, yet intellectually rigorous, deconstruction and lashing from Finlayson in the *London Review of Books*, you know it is time to rethink why we are not deconstructing pornography and BDSM in the fields of Literature and Writing. While many readers may not choose to read or engage with pornography or BDSM activities, and by no means do I mean to dismiss the complicated harms, damage, and misuse that can arise out of either, there is a real danger in ignoring where and how the anti-pornography, sex panic argument fuels restrictions and silence directly related to human rights, equality, and freedom. In the words of Finlayson "the recognition that anything could in principle cause anything else … would be pretty useless as a guide to activist practice."

Many decades of confusion and fear-based reactivity around LGBTQ sexuality, pornography, and BDSM have served to produce a two-fold effect: *the first* is to elicit a political and social agenda that is remarkably anti-sex and restrictive of personal choice, freedom, and action. The fact that queer and gay men cannot donate sperm or blood in Canada and that same-sex marriage and adoption is still illegal in many countries in Europe and elsewhere speaks volumes about how we view sexual difference as abnormal and unhealthy: "perverse." Same-sex sexual activity is still illegal and punishable by way of prison terms in seventy-two countries, ranging from Western Africa and Western Asia to the Caribbean and Central America. Suria and Islamic law in eight countries ask for the death penalty. The number of age-of-consent laws is increasing, rather than decreasing, in both Canada and the United States despite the fact that teens are having sex at similar rates and ages as they always have. Access to the Internet, apps, and texting, with their fast and easily available sexually explicit and X-rated material, is certainly not driving those numbers lower.

Sexism, racism, paranoia, and fear of the unknown are subtle when countries like Canada, England, and the United States support anti-erotica, pornography, and BDSM censorship legislation and laws that, effectively, make adult consensual acts and choices illegal; consent has become "immaterial"[14] and pro-sex arguments are "degrading and dehumanizing." Consent laws in many US states, Kansas and Georgia for example punish young people for consensual homosexual acts with far greater penalties than for consensual heterosexual acts. Concurrently, fourteen US states are taking a stand for a responsible safe-sex education program, refusing federal funding for sex education owing to the federal requirement that schools only teach abstinence. The "don't ask, don't tell" and "just say no" policies and laws stifle sexual and gender identity and expression as our North American legal and legislative system punishes mothers and women especially, but also fathers and gay men, who are LGBTQ and deemed deviant. Countless political scandals and dismissals, military discharges, corporate and educational firings, school ground beatings and murders, and a long, historical, medical, political, legal, and cultural record of the suppression of sexual and gender "deviancy" and "perversion" have produced a pervasive culture of fear and cover-up, closeting and secrecy.

The second effect, of course, is that consensual, pro-sex, BDSM, and alternative gender and sex communities and activities are pushed underground. Isolation, repression, silence, shame, addiction, and a loss of visibility and community are the results. Peruse the "casual encounter" advertisements of any city's Craigslist site, and you will find a plethora of perverse, subversive desires seeking "intimacy." The free, cultural newspaper of any big city, such as *The Village Voice* in New York, offers similar advertisements and searches: many originating from and/or geared to relatively "conventional," middle- and upper-class men. Still legal, sugar baby websites serve to link young college women who are financially struggling with older, wealthy men. While the sites ask each member to agree to not engage in "pay for visit" activity these sites exist as havens for older men, often married, to meet very young women and pay for sex, which is illegal in many countries, such as the United States and Canada. Women are asked to click a box and attest to being over eighteen yet are asked for no identification to prove it. One could also visit a bathhouse or rest stop to find heterosexual, married men seeking out same sex, casual encounters (while insisting they are straight) or walk past a street corner where sex workers stand each evening waiting for their next customer to take a detour on his way home from work.

From online to on the street corner, a plethora of mostly married, "straight," and otherwise conventional men are looking for something very much outside of their "normative" lives. The seeking out and/or supplying of such experiences—and the risk, harm, and addiction that accompany them—are not as rare or uncommon as people may want to believe. In a culture that deems "non-normative" desires deviant, it is no wonder that secrecy, shame, addiction, and harmful behaviours and actions result from suppressing conversations around variant sexuality and sexual expression.

Within this pervasive misogynist, homophobic climate feminism is considered an "f" word and women's and gender studies as an over-funded, illegitimate department run by man-hating, angry lesbians. While interdisciplinary feminist scholars have been on the front lines of pushing for the inclusion of gender, sexuality, race, and other marginalized topics to be included in our institutes of higher learning, LGBTQ people continue to be seen as *queer* in the 1920s connotation of the word: gay men continue to be the brunt of purse jokes, flips of the hand, and raising the octave of the voice until a suitable amount of laughter is heard; lesbians and queer women are at the butt end of bulldagger, not man enough, trying to be or act like a man, not attractive enough to get a man, can I get in the middle, who wears the pants jokes, commentary, and affronts.

The hostile, violent, offensive, and accusatorial interactions that many genderqueer, non-binary and trans people experience is a daily occurrence. Genderqueers experience random demonstrations of fear, anger, disbelief, and questioning when they leave the house, use public transit, or a public restroom. The lack of safety when faced with these daily confrontations take a great deal of social agility and courage. Policing, enforcing, and living from the stereotypes and norms of what our gender *should* look like, ought to dress, appear, act, and/or be, limits the world for everyone. Ought the same not apply to our sexual desires and choices?

There exists North American and European access to pride days, LGBTQ centres and organizations, human rights legislation, same sex marriages in some states, provinces, and countries, and a visibility and acceptance that no other decade has witnessed. Further, legislative and social reforms are continually being sought. For example in September of 2011, the addition of an "X" category of gender/sex (the terms are used indiscriminately) to identify intersexed and transsexual people (for which a person must have a doctor's note and/or be undergoing "clinical study") on passports from Australia was approved. Yet, a network of large-scale walk-in closets and silence abounds as North American undercurrents of anxiety and fear surround "deviant" LGBTQ sex and proclivities.

While the larger society often seems overly committed to upholding these sorts of moral policing's and enlists shame, embarrassment, and the fear of being "abnormal" when one operates outside of the "normal" values, ideals, and standards of gender and sex, it would be a false claim to assert that queer (sub)cultures—academic and non-academic—are immune to this policing; in fact, our subcultures have become very good at it. Sexual and gender switching, most especially, are often met with discomfort, confusion, confrontation, and/or disbelief.

If it were not for a friend of mine quizzing me in utter disbelief: "Are you wearing *a dress*?!" in New York nearly twenty years ago, this theory would never have been born. We were in a dyke bar, in Brooklyn when her face contorted in puzzlement and disgust as she questioned me. We were standing in a small circle of six people and everyone turned silent as they all looked to me to answer. When I left the house that night I felt both sexy and comfortable in my slip-dress and black combat boots. My pompadour was at a respectable height of 2.5 inches and perfectly coiffed, and my accessories were of leather and metal. Back then, there were only a few of us lesbian women who were rocking this hair and queerly revised, rockabilly, greaser, punk rock, New York aesthetic; two of us, to be precise. Myself and Elizabeth Streb—and Elizabeth wouldn't wear a dress. Like me, most of the time, she wore tight, form-fitting pants. I, on the other hand, was embracing being both a genderqueer and a switch (both in public and in private).

The friend who was seemingly confronted and bewildered by my wearing a dress was, like me, involved in numerous subcultures that operated outside of the heteronormative, patriarchal mainstream. Subcultures we were deeply committed to and involved in. She was a professional, well read, and educated, regarded herself as a feminist, was a regular and visible member and participant of the dyke/lesbian/queer scene of Brooklyn and Manhattan, and part of the small, queer punk rock subculture. She was similarly experienced in life and considered a bit of a veteran in our circles. Yet, in that moment, I was seen as operating outside of the gender and sexual norms of all of our LGBTQ subcultures. I was deviating from the script and needed to be questioned. While known as being one of the more fashionable and cutting-edge members in our various subcultures, I needed a course correction; I needed to choose a gender and sexual box and not deviate. I needed to be brought back into line with who and what I represented. I was shamed and felt ostracized and made wrong for my choice of gender and sexual expression. In this dyke, queer bar in Brooklyn, surrounded by queer, feminist, women punks, I was a deviant.

Those who occupy variant or non-normative combinations, even within the don't-box-me-in subcultures, do not always experience inclusion and visibility. In my case, while nothing had changed for me as far as my self-concept of identity, I felt like an outsider for my gender and sexual presentation and expression. As much writing and research has shown, individuals who challenge societal and cultural norms and concepts of gender and sex binaries, who may live between genders, be fluid, and/or express unfamiliar, switchable, or new gender expressions, are likely to be questioned, ridiculed, and stigmatized.

Since that defining moment, I have continued to be questioned for switching and found that variancy and switching within the many subcultures and communities I have been an inclusive part of continues to be kept on the margins and fringes, including within some of our treasured LGBTQ communities, movements, and activisms. Understandings of "normal" versus "abnormal" embodiments in regard to gender and sexuality can be subtle and internalized: one is either butch or femme, queer or straight, boy/i or girl, feminine, masculine *or* androgynous, man or woman, top or bottom, sadist or masochist. Those who switch can be categorized (and treated as) confused, wrong, weird, or abnormal and this needs to change.

Living a life on guard can take a serious toll on one's internal world of self-acceptance, integrity, and place in both group, community, and society. As many personal narratives have recounted:

> I don't live without gender. Every day I'm forced to make a conscious choice about what part of myself to reveal on that specific day. How vulnerable am I willing to be? How strong do I feel? Somedays its great fun and sometimes it's a real drag. It's never not an issue, but it makes me who I am.
>
> (Justin Bond in Kate Bornstein's *My Gender Workbook*, 283)

Constricting and policing authentic displays of gender and sexual variancy create divisions that divide intersectional aims of equality and also thwart people connecting across both our commonalities (humanness) and our differences. Those who make up LGBTQ, feminist, and social-justice communities, including our allies, are called upon to be alert and aware of both our tendency to over-simplify and/or constrict gender, sexuality, and identity. We do well to consider where we box in ourselves and others. To consider our multiple privileges, how they interact with others, *and* how privilege and normative binaries inform public spaces. Being willing to be aware and notice, and possibly say something, when witnessing or experiencing a challenge or difficulty in public and shared spaces is critical.[15] If we consider that educational institutions and arenas are public spaces, how might integrating a theory of switching in our daily lives *and* into appropriate curriculums benefit our intellectual contribution to gender and sexual social justice issues?

Gagne, Tenksbury, and McGangley's research corroborates the reality that "gender is not a natural and inevitable outgrowth of sex." They conclude, "[T]hose who are not comfortable expressing gender that is congruent with genital configuration experience an overwhelming urge to experience gender in alternative ways. Nonetheless, the vast majority stay within the gender binary as masculine men and feminine women" (247). The tendency to "stay within the binary gender system is so strong" that researchers[16] have asserted that "gender determines sex, rather than the reverse. Given the limited range of identities available it is interesting, but not surprising, that the overwhelming majority of transgendered individuals adhere to traditional conceptualizations of sex and gender" (247).

Many academics, feminists, progressives, LGBTQ folks, medical and psychological professionals and their theories have, to varying degrees, sought to disrupt polarizing, gender binary systems, conservative sexual judgements viewed as "normal," and the real fears that accompany appearing deviant or transgressive continue to be socially and culturally ingrained in most aspects of North American society. These theories and ideas continue to be highly contentious and often marginalized. Fear and paranoia are behind such policing, and while sometimes the need to control "deviance" is based on a past traumatic or isolated experience it is most often fuelled by unfamiliarity and disinformation. One might argue that having to defend sexual pleasures and choices is only as unreasonable as attacking and problematizing consensual, adult-based, sexual pleasure choices.

When the historicity is distinguished, most people would assert, at a basic human-rights level, that each of us has the moral and constitutional right to choose and name what brings an individual pleasure and happiness so long as that pleasure is consensual and no one is hurt or damaged in the process. If we accept the fact that there never has been, nor could there ever be, any humanitarian basis for "conventional" sexual norms, despite the fact that many folks attempt to have it otherwise, the notion of subversion or perversion becomes illogical and preposterous. Sexual convention could thus be deconstructed as a lie, and wherever there is a lie deception, manipulation, and a lack of integrity lurks. The sooner we bring the falsities of our past-based, conventional "norms" to light, the safer, healthier, happier, self-expressed, and more joy-filled our society will be (no matter how conservative or traditional one's values or practices may be). The freedom that comes when one chooses to be open and honest about one's gender and sexual preferences is truly remarkable and affirming. Why else would pride parades be such jovial, celebratory events?

On the construction and realm of (variant) sexualities and identities

In *Public Sex : The Culture of Radical Sex*, Pat Califia, one of the early, influential writers and activists for a more expansive freedom in sexual and gender variancy, asserts that our dependence and belief in sex differences is primarily driven by sexual pleasure; this pleasure thus becomes the most common perversion. The fact that eroticization of the other clearly drives our society allows only two genders; it is a system that works effectively and often fanatically, to keep gender and sex differences polarized. Califia asserts that,

> Strict gender division is so important to people's sexual pleasure that they want to disguise it as nature or biology, so nothing will threaten to change it. The differences between men and women are seized upon, encouraged, artificially exaggerated, and even lied about to create a distance and a tension that give heterosexuals [and those finding heterosexist, male/female modalities sexually pleasing] something to struggle with, a strange territory to explore, a mystery to apprentice themselves to and celebrate.
>
> (178)

Califia argued that rather than celebrate gender diversity, the eroticization of the other, combined with the fear of losing the object and source of one's sexual desire, drives institutional sexism and heteronormativity. This pattern is "so recalcitrant" Califia writes, "because even people who realize how bad it is are afraid that getting rid of it would mean getting rid of the pleasure they obtain from the dual-gender system." Homosexuality "both challenges and reinforces this system ... the dialectic—the fact that homosexuals are challenging and resisting, yet simultaneously dependent upon and deeply attracted to gender differences" contributes to a relatively closed and coded gender and sex system (178–179).

Looking at the dual-gender system from another angle in *The Five Sexes: Why Male and Female Are Not Enough*, biologist, feminist, and historian of science Anne Fausto-Sterling states that during the twentieth century the legal and medical communities completely erased "any form of embodied sex that does not conform to a male-female, heterosexual pattern." She notes the irony of "a more sophisticated knowledge of the complexity of sexual systems" leading to "the repression of such intricacy" (41). If we are to think about how can we actively choose to be in progressive action(s) with fully accepting and honouring the ever-evolving ranges and continuums of gender identities and sexual variances—regardless of how different they may be from our own experiences or how *seemingly* antagonistic or threatening they may occur—it seems incumbent that each of us ask

> why should we care if a "woman" defined as one who has breasts, a vagina, a uterus, and ovaries and who menstruates, also has a clitoris large enough to penetrate the vagina of another woman? Why should we care if there are people whose biological equipment enables them to have sex "naturally" with both men and women? The answers seem to lie in a cultural need to maintain clear distinctions between the sexes.[17]
>
> (41)

Probing questions, indeed. Even the most feminist, progressive and educated among us can be influenced by the powerful and seductive heterosexist patriarchy we swim in—and so subtly wedded to maintaining singular or clear identity distinctions that do not fully serve us or encompass the full spectrum of possible gender and sexual variance within ourselves, the people we may know, or our communities. What has us continue to stay committed to notions of identity as fixed and stable when we experience, witness and/or are made aware of degrees of variancy? Especially if we are students or teachers who highly value curiosity as a vital component to education. Or experienced and wise enough to know (and accept) that change is both certain and inevitable with time? Questioning ourselves, as well as the various groups and segments of society that we are a part of, as to where we benefit from the attachment or enforcement of systemic patriarchal and heteronormative standards concerning sexual and gender difference is important. So, too, is questioning how and where we may reinforce singular, uncomplicated categories and distinctions in the first place.

Fausto-Sterling contextualizes the increase in surgical interventions (which is not new) with intersexed and differently gendered people with societies "mandating the control of the body": because those of us who are different "blur and bridge the great divide"; by challenging traditional beliefs we "possess the irritating ability to live sometimes as one sex and sometimes the other" thus raising "the spectrum of homosexuality" (41). Fausto-Sterling asks,

> [w]hat if things were altogether different? Imagine a world in which the same knowledge that has involved me to intervene in the management of intersexual patients [or any sexually or gender variant subject] has been placed at the service of multiple sexualities. Imagine that the sexes have multiplied beyond currently imaginable limits … oppositions and others would have to be dissolved as sources of division. A new ethics of medical treatment [as well as laws, education, social systems, and structures] would arise, one that would permit ambiguity in a culture of divisions. Conforming to society would no longer be the medical issue.
>
> (41)

These imaginings and questionings are important because—despite many decades ripe with scholarship, education, and activism around gender and sex equality—we continue to live in a dualistically based (us versus them) world. It's been years since forward-thinking, widely popular books like Kate Bornstein's *My Gender Workbook: How to Become a Real Man, a Real Woman, the Real You, or Something Else Entirely* have been published; medical plans have been modified to pay for gender-based surgical procedures and reassignments; universities have expanded their women's studies departments to include gender studies and sexuality studies; countless personal narratives and organizational actions have made it to mainstream media to challenge what it is to be a "real" woman; and trans-gendered people have gained increased visibility, rights and protections, *and yet* variant genders and sexualities that don't conform to heteronormative, singular categories and generalizations continue to be ignored, silenced, misunderstood, and/or hyper-eroticized. The process of educating and bridging people's lives and experiences with the various progressive theor-etical conversations *and* intersectional, social justice movements that seek equality, inclusion, respect, acceptance, imagination, and compassion have a long way to go.

Jonathan Ned Katz proposed an additional way to challenge the "histor-ical relativity of sexual behaviors … identities, meanings, categories, groups, and institutions": he asks us to consider

> if sexual behavior is more than just a conjunction of organs, if it is always shaped by the partial system within which it functions, and if it always includes a mix of socially defined feelings and meaning, behavior is just as historically related and constructed as [identity].
>
> (44)

To speak of heterosexuality (or homosexuality) as having a historical, various past and thus an undetermined future "challenges our usual, implicit, deterministic assumption that heterosexuality [or homosexuality] as fixed, timeless, biological" and synchronous with female and male bodies (44). Katz sees this challenge as "subversive when applied to erotic and gender history, for it challenges our stubborn, ingrained idea of an essen-tial, external heterosexuality and heterosexuality." He involves Karl Marx's idea that "people make our sexual and affectional history," and that we are "given by the past and altered by [our] political activity and organizations … [our] visions of a valued future."

Creating a clearing for gender and sexual identities and relations to have the freedom to be in a mode of construction and revision, of morphing and change, is a step. Katz argues that moving away from a history of "homosexuality and heterosexuality *to* a history of eroticism and gender … empowers a pragmatic, strategic, conceptual advance, allowing us to ask new questions." The notion that heterosexual or homosexual feeling, actions and so forth are "not omnipresent, not a biological fate;" gender, affection, and eroticism are historically diverse and historically varied (45–46).

Katz asserts that we need to become neutral, technical observers of sexual behaviour, which is difficult in a "world where no one escapes pressure to monitor personal sexual standards and desires" (49). Certainly, most of us would agree to be wary of universal truths and of fusing our cultural, historical, and personal beliefs and concerns as we take on best practices in our research. That said, progressives, feminists, and activists help bridge conversations when we pay attention to how post-modern identity theories work and/or appear in our day-to-day lives. If desire is part of a "continuing process of creating the self" by allowing multiple experiences of satisfaction, then what may be

> required more than anything else, if a promise of a postmodern sexuality is to be realized, is a self-conscious effort to free the sexual from the intellectual isolation within which the modernization of sex originally prospered ... no easy task. At a minimum it requires that we place all sexual behavior in the larger context of the lives lived by those having these experiences and that our "theories" of sexual behavior is made responsible to our sense of the human.
>
> (William Simon, *Postmodern Sexualities*, 38–39)

Allowing and accepting each person's freedom to define the gender and sexual behaviour and choices that are most appropriate and healthy, without influencing a scripting or conforming, is one "responsible" way to validate both our humanness and offer a praxis in academia and scholarship that could serve more fully and expansively. Actively choosing a daily cognizance—personally and in community with others—that reflects challenging sexist gender stereotypes, and heteronormative sexuality is powerful. Choosing to dwell in a more consensus-based framework for creating our identity and sex-based conversations, we could challenge the given scripts: from gender and sexual scripts to racial and consumer ones.

In *Postmodern Sexualities*, Simon asserts, "[F]ew instances of human experience are more fully reflective of the dialogical character of human existence than is the relationship of object choice to sexual identity and of the relationship of both to social life" (43). It is precisely the intersection of object choice and the standard, socially acceptable sexual and identity scripts that he delineates in the following:

If I am a Y, I must desire an X.
Or
If I desire an X, I must be a Y.
If I want to be a Y, I must desire an X.
Or
Z wants/expects me to be Y, so I should try to desire X.

Or

If I am X, I should have to be $X_1, X_2, X_3 \ldots X_n$,

Or

Being X, it is easier to be $X_1, X_2, X_3 \ldots X_n$.

(43)

The scenarios above leave little room for variance, yet isn't that part of what our postmodern theories are grounded in? Simon articulates that the logic(s) above "allow individuals to volunteer for standardized identities that organize standardized scripts in order to avoid a crisis of individual cohesion occasioned by a failure of societal integration" (43). Recognizing standardized scripts as operative challenges what are often socially proscribed "beliefs" rather than actual "truths." Following laid out, socially acceptable, gender and sexual scripts is the easiest and most convenient path: failing to integrate within society, at any level, is often a huge concern that parents and individuals worry about: wanting to "fit in," avoiding a "crisis of individual cohesion," and the fear of failing to integrate with society keeps many people confined, closeted, and silent (in one way or another). What is often not publicly discussed—until a LGBTQ murder or suicide makes the front page of the mainstream press—is that the consequences of following predetermined, generic identity-based scripts that *don't authenticate* who a person is can also be lethal.

We need to diligently continue to educate, read, and think outside of these unoriginal scripts and boxes. We can revisit the invitation of the activist group Radicallesbian's to transform who and what our identity is into and through a fluid and non-linear language; we can acknowledge that while identity categories can often be useful, they can also be limiting, and in the case of gender, deeply invested in rigid, limited sex-role definitions and constraints that do not serve those who are more fluid.

Most readers will be familiar with philosopher and theorist Judith Butler's exploration of the concept of gender as a social, performative construction; her theories are generally regarded as helping to birth the notion of gender fluidity in academia. Butler addresses how power, heteronormativity, and social standards influence one's gender, and some conclude that her theories call for a total dismantling of gender categories. Her groundbreaking work in *Gender Trouble: Feminism and the Subversion of Identity* (1990), while not easily accessible to those outside of academia, ushered in both a new language and new concepts/tools in the arena of understanding and living queer theory. Butler's work is highly revered and valued as well as debated and criticized. Judith Roof would write that, even as appealing, the notion of performativity and the term itself is "vexingly ambiguous (and hence attractive in its elasticity) … identities, like genders, are multiple, changing fictions of position, desires, and unification" (*What Gender Is, What Gender Does*, 30).[18] The questioning and disengagement with the influence and flux of both external and internalized conditioning continues to be a foundational point of exploration and debate in queer theory, as well as at social justice intersections, and is especially relevant in the lives of variant, queer, trans, and intersex folks.

In *What Gender Is, What Gender Does*, Judith Roof asks us to consider that

> what we might understand as gender itself in all of this is that gender signifiers function as a mode of regulation and organization, harnessing the energies that fan isometrically from the various vectors of consciousness, a vertiginous gender regime ... not only reiterates gender signifiers, it also makes visible what binary taxonomic regimes do.
>
> (180)

On gender fluidity, she writes that "belief in the one (masculine or feminine) (or not) is ultimately an unconscious positioning in relation to the intersection of knowing and being—an epistemology," asserting that

> the fluid assaults the crystalline character of this epistemology by suggesting not only that knowing is not everything, but that everything knows, but not everything. Not only is there no one who has all, there is no one who knows all, and there is no all to have or know. Evoking the uncapturable, the fluid, supple, unlocatable, and changeable as an economy the evades the crystalline, bifurcating apertures of structure.
>
> (173–174)

In the ever-changing and contested areas of theories of gender variancy and fluidity the notion of evading the crystalline is beautiful and apt, especially for those who switch. It follows after what the Radicallesbians would assert is a necessary step in the "revolution to end the imposition of all coercive identifications, and to achieve maximum autonomy in human expression" (399). Thus, key to my theory of switching is Kinsey and Butler's argument that there are no "true" or ideologically sound sexualities to which we can add gender or any aspect of human "nature" categorization; the location of switching encourages us to give up toxic staticism, as well as fixed notions, judgements, and senses of right and wrong concerning the gender identities, sexual practices, fantasies, and desires of others.

In *Michel Foucault : Politics, Philosophy, Culture : Interviews and Other Writings*, Lawrence Kritzman offers that a truly radical Foucault-inspired position seeking to

> destabilize our ability to decide about the 'typical' or 'unusual' in sexuality, or draw any conclusions about frequency or infrequent phenomena. If sexuality and its meaning is entirely dependent on the context in which it occurs, so the argument might go, what significance can we attach to its vanity or commonality?
>
> (6)

This radical departure would allow the Buddhist concept of "empty and meaningless" to drive a fearless self-expression in our sexuality and gender. Conclusions would be mute, redundant. The context would be decisive. The experiential would be valued as well as grant us an immediate, temporal, ever-changing context that could be very liberating.

Philosopher and theorist Foucault wrote, "[G]ood critical historical method involves 'making visible a singularity at places where there is a temptation to invoke a historical construct', so that 'what reason perceives as *its* necessity, or rather, what different forms of rationality offer as their necessary being can perfectly well be shown to have a history … the network of contingencies from which it emerges can be traced." Through getting present to the historical trajectory of singular instances of occurrences that have formed our points of view, we can proceed to the incredibly opening place of recognizing that "since these things have been made they can be unmade, as long as we know how it was that they were made" (Michel Foucault, "Critical Theory, Intellectual History" in *Michel Foucault: Politics, Philosophy, Culture: Interviews and Other Writings*, 37). The art of acceptance and allowing thus begins when we clear the present of the past and come from a place of no-thing interfering in our self-expression: gender, sexual, or otherwise.

For example, through the tireless work of Foucault and Weeks in unpacking the essentialist tendencies and theories and the social construction of identity categories, the "'axiomatic' distinction between sex acts and identities" is now relatively accepted in the field of Sex Studies (Beasley, 146). Sexual identity is something that *can be* reinvented, independent of the physical body; further, sexual identity can *alter and change* pre-existing historically based views and interpretations of sex acts.

On expressive subcultures

The reality is that LGBTQ women, like any other outsider, marginal, or non-dominant group, have long established subcultural practices, language, and community spaces to serve the individual and community needs. These needs take the form of relationality, creative outlet, community building, and activism. The closets mainstream society has constructed wherein to place that which is offensive, different, or feared have given rise to a plethora of spaces in which to play. In her excellent discussion of how lesbian and androgynous female-coded fashion and constructs have proliferated mainstream media and advertising, Danae Clark claims that lesbian readers are no longer outside heterosexual/heteronormative culture, but rather "insiders privy to the inside jokes that create an experience of pleasure and solidarity with other lesbians 'in the know'" ("Commodity Lesbianism," 194). She relates Elizabeth Ellsworth's very accurate articulation that lesbians "'have responded to the marginalization, silencing, and debasement' found in dominant discourse 'by moving the field of social pleasures … to the center of their interpretive activities' ... reinforcing their sense of identity and community" (187).

The importance of LGBTQ people having developed subcultures and codes of our own making and thus creating liminal, fluid, and dynamic communities and spaces that serve and affirm them cannot be underestimated. They can be found in a variety of locations and at events that centre around supporting the LGBTQ culture via writing, art, music, film, education, activism, and other social and cultural forms of visible production and sharing. Another fluid subculture, which holds space for variant LGBTQ women's sexuality, is the BDSM community, which exists in most large cities through events, parties, and online social networking sites. Because the state and society regulate, control, and monitor homosexual and variant sex to such a high degree, same sex, pro-sex, and BDSM communities are vitally important spaces that serve to offer sites of sexual freedom and expression, belonging, and affinity. These structured spaces and sites hold "safe, sane, and consensual" as a mantra thus creating a safe environment for gender and sexual variants.

It is here, in feminist pro-sex communities, that LGBTQ women especially can come together for convivial community through sexual belonging, regardless of their cultural, racial, ethnic, political, social, economic, or class affiliation. These special and rare communities welcome people with variant, switch-like identities (sometimes seemingly conflicting), who most often engage in multiple communities to support their various identities. The "concept of the neotribe," writes Darren Langdridge, can especially be applied to LGBTQ and BDSM communities and has

> increased in popular culture studies as a heuristic for understanding the ways in which nebulous communities might serve the needs of their members in a time still dominated by a culture of individualism.
> ("The Time of the Sadomasochist: Hunting With(in) the 'Tribus,' " 375)

Similar to how the word *queer* has been reclaimed (as discussed previously), some LGBTQ folks and neotribes find it empowering to use words like *pervert* or *perverted* in the need to name, identify, and sex-up variant, consensual, playful practices outside of mainstream, conventional, vanilla sex practices and culture.[19] Thus, throughout this book, I use words like *pervert* and *perverted* in a positive, queerly informed, pro-sex context: a pervert moves from being a shunned degenerate to someone committed to "allowing imagination, intelligence, and choice to create sex for pleasure, as opposed to restricting ourselves to instinct, hormones, and religion, and limiting sex for procreation" (Califia, 178).[20]

Where can we go from here, queer theory?

As the writing and research around gender and sexuality have increased, especially trans awareness and studies, so too has writing on the subject of genderqueer genders and sexuality; *however*, the degree of awareness, visibility, and scholarship around genderqueer women and LGBTQ women continues to remain quite low. For example in June 2016, while there were 2,247 scholarly scientific articles on transgender research located on PubMed (publishing life science and biomedical literature and research) there were only 12 on genderqueer, 7 on non-binary, and 1 on gender fluid identities. For perspective, there were 28,426 scientific and scholarly articles on homosexuality.

As most new scholarly writing on gender variancy is published in the form of articles and journals, which often doesn't make it into the mainstream, it's important for us to ask, Where and how is our scholarship impacting people's actual lives? We have a great deal of discussion on identity *and yet* narratives, scholarship, and activism that include genderqueer identities and gender and sexual variancy—*and are from a LGBTQ woman's perspective*—continue to remain subcultural and marginalized. A few exceptions: Meg-John Barker writes refreshing and empowering work on gender and sex from a psychological and mental health perspective; Joan Roughgarden, an evolutionary biologist, has written on gender and sexuality diversity from an evolutionary, scientific approach; and Judith Butler's latest book on the subject, entitled *Undoing Gender*, argues for the witnessing of social and cultural norms and constraints of the self and one's gender that make life "unliveable." We also have an increase in self-help/awareness books that help many gender-variant folks gain clarity, an increase in memoirs of people's experiences as gender variant, many wonderful new children's books geared towards understanding gender variancy and trans children, and a marked increase (when before there was none) in LGBTQ and genderqueer visibility through television and film.

While room continues to be carved out to include gender, sexual, and identity variancy in feminist and queer theory and activism, both gender and sexuality studies, as well as the broader areas of academic discourse, show a need for a *bigger capacity* of continued inclusion, dialogue, and acceptance of that which is *variant*. No doubt the last two decades have seen a good deal of excellent writing, scholarship, and activism arise for LGBTQ people and variant identities: for femmes, butches, genderqueers, and transsexual genders, sexualities, and identities. Yet, there exists no real oeuvre, inside *and* outside of scholarly discourse, for North American gender and sexually variant women and people who choose to embrace all of the following: (1) Identify outside normative/heteronormative identities of gender; (2) Identify and play with variant LGBTQ sexual roles and desires; and (3) play with these variant gender and sexual identities by way of switching.

The visibility of this location of desires, roles, and identities is hazy and relatively invisible outside of marginal subcultural, pro-sex, BDSM[21] circles; and even within them, genderqueer women who actively identify and embrace switching are rare, *especially* if switching occurs with other genderqueer women (or men!).[22] Switching, even amongst informed, educated, and open-minded LGBTQ progressives, continues to be regarded with perplexity, confusion, scepticism and, at times, hostility. Women and/ or LGBTQ folks actively switching identities and roles is still a marginalized concept and identity in its infancy: in part because the narratives and writing have not been widely read as such and so they have not been given serious scholarship and inclusion they deserve.

Switching is not an either/or, easily identifiable identity or category: it resists static, either/or, polarized, binary frameworks. While LGBTQ subcultures and progressive feminist and queer movements and communities continually strive to challenge gender and sex stereotypes and binaries, they most certainly still exist and are reinforced. The absence and resistance to both sexual *and* gender deviancy (without labelling such deviancy as "other" or "perversions") opens up a site for research, scholarship, and theoretical proposition. This book exists to offer a serious scholarship on switching to augment and inform new feminist and queer theory, scholarship, and activism.

Editors of *After Sex: On Writing Since Queer Theory*, walk a tightrope when claiming an "after" in the queer, theoretical present, asserting the concept that legendary queer theorists (such as Eve Kosofsky-Sedgwick and Judith Butler) are no longer writing about queer theory because it is no longer interesting and/or they are "distancing themselves from their previous work" (2). While we may get to an "after," I also value granting all theorists, writers, and people the right to move into new creative ventures that inspire and speak to them. I know personally that while Kosofsky-Sedgwick turned toward making art, Buddhist writing, and philosophy (among other interests) she *also* most certainly held the solid ground and space for a *living* queer and feminist theory and progressive academic and social culture. For me, finding queer and feminist theories *embedded* in *unlikely* places is incredibly evocative and powerful—and speaks to our various movements' successes.

The idea that each new wave of theory or creative output needs to distance itself from the past, that new, progressive shifts in theory and practice is somehow unrelated to previous work and/or no longer relevant to current work, resonates as problematic to me. We have a rich, critical tradition that, fused with experiential, genre-challenging texts *and* new, variant deconstructions and theories (that are different and can sometimes be conflicting and uncomfortable) becomes even stronger. We agree, we diverge and disagree, experiencing difference and frustration, and political/personal conflicts, while also experiencing affinity and a hope for renewed scholarship and activism. Apropos is Mark Twain's idea that there are no new ideas, just different methods of discovery and delivery.

Feminist and queer theory is still interesting and relevant; there is no "post," or final wave if we choose to dwell in both our differences and our commonalities differently. In *Touching Feeling: Affect, Pedagogy, Performativity*, Kosofsky-Sedgwick questioned "the strategic banalization of gay and lesbian politics," wondering, or perhaps lamenting, if "the moment may be past when theory was in a very productive relation to sexual activism" (13). For many of us, our theories and activism concerning progressive possibilities coexist in various unconventional, interdisciplinary relations (sex and religion would be great examples here). What we need to utilize, and grow our capacity for, is our strategic activism and theorizing: we require cultivating a greater openness and radical acceptance for both subject and object while also not dismissing some of the identities and contexts of people's experiences.

Lauren Berlant similarly questions the state of queer theory and postness:

> [I]s *everyone* beyond sex (not just the queer scholars who might have, you know, been there and done that, aged out, made art, bought property, endured AIDS, forged a couple, taken hormones, had events, reproduced, got tenure, had episodes, done new research, said what they had to say, heard what there was to hear, looked around the room, gotten bored)?
>
> *(After Sex*, 79)

While we do change our priorities as we age, for those who still see the benefit in exploding a hinder-less, gender and sexually free politic in our personal and theoretical lives, there is an urgency in bridging theory, scholarship, and academia/teaching and sex practices. To do this, we may be called to abandon some of the conversations that limit what is possible.

Carla Freccero's first chapter of *After Sex* tenderly echoes this desire:

> I want to preserve sexuality's importance to the notion of queer mostly because there are other concepts that convey the work of denarrativization, broadly conceived, for other domains. Queer, to me, is the name of a certain unsettling in relation to heteronormativity. It can be thought of as, and is akin to, the "trace" in the field of sexuality.
>
> (17)

It is this "unsettling" of our preconceived notions and "beliefs" in regard to gender and sexuality that is still so very much needed and necessary. Freccero summarizes a foundation of Foucault's philosophy quite well, writing that "historical time was multiple and that multiple temporalities could be seen to *coexist synchronically in any given historical formation*" (19, italics mine).

A project concerned with the erotic life

This book is primarily concerned with switching that occurs at the level of language, action, and practice. While switching can occur in many locations (in culture, film, media, etc.), I am predominantly engaged with illustrating my theory via a small selection of twentieth-century modern and post-modern experimental, avant-garde narrative texts, including selected fiction, poetry, memoir, letters, and essays. Throughout this book, I examine crossovers of the personal and memoir with the performativity of the authorial voice and narrative text to illustrate how switching—for example in occupying a gendered body, versus not occupying a gendered body—complicates notions of gender and identity. Through this active phenomenology, I unpack and connect a wide range of genderfluid, genderqueer, gender-variant, and sexually variant "switches" with the intention that narratives of switching and the expanded continuums of identity and play they create can newly enter the study and reading of literature, women's, gender, and sexuality studies and theory in accessible, visible, and meaningful ways.

My chosen authors, Gertrude Stein, Jeanette Winterson, Kathy Acker, Eileen Myles, Anne Carson, and Sappho, all write in a verse that employs innovative and unorthodox uses of punctuation, line spacing, and grammar that prove a key way to home in on a subject's ambiguity via creating the physical space to allow alternative makings and meanings to present themselves. All actively employ switching gendered bodies, gendered identities and/or sexual identities and sexual roles to such an elevated degree that stable notions of any of the above are continually, and very wonderfully, destabilized. Rather than this destabilization creating chaos or mayhem, what opens up is a space for inquiry and accessibility: curiosity about constructions of the self and a playful switching with identity, roles, and desires allows for an unfamiliar wonder where unlimited and unrealized possibilities are made available.

This book deliberately opts *out* of a "one model fits all" book where all genders, sexualities, or identities are covered to surfacely illustrate my theory and idea of switching. Rather, I have chosen to focus on five exceptionally prolific, brilliant, experimental, avant-garde, genre-pushing, twentieth-century women/LGBTQ authors. I have chosen these authors, and not others, for a number of reasons. While the footnotes of this chapter go into much more detail, it's important to note that my selection process is based on a few criteria. While there is a small jump from Stein to my other authors, and a larger one with the translations of Sappho, narrative writing that dwells in variancy, desire, and identity is not confined to or limited by a generation or century. All of my authors use *language* as a site of identity creation and resistance. Each of them pushes against the boundaries of genre, topic, form, and style—and they push hard. All of them create new, complex identities through experimental pathways: worlds of freedom are created through their experimental topics, words, *and* forms.

All of my authors were and/or are exceptionally prolific 20th Century masters and yet all of their texts are lamentably marginalized and wrongfully under-read. Over the decades, in both teaching and discussing these authors and their texts with thousands of educated and informed people, from students to professionals, I still find myself being both disappointed and shocked that the names of so many legendary women writers, especially LGBTQ ones, are unknown. While Sappho, Gertrude Stein, Kathy Acker, Eileen Myles, Jeanette Winterson, and Anne Carson are rightfully lauded and revered in various small subcultures, literary circles, and/or academic communities,[23] not many students graduating from a four-year university or people outside of specific literary circles and subcultures know these six authors or their work, and they *should*.

All of my authors are tenacious, driven, cutting-edge, *prolific* producers of *timeless, powerful narratives of identity and desire*. All of their writing is concerned with valuing freedom in gender, sexual, and identity expression and uses language as a pathway. I am thus passionate about their writing being included in the canon of English literature further, I am excited about the impact that all six of these authors can have for a much broader and progressive literary, gender, sexuality, and queer studies, theory, and activism that ripples out and makes a profound difference in how we understand gender, sexuality, desire, and identity.

Due to all of the above criteria and aims, what is missing is a truly inter-disciplinary reading, deconstruction, and theoretical proposal of switching, which would include race, ethnicity, and class. Earlier in my footnotes I noted some of the exceptional indigenous women and women of colour who have contributed to lesbian and feminist scholarship and theory being intersectionally informed. When the work of many indigenous and black women has greatly informed my own life and work, it is a missing that none of my five authors are women of colour or indigenous. Having specialized in bridging the interlocking oppressions of sexism, heterosexism, racism, classism, and elitism for the better part of thirty years, this missing is felt. While Audre Lorde fits some of the criteria and most certainly warrants being added to the canon of English Literature, she did not meet other criteria (she's not experimental or avant-garde, and her locations of switching do not occur in gender and sexual locations for example) and so my specific focus, lens, and theory could not be deconstructed in her work.

Similar to Alice B. Toklas's approach of thoroughness ruling everything in the kitchen, this book has chosen to be very narrow and specific with my subject, selected writers and theory criteria *and* intention. There is loss in this approach—and there is also something offered that, even if imperfect, can be used as a template and map. It is my intention and hope that my theory of switching will filter out into a much wider audience and *be applied and used* in new scholarship that addresses, deconstructs, and makes visible switch moments in locations of race, ethnicity, and class. Most certainly, the intersections of race, ethnicity, and class are vibrant, ripe, and *needed* areas for future study and scholarship that demonstrate and deconstruct switching. Other work I've written, for example, demonstrates switch moments in subcultures and in multi-ethnic locations. Suggestions for future research, as well as questions and ideas to inspire it, follow. For now, this book advocates that we begin to understand and apply my theory of the switch via the deconstruction of six fabulous experimental, avant-garde authors who push us to understand, in *radical* new ways, contested and complex locations of sexuality and desire, gender and the body, language and writing. Further, it acts as a springboard to start reading, teaching, and integrating their writing into our classrooms and advocacy while some of them are still living!

Gender and Sexual Fluidity in 20th Century Women Writers: Switching Desire and Identity is organized as follows: Chapter 2, "And The Tickertape Reads 'A Fraction of a Shudder'; Hidden Spaces and The Switch: Gertrude Stein Does Man-Space and Girl Pink," brings to light the gender, sexual, and BDSM switching in the now-published private letters of Gertrude Stein and Alice B. Toklas, and in some selected writings of Stein. In Chapter 3, "Theory Must Be Doing: Jeanette Winterson, Eileen Myles and Kathy Acker Switch in the Spaces and Language of Non-Normative Identities and Desires" I focus on how these gender and sexually variant authors practice, evoke, create, and play with ideas and concepts of desire that truly encapsulate subversive sexual and identity practices. Chapter 4, "Memoir, Girl and Teen-hood— The Body and Deviancy in Kathy Acker, Anne Carson, and Sappho" maps out a rampant perversity: gendered and sexualized perspectives, locations, and boundaries are seen from a young person's perspective. Anne Carson's *Autobiography of Red* read along with Anne Carson's reading of Sappho in *IF NOT, WINTER: Fragments of Sappho* creates and displays desire, how the characters shift in roles and identities, and thereby how they birth a reinvented language and meanings that are acutely subversive. Chapter 5, "Concluding Possibilities For Switching: Gender, Sexuality, and Identity Freedom" brings together the patterns of non-normative and subversive genders, sexualities, identities, and desires, bridging the texts and paving the way for future inquiry, research, and activism in examining the language, agency, and locations of switching and identity freedom in contemporary writing, activism, and scholarship.

Method and audience: A third way between any two sides that tend to divide

My writing and teaching methodologies are grounded in postmodernism, deconstruction, feminist, and queer theory; further, my readings, approach to literature, and theory of switching are firmly based in the progressive feminist and queer theories and practices of intersectionality. I find that deconstruction serves to bridge new readings and understandings with the complexities of gender and sexuality in productive and impactful ways. For it is these theories, used within an intersectional, deconstructionist framework, that best serve the marginalized writers and topics in this book. My author's narratives are a way to both newly understand the topics of variant gender, desire, sexuality, and roles, *and* to demonstrate my theory of switching through deconstructing where my authors and their narratives traffic in pushing boundaries and destabilizing the identity scripts of gender, desire, roles, and sexuality.

I also deconstruct and conceive of switching, gender, and sexual identity and variancy from an *experiential* methodology. Murray S. Davis takes a similar approach in *Smut: Erotic Reality/Obscene Ideology*, wherein he treats sex as "an *experience* that the individual wants to undergo and that society may encourage, rather than as an *instinct* that the individual wants to express and that society may repress" (xv–xvi). I agree with Davis when he notes that the general acceptance of instinct theory, to explain sex and sexual expression, has "reduced its potential to generate the intellectual excitement necessary to stimulate further explorations of the unknown" (xv). Elizabeth Meese would write that "the transformation of literature and criticism as cultural institutions demands a language of defiance rather than the silent or unquestioning mimetic complicity expected of us in order to sustain phallocentrism (*Crossing the Double Cross: The Practice of Feminist Criticism*, 17). As my theory and book are concerned with new readings and explorations of under-researched and marginalized topics in literature, gender, sexuality, and identity studies, I have deliberately chosen not to neutralize my sexy and potentially transformative subject matter.

My method is thus not one of scholarly detachment, uninvested subjectivity, or highly abstract vocabulary or theory. While my audience includes scholars, students, professionals, writers, and activists, this book is not filled with intellectual jargon that is only applicable to rhetorical, academic discourse and elite classrooms. One reason for a more accessible approach in language use is readership. One of the main goals of this book is to contribute and make a difference to a larger conversation among and between queer folk, activists, progressives, and allies. From undergraduate to graduate students, scholars and teachers, professionals and intellectuals, writers and activists, my work exists to open and *expand* how we theorize, read, talk about, witness, associate, connect, and dwell in literature, writing, language, and constructed spaces/locations that discuss and take on variant sex, gender, and identity. Marginalizing readers with highly academic, theoretical language serves to keep academic thought and theory insulated, which is the opposite of my project's goal.

While there is value in theoretical complexity, and in the language in which many of us academics have been exceptionally trained, there is also value in disrupting academic class barriers and writing theory so that larger audiences can understand and receive it. Thus, another reason for my broadening academic writing and style to include accessible deconstruction, feminist, and queer theory is that doing so is an action that pushes for a decolonization and displacement of hierarchies. My work seeks to expand the canon of English Literature to include *both* experimental, boundary-pushing, and/or women authors currently regarded as "niche" and who have been excluded from academia *and* the topics of variant sexuality, sex practices, gender, desire, and identity in writing. My work *also* seeks to expand and contribute to a vibrant, ever-growing, alive, and impactful intersectional feminist and queer theory. Thus, an inclusionary and access-ible language and approach are necessary.

We need penetrable and accessible theories to accompany our progressive pedagogy. We need bridges that link academia with activism, that close the gap between the personal and the political. As the canons of both English literature and criticism and theory slowly expands, so too must our ideas of what is canon-worthy and theory-worthy. If our narratives *and* our theories, which are avenues by which we make sense of both words and the world, are to expand, so too must our audience and readership.

If we are committed to challenging sexist, racist, heteronormative, and homophobic pedagogy, we must also challenge elitist and classist peda-gogy and language. A living and breathing feminist intersectional pedagogy, especially when trafficking in complex identities, requires an axis that is approachable and available. While there are risks to such an approach, nevertheless, as Davis notes, "the intellectual benefits derived from drawing on direct subjective resources in the study of sex far outweigh the personal risk involved" (*Smut: Erotic Reality/Obscene Ideology*, xxi).

I seek for my theory and work to make a real difference in the lives of readers. Most especially to women, those who identify as gender or sexually variant, and our allies, and I hope that my offering bold readings and a new theory of switching will serve to increase the visibility, acceptance, inclusion, and freedom that is possible for variant, switching identities. More broadly, I seek a de-closeting, birthing, and celebration of the beautiful, multi-faceted, realities of switching that can occur when we read these narratives *regard-less* of gender, sexual preference, or identity.

Kate Bornstein asserts that when the majority of people transcend gender and say:

> "Yeah, I transgress gender," then gender will be relegated to the status it deserves: a plaything. When that happens, there won't be any value to the term "transgender" and a new challenge will have risen up, new political identities will raise their heads, and the transgender movement will be shown to its proper place as some historical oddity, back in the days when people thought there were only two genders.
>
> (*My Gender Workbook*, 280–281)

This book is grounded in, and encourages, such play. My chapters decon-struct how, when, and in what contexts and spaces my writers and their subjects illustrate transgressing, ambiguity, shifting and switching: in the being, language, and slippages of sex, gender, identity, roles and desires. My work aims to create a stage to witness and bring about enriching possibil-ities that will deliberate, discuss, and address gender and sexual variancy, identity, and desire in diverse, fluid, switchy forms and as worthy of our fullest unveiling, presentations, representations, and manifestations of what those possibilities might look like or be.

My work with these authors is an invitation to consider that no matter where or how we dwell on the gender and sexual spectrum, we *can* allow, understand, and respect different and complex gender and sexual identities and practices—to the degree that our teaching and learning are influenced and expanded. My work calls upon all readers, as intelligent, complex human beings, to consider understanding gender and sexual identities and practices as constructs to be played with and (re)invented (regardless of our experience). How can each of us be open to creating and allowing space for challenging and complex sex and gender differences? Asking this question ongoingly serves to allow one to move from protectionism and fear to an acceptance (which is much more than a tolerance) in regard to having more than one, static, gender, or sexual role and/or identity existing; it also serves to have switching identities seen and accepted as "normal." A primary question that drives this book is: Where in the schema of feminist, queer, sexual and identity writing, reading, theories, and practice do the subversive and perverse desires of gender and sexual variants that switch have visibility and room to play?

At every level and in most disciplines, colleges and universities that offer courses that centre around variant gender, sexuality, and multi-ethnic narratives are confined to being taught in *specialized* women's, gender, or sexuality studies classes. As they are not represented in the main body of canonical Literature, they are also not included or taught in elementary, high school, or first and second-year survey courses (please see my extensive footnotes for more on this). Isn't it time for some of these writers to be moved to the core of the cannon in our educational systems, instead of being relegated to the margins? A great many multi-ethnic, hybrid-cultural intellectuals and thinkers—from writers and artists to musicians and philosophers—have been creating and sharing narratives that illustrate small, brief switch moments in gender, sexuality, ethnicity, race, and/or class. In Literature, Gloria Anzaldúa, Audre Lorde, Lee Maracle, Leslie Marmon Silko, Buchi Emecheta, Alice Walker, Julia Alvarez, Cherie Moraga and, more recently, Zadie Smith, Rebecca Walker, and Andrea Levy are all very good examples of women writers who have received acclaim for their intersectional writing, yet they have not sufficiently broken through the glass ceiling of Literature, criticism, and theory to be known and read *outside of* "specialty" courses.[24]

I have thus chosen to deconstruct women and/or LGBTQ authors who have extensively and quite prolifically written gender *and* sexually variant writing to map out my theory of the switch and switching. I invite you to consider that this project is not just solely concerned with, and for, women or LGBTQ people—like the majority of male theorists, thinkers, and authors who would not want their scholarship and ideas (which often focus on male authors without any mention of gender) to be regarded as *only* for men: it is not. Plainly put, it doesn't really work to think that women writers, like male writers, do not have something to offer to everyone: we do. This book offers new deconstructions and a new theory, and the ideas within are something to *try on and consider* regardless of the writer's gender, character's gender, or your gender/sexuality.

Similarly, while the primary directive of this book is queerly and subversively focused, the theory I am introducing is one that can readily apply to discussions pertaining to other variant sexualities, roles, desires, and preferences. This book offers a *template* for variancy, my deconstruction of the texts *a map* by which to navigate the terrain. I am illuminating a fairly invisible population: women and gender-variant writers, and it is my hope that by the time you reach the conclusion you will see that my concept of the switch—and my intention with the theory—reaches *into and through* sexual preferences, genders, and identities, thus providing a whole new lens by which, not only sexuality and gender, but identity itself, can be further understood, explored, and expanded.

Notes

1 An invitation to the reader: please do not get hooked on any of the material or terminology that may not fit your lifestyle, preferences, values, or identity. My work is premised on the reader being open and curious in their intention to increase their knowledge and understanding of (1) some of the ways that gender, desire, sexuality, roles, and identity exist and can be expanded and (2) how my authors and the selected works of literature can be newly read. Further, my work is not arguing against anything, rather it is demonstrating *something for*. My theory and readings *are one lens* by which to look at the subjects and my selected authors. I do not claim to know or offer "the truth"; rather, I am offering readings and a theory to contribute to the conversation on illuminating the possibilities for a future free from pre-determined, rigid, and unchanging identity boxes.

2 I will briefly look at the social constructions of gender and sexual norms further on in this introduction. Throughout my work, biology is irrelevant unless I make a point of it being relevant.

3 Why primarily women writers you may ask? Some LGBTQ readers may also add: Why even make note of the gender when gender is being increasingly obscured and accepted as undefined, especially by those working in the fields of variant gender/identity studies? Other readers might respond to the question with, "Why not? Are women not worthy enough to take up an entire book," or "because we are so often silenced." Elizabeth Meese would write that "because the motive of feminism, including feminist criticism, is political, it is automatically in the business of explaining itself to someone" (*Crossing the Double Cross: The Practice of Feminist Criticism*, 137) and, as the subject is a knotty and contentious one, a long note that covers a few of the reasons follows.

First, a quick diversion: there is a 1990s slogan that harkens back to many decades of tireless work, begun at the turn of the twentieth century and at its height in the late 1960s and 1970s, one that advocates for a world of equality and that still resonates as strongly today as it has in the past: "I'll be a post-feminist in the post-patriarchy." *Oh patriarchy*: that tired, heavily laden word that evokes photographs of "angry women" holding placards advocating for "votes for women." For over a century, women have made great strides to secure "equal rights" as men—and to live freely. While 78 per cent of men think we've done a good job of this, 71 per cent of women disagree. Within our first-world society of women's right to vote, work, and live there also exists a culture and sociopolitical climate patriarchy.

The annual VIDA: Women in Literary Arts counts reveal where and how women and gender minorities are represented in the literary world by the numbers: articles, magazines, books published, bylines, and reviews are all counted. They also look at the numbers as they relate to intersections of race, sexuality, age, ability, and education. According to VIDA, out of 15 print publication journals, "8 out of 15 publications failed to publish enough women writers to make up even 40 per cent of their publication's run in 2017: *The New York Review of Books* had the most pronounced gender disparity ... with only 23.3 per cent of published writers being women." For *The London Review of Books*, their gender disparity in 2016 was worse, at 21.9 per cent. These numbers are average from year to year. VIDA notes that while the rates are low, women of colour have more articles than women who identify as anything outside of heterosexual or bisexual and also more than those with different abilities; people who identify as non-binary have remarkably low rates of publication, and women who identify as trans have numbers that exceed those of women of colour. They note there has been a decline, where we might have expected an increase, in the "representation of bisexual, queer, and lesbian writers who are women or nonbinary."

Is one surprised by this representation when, in the United States a businessman who finds power, control, and humour in "grabbing women by the pussy" is rewarded for his misogynistic values by being freely elected to the office of the president in the largest first-world country, whereas the educated and experienced woman who ran for the same office was criticized more often for her wardrobe choices and held to impossible "good woman/mother/wife" standards rather than noticed or appreciated for her articulate language use or well-thought-out domestic or foreign policy agendas? The fact is that many North American families sitting around the evening news prior to the election did not notice *anything different* in the reportage. Patriarchy is ingrained—and sexism normalized. The average, educated, middle-class woman voted for him: "boys will be boys" after all.

Perhaps instead of asking "Why women?" we could ask: Why are only 5 out of 150 historical figure monuments in New York's outdoor spaces women? Or why is the ratio of male to female characters in children's television three to one? Or why do women make up only 23.3 per cent of all clergy (Catholicism not included as women are not permitted to lead) with white women making up 21.7 per cent of that number? Or how is it that a black woman earns only 64 cents, and Latinas 54 cents, for every dollar a white man earns? Or why white women earn about 78 cents to every dollar a white man makes?

While efforts to include the narratives and experiences of women, LGBTQ, and people of colour into a visible, intellectual, and socio, political, economic climate has decades of traction, the reality is that white, supremacist patriarchy is not willing to give up its power, dominance, and control easily. Progress has been made, and will continue to be made, no doubt, and yet in every sector there is backlash. One example, in the area of government and social structure, is the current United States cabinet and administration of President Trump, which influences every sector of domestic and foreign decision-making and policy, and is regarded as the "most conservative cabinet in United States history" by *Newsweek*.

Another example is the sexual assault rates: 39 per cent of all Canadian women report having at least one experience of sexual assault, 99 per cent of all sexual assaults are perpetrated by a male, with 997 out of every 1,000 sexual assailants in Canada walking away with no penalty. Sexual violence costs the Canadian economy $4.8 billion as compared to gun violence, which costs $3.1 billion annually. In the United States, an American is sexually assaulted every 92 seconds, with 5 out of every 1,000 ending up in prison; 82 per cent of all juvenile, and 90 per cent of all adult, rape victims are women. Girls between the ages of 16 and 18 are most at risk and four times more likely to be raped; women between the age of 12 and 34 make up 69 per cent of sexual assault/rape victims. Native Americans are twice as likely to experience a rape/sexual assault compared to all other races. Transgender college students are also slightly more vulnerable to sexual violence, with 21 per cent of transgender, genderqueer, and gender-nonconforming college students having been sexually assaulted compared to 18 per cent of non-TGQN females and 4 per cent of non-TGQN males.

Perhaps instead of asking "why focus on women?" we could reconsider the slogan, "I'll be a post-feminist in the post-patriarchy." Just as many activists and educators who are committed to challenging systemic racism assert that "black lives matter," intersectional-minded women and men who seek to challenge sexism could assert that women and feminism matters, and that a white, supremacist, heterosexist patriarchy does not work for the majority. From the #metoo movement to the Women's March—both *global* movements—women *and our allies* in equality *for all* continue to be needed voices and educational activists; joining together in support and solidarity with diverse voices as they share: "this is my perspective/idea/experience," "hear my story," "my/your voice matters," and "I am *listening*" continue to be important. This speaking, from the classroom to the courthouse, requires vulnerability and takes enormous courage and strength— and so does the listening.

The invisibility, dismissal, and erasure of women's voices (perspectives, stories, ideas, opinions, experiences) is global and insidious; the request (and sometimes demands) for LGBTQ and women's voices to be regarded equally and with respect in every area of the law and society has a very long, recurring dialogue of dismissal. Lives and laws continue to be steeped in decades of "tolerance," which is not the same distinction as being "accepted." Our choices, like our language use, inform our world: both internally and externally. Clinton was described as "shrill" and "unlikeable" whereas Trump was described as "alpha" and "powerful." Women leaders, like Clinton, who are courageous in standing and speaking up, are often labelled with negative, limiting, *female-use-only* adjectives and connotations, such as "difficult," "a nag," "whining," "too pc," "a prude"; a woman is "too tough" or "too weak," "emotional," "angry," "bitchy," "bossy," "pushy," "frigid," and "feisty."

It should thus not be surprising that women authors are not regarded or respected as serious, heavyweight, *literary* figures. Women writers are often added as a "token" of diversity in similar ways that people of colour are. Women writers are still under-published and underpaid, under-read and under-publicized, far less discussed in the mainstream media and taught in our schools than our male counterparts. Most North Americans know far less women writers by name or poetic stanza than they do our male counterparts, and women continue to occupy a minority percentage of academic and mainstream intellectual conversations despite *over six decades* of activist feminist scholars both politely asking for and rigorously demanding that women's voices be included and regarded as equal. Equal rights and feminist policy/change are still very much needed in every corner of the world, from large cities and university classrooms of affluence to the poorest of villages and most remote rural schools—and academia is not immune to this effort.

In education, for example, the average English survey course syllabi—which is regarded as a relatively progressive humanities subject area—will have roughly 70–80 per cent male authors on the reading list, *unless* it is a *specific* women's-topic course and/or a feminist is teaching the course. Disciplines like History, Psychology, and Science have a ratio closer to 90 per cent. This is not because male writers write more prolifically or produce more worthy scholarship, although some male scholars and writers would argue that they do, rather, it is in part due to the mostly unconscious, ingrained pattern of regarding white, male knowledge, understanding and points of view as the epitome of rational, human intelligence (which is a cornerstone ideology of patriarchy). Systemic systems such as patriarchy, white supremacy, and heteronormativity are so ingrained that to venture outside the stream of them one must tenaciously hunt down alternative readings and knowledge. More on this will be said later.

It is thus a powerful and important feminist action to use women and gender-variant authors and voices to demonstrate a theory and idea. Doing so challenges the underlying sexist, patriarchal assumptions and contexts that academia is unfortunately still embedded with. We have *always* had a plethora of diverse female writers, thinkers, doers, and creators, and yet so many of them have not been included in our learning so that they are known and have influence. We have wonderfully rich and diverse voices to add to the canon of English Literature that benefit *all* to read and dwell upon and, sadly, some of the great books and ideas written by women and other marginalized communities have been so severely under-read or stigmatized that they are difficult to locate, find in print, or purchase, with some going out of print for decades until rediscovered: Zora Neale Hurston being just one good example.

Might Gertrude Stein be taught to Grade 5 English students and quoted as much as her contemporaries, T.S. Elliot or William Carlos Williams? Might Anne Carson, upon being the first woman awarded the first T.S. Elliot prize in poetry, rather than be criticized and demoralized publicly by many male writers and colleagues as being "too different" or "*too difficult,*" instead be celebrated as a welcome challenge and her poems taught in every high school writing class across Canada and the United States? Might Adrienne Rich's death notice in the *New York Times* not start by describing her as a poet of "towering *rage*" but as a poet of towering brilliance and courage? When might Audre Lorde and Gloria Anzaldúa, Leslie Marmon Silko and Lee Maracle, Jean Rhys and Janet Frame be included in the syllabi of *regular* high school English classes and first- and second-year university English classes, taught *in equal numbers to their male counterparts,* and not just reserved for courses specializing in women or race?

While we are discussing language: consider that most often, and even amongst the conscious or educated, the gender of most people and things is often assigned as male without much thought. From the authors we talk about and read, to how we reference an animal, "he," and the masculine versions of "he," are the used and preferred pronoun and lens through which "we" see the world, regardless of if we identify as a "he," "she," "they" etc. You can test it out very quickly for yourself in three easy ways: the first is to point to any animal when in conversation with someone. Dogs, cats, and birds are especially easy examples. Within a sentence or two if the gender is not apparent, "he" will be most often be used to refer to the animal. Sometimes this happens *despite* the gender being obviously female (as with birds or dogs for example). The second is to pay attention, over the course of a day or two, to conversations when a gender is *not known*, such as; "I read a great article by a British-based journalist today" the gender of the person will *most often assumed* as male, and "he" is used to refer to the person.

A third, and perhaps the easiest method, is to walk into any clothing store that has a greeter stationed by the door *or* take a seat in a café or restaurant with another person. Observe the greeting you most often will receive, regardless of your or the other person's gender. Most likely it will be something along the following lines: "Hi, guys," "How are you guys doing today," "Let me know if I can help you guys find anything," and/or "Can I get you guys anything to drink?" "Guy" is the informal word to refer to "man," and came from Guy Fawkes's death, after which "guys" were burned on Guy Fawkes Day. Masculine pronouns and words such as "guy" are now so commonly used when referencing a group *regardless of the gender* and so insidiously ingrained and permeated within our culture that *a woman server* will greet *a group of women or an entire table of women* with "Hi, guys" *without even thinking of her language use as gendered*.

If you take issue with this point of view in considering patriarchal language use, please consider that the adult, feminine version of "guy" is "gals." With the alternate, child or young adult version being "girls," (which still can be patronizingly used by a man when talking to a group of women. Not surprisingly, a woman will very rarely call another group of women "girls" unless she is being playful and fun). Thus, consider: would it not seem nonsensical (as well as demasculating) to greet two men with "Hi, gals," or "Let me know if I can get you gals/girls anything to drink?" How would it occur to refer to a group of men or mixed gendered people (without any prior conversation as to pronoun preference or gendered identity) as *"gals" or "girls?"*

Yet "guys" is pervasive and prevalent in our daily-language usage. Why is that? Why are male pronouns normalized as a fill-in for "human?" And female pronouns not? Why is sexist language *normalized*? Patriarchy essentially means that the white, male, upper-class viewpoint informs the lens by which we know and experience our world. This lens controls the majority of our mainstream cultural world and landscape: from the writers who author most newspaper articles to the characters most known and quoted in the Bible. Quite bizarrely, while women's and alternate voices make up the majority, male dominance draws little attention to itself and seems "normal." We might ask: Why and how does the male speaker and writer speak and write for all of "man"/humankind? How, where, and why does the white male writer and intellectual still continue to speak for and on behalf of women's experiences? This is a critical issue and inquiry and applies not just to gender—to which I will return subsequently.

Another point to consider here is agency, and what it is to be an ally (a person chooses to actively cooperate with and support those who are marginalized and seeking equality while not directly being a member of that particular group/

identity). The authenticity that comes when one speaks about what one knows and has experienced—deeply and personally, as well as intellectually—is without parallel. For now, it's worth considering that in a culture in which we have become so conditioned to an authority speaking for and on behalf of us (and I'm not just referring to women here), to retrain the mind to speak only about one's own thoughts, needs, and feelings—and for the authority to stop speaking for others and instead take on listening—is a radical act of ownership, responsibility, connection, *and* inclusion. An ally does not speak *for* others. An ally actively listens, asks questions, and stands with and for the visibility, inclusion, and respect of others (among other things). Allies in all intersectional thinking of social and political activism are most welcome and needed. My humble and heartfelt thanks for being here.

And so, to return to the question: Why mostly women? What about the men? Well, in a climate where to be an "SJW" (social justice warrior) is a new pejorative that appears on the front page of daily newspapers, and the hashtag "fuckfeminism" has 92,000 posts and many accounts on Instagram, a new wave of #metoo feminist thinking and activism has embraced the word "woman." There is a new wave of interdisciplinary solidarity as activists re-ignite some of the 1970s placards that are still applicable, sadly. From the classroom to the airwaves, from the streets to the sheets, those of us who have spent decades advocating for women's, LGBTQ, people of colour, and other marginalized voices and narratives to be included and valued in all levels of our society are in good company with a resurgent conversation that is consciously choosing to focus on these issues.

The prolific misogyny, unthoughtful use of language, and the marginalization and dismissal of brilliant women thinkers, creators, and makers in our society and culture are just a few examples of why a book that chooses to focus on (mostly) women's writing, as well as feminist and queer theory and deconstruction, to illustrate both progressive inclusion and theory, is important today: variant women's perspectives, voices, and visibility continue to be needed additions to the theory and scholarship we currently have and use. "I'll be a post-feminist in the post-patriarchy" speaks to the need for specifically female experiences and contributions—across every discipline and field—to be accepted, regarded, heard, and included, equally. Please see Gerda Lerner's *The Creation of Patriarchy* for a more comprehensive history.

4 It should be noted that in addition to the open-ended usages noted above, some individuals may adopt the terms *queer* for socio/political reasons, to identify themselves outside the mainstream (as progressives) and/or as allies of the LGBTQ movement; others take on the term to queer their gender expressions and have their gender expressions live outside the traditional, conservative female/male determinants.

In active LGBTQ subcultures since the 1990s the term *queer* has been reclaimed by politically active, younger progressives and leftists, sometimes sexually variant and/or pro-sex, LGBTQ folks to differentiate themselves from mainstream lesbian, gay, and bisexual movements. It was a similar reclaiming as the word *dyke* was in relation to the word *lesbian*. *Queer* also came to be used as a replacement for the term *bisexual*. This occurred for a number of reasons: first, bisexual was an identity that was somewhat accepted in the mainstream when it pertained to women; the identity lost some of its self-agency and edge when associated or seen to be rooted in the male gaze and fantasy; second, to be bisexual became rather passé for sexual and political progressives who were allies of the trans movements, as *bi* came from the root words meaning two or double, and thus related to a spectrum/polarity of two, female or male, and thus could be viewed as confining and not inclusive of a larger, variantly gendered spectrum or more complex identities. Interestingly, while it never went entirely out of fashion as a term, *bisexual* seems to have made a recent resurgence among millennials who are in the early stages of questioning heteronormativity and/or their own sexuality. The term *pansexual*, which refers to those not sexually or romantically limited in any way by the biological sex, gender, or gender identity of another, can also be used and more accurately disrupts the either/or binary.

Around the mid-2000s a new evolution of the term *queer* emerged: some progressive, queer allies moved to adopt the identity of *queer* as a catchall to identify their political and social allegiances. *Queer* became a powerful and, albeit "cool," identity among younger or newly progressive folks who were active in feminist, LGBTQ subcultures, be they sexually curious, exploratory, a gender bender, or sexually LGBTQ practicing (some might assert that this line of thinking now applies to gender as well). Thus, for some, the term *queer* did not function as powerfully as it once did: as a descriptor and code for gender and sexually variant people who were also active in progressive, leftist politics.

For those queers who used the term to identify themselves as radical gender, sexual, *and* political beings, this conflation was seen by some as blurring important lines of individual and community (tribal) identification. At the most extreme, it seemed an appropriation. That said, as the term *queer* became delineated and more of a lucrative catchall, the larger, the ultimate goal for some: LGBTQ inclusivity and acceptance could be seen as becoming more real. LGBTQ communities and spaces may no longer be as isolated: differing locations of sexual identity have been moving into the spotlight and with them has come the slow, gradual acceptance of sexual fluidity and identity. If the long-term goal for progressive activists is a society that is equal, free, and respecting of people across all spectrums—gender, sexuality, race, ethnicity, age, ability, etc.—some consider that it may no longer be necessary to use identifiers to the extent that we do now: we may gather as humans instead of by our various identities. Of course, many also advocate that we continue to need separate, identity-based language and spaces for marginalized and/or oppressed identity groups. Certainly, the use of language and identity descriptors is a ripe location for both bridging and erecting barriers: these discussions are complicated and not new, nor are they going away. Endless is the rapidity with which language changes, is adopted, and used, and then revised, yes.

5 Similarly, some readers may remember the fashion industry having four seasons, where before there were only two. Today there are 52 micro-seasons, and we do our best to "keep up" rather than be labelled prehistoric, dinosaurs, or "not woke."

6 For cross-disciplinary, historical approaches to Western sexuality from the ancient world to the sexual revolution and into the early contemporary present please see: Ed. Robert A. Nye. *Sexuality.* New York: Oxford UP, 1999; Mark Blasius and Shane Phelan, Eds. *We Are Everywhere: A Historical Sourcebook of Gay and Lesbian Politics.* New York: Routledge, 1997; and Henry Abelove, Michele Aina Barale, and David Halperin, Eds. *The Lesbian and Gay Studies Reader.* New York: Routledge, 1993. I would offer that Jeffery Weeks's question, "So what is a history of sexuality a history of" ignites each of these anthologies. For more biological based discussions, see Anne Fausto-Sterling's books and publications,

specifically "The Five Sexes: Why Male and Female Are Not Enough," in *The Sciences*, March/April 1993 as cited in *Sexualities: Identities, Behaviours, and Society*. Ed. Michael Skimmel and Rebecca F. Plante. New York: Oxford, UP 2004.

7 See Pat Califia, Gayle Rubin, Eve Kosofsky-Sedgwick, Jeffery Weeks, Annie Sprinkle, and Dan Savage to name a few. Surprisingly, a quick Google search of "sex positive feminism" brings up a surprisingly excellent Wikipedia entry that includes well-researched paragraphs on gender, sexual identity, and BDSM (including a very accurate, dyke-centric photo of a BDSM scene).

8 This topic, as well as both authors noted, will be discussed further on in this chapter. See also Lisa Duggan "Queering the State" in *Sex Wars* and Jyoti Puri's "Sexuality, State, and Nation" in *Introducing the New Sexuality Studies*.

9 Hekma's article is specifically concerned with looking at the fact that counter to the notion of Amsterdam being a place of sexual rights, freedoms, and acceptance, the Dutch are as repressed and restricted as any other country. Strong state controls around the Dutch red-light districts, public displays of the erotic, sexual advertising, and homosexuality are severely policed and geared toward a tourist market. The "filthification" of public culture with erotic postcards, for example, is noted as forbidden. To add, gay and lesbian parades have strict rules, routes, and regulations: sex shops and cinemas have been closed down, and cruising walkways have been curtailed and restrained by changing the city's infrastructure via adding buildings and bicycle lanes (218).

10 I add and amend Rubin's wheel in later chapters in the hopes that this visual tool (and her analysis in "Thinking Sex") will (re)enter into current gender and sexual theory, discussions and analysis. Fausto-Sterling's diagram of sexual and gender continuants, in *Sexing the Body*, is also an incredibly rich place to situate bold new queer theory.

11 Regardless of the fact that within legal marriages, especially the criminal marriages of underage girls and children as young as 12, where sex is granted by the parents/guardians and these young girls have no agency or rights of consent, and are raped by their much older husbands, usually old enough to be their grandfathers. The global organization Girls not Brides cites that "12 million girls under the age of 18 are legally wed" that's 23 per minute. This is a global, and local, problem of consent within the marriage system, with only two American states, Delaware and New Jersey, having over 18 laws in place to protect underage girls.

12 For example, the Occupy began as a political/economic equality movement and now links systemic oppressions in the effort to create a world of equality for all. Similarly, the Women' March movement, which at first looked at gender equality, quickly incorporated and included the systemically similar movements of ethnic, economic, class, and sexual equality. Occupy has been the only *recent global* example of a community group and movement wherein the main tenant is accepting, valuing, and honouring *all* differences and *all* people as equal regardless of how difficult or problematic those differences may be. No doubt it is a movement that is born out of decades of coalitional activism and theory working for sex, race, economic, and class social justice and equality. The bridging of grassroots movements that advocate for equality, justice, and acceptance, be it racial, gender, sexual, or environmental equality, forms the roots of the Occupy movement and much of the current social justice activism and theory. Occupy and The Women's March courageously aim high in their notions of freedom

and inclusion, recognizing, as many do in social justice coalition work, that each effort towards human rights, equality, and justice is interconnected. While my book specifically looks at gender and sexuality variancies, deconstructing how characters and readers can dwell in the freedom to shape our identity and erotic lives, my work is intrinsically connected to the interdisciplinary social justice movements; the core values of these activist movements are founded on honouring all human beings as equal, in all of our diversity and variancy, and further, being committed to creating a world in which the spectrum of human rights are equally regarded and respected.

13 The landmark Canadian Supreme Court cases of R. *v. Butler* and R. v. *Scythes*, which labelled lesbian BDSM sex obscene via the magazine *Bad Attitude*, is a brilliant example of heterosexual norms controlling and dictating LGBTQ rights and freedoms of sexual agency. These legal cases set a dangerous precedent, which has fuelled and influenced ruthless and continued censorship in Canada for decades. LGBTQ communities and subcultures, which find visibility and support in LGBTQ specific art and culture, have felt the anti-pornography battle severely: patrons as well as the owners of bookstores Little Sisters Book & Art Emporium and Glad Day Bookshop suffered greatly when LGBTQ sexual content publications were confiscated when crossing the border into Canada due to these legal decisions. Years of legal battles resulted. In fact, Brenda Cossman in "Feminist Fashion or Morality in Drag? The Sexual Subtext of the *Butler* Decision," cites that the legal court founded "*heteroswitching*" to support the legal decision against Butler, where "gay sexual representations can always be transformed by replacing a man with a woman; and lesbian sexual representations transformed by replacing one of the women with a man" which works to support heteronormative agenda through legal means (136). For a very thorough reading on this legal case and the consequences that followed please see: Brenda Cossman, Shannon Bell, Lise Gotell, and Becki L. Ross, Eds. *Bad Attitude/s on Trial: Pornography, Feminism, and the Butler Decision*: University of Toronto, 1997.

14 From the Court of Appeal ruling in England, February 1992, wherein fifteen men (none of whom brought charges) had home-made sex videos confiscated and were given prison sentences up to four and a half years. See "Sado-masochists jailed for 'degrading' sex acts" in *The Guardian*, December 1990.

15 We are given these opportunities when someone who is read as a female or woman shares that they are a gender-variant, trans or non-binary person, or when a cis-born and/or read-as-male person asks to be referred to as "they." While we may not understand or relate to their experience, we can ask for clarification around which pronoun to use and begin to adjust our language accordingly. When referring to gender identity and presentations, educating oneself on what gender-variant people prefer, being willing to (re)consider the language we use, and bringing mindfulness to our word choices, serves to provide an inclusive and safe space for all people, not just gender or sexual variants, to self-create and be respectfully seen, accepted, honoured, and peacefully coexist. And while some of us may take responsibility for sharing our experiences, as we feel comfortable, with those we care about so that they may better support and understand us and/or to educate others, *it is also* not up to those that have been marginalized as "different" to educate the masses. It is up to *all of us to educate ourselves* on how systemic oppressive systems work: how they are structured and supported.

It is also up to each of us to root out and challenge our various privileges, and further, to support and create space for marginalized voices to be heard and respected equally.

16 Gagne, Tenksbury, and McGangley cite Bernice Hausman. On Hausman fitting into Sex Studies, see *Gender and Sexuality: Critical Theories, Critical Thinkers* Ed. Chris Beasley, Sage Publications, 2005. See also: Bernice Hausman, *Changing Sex: Transsexualism, Technology, and the Idea of Gender.* Durham, NC: Duke UP, 1995; and Christina Lammer, Ed. "Cosmetic Surgery and Transgender Discourse in the Twentieth Century," *Digital Anatomy*. Vienna: Turin and Kant, 2001 (86–97). In these texts, Hausman is mostly concerned with trans sexuality as a way to unpack the historical and social constructions of our sex-gender systems. She critically examines the relationship between trans sexuality and the medical field and practice of sex reassignment surgery.

17 While I will not embark on the debate of the historically complex and excessively debated topic of the womyn-born-womyn attendance policy of The Michigan Womyn's Music Festival, which was the first and longest running North American all women's music, culture, and arts festival, which ran from 1979 to 2015, to not mention the exclusionary admittance policy would be remiss. Sadly, the policy of the festival is a very clear example of how some progressive, feminist, LBTQ women can place and value the gender identity assigned at birth over chosen gender identities (and vice versa); further, it is an example of how hostility, fear, antagonism, and threat can undermine (and dismantle) the progressive and activist aims of a disenfranchised group who other marginalized groups could be in solidarity with, despite our differences. The MWMF was built on a very progressive, inclusive, and liberating value system. Groups of women who were marginalized and discriminated against, such as women of colour and indigenous women, elders as well as youth, people with disabilities of all kinds, and every social and economic class of women found a place of belonging, refuge, respect, visibility, and community at the festival. It's important to note that transsexual and transgendered womyn *did* attend the festival: often with full disclaimer when purchasing their tickets and/or by sharing their male-born womyn identity during the festival. Despite this, the festival came under years of attack and protest for not being "open enough." The Michigan Womyn's Music Festival was an example of a very progressive, intentional, and in many ways utopian community that was committed to stay in open and active dialogue with attendees, workers, and staff in the effort to honour and maintain the original intention of the festival while being open to the evolutionary, progressive thinking and activism on gender. Much has been written on the importance and need for women's spaces, especially lesbian spaces. A 2014 article by Patricia McFadden titled "Why Women's Spaces are Critical to Feminist Autonomy" published by Isis International, shares some of the main arguments to support and maintain women's only spaces.

18 Judith Roof would also write on the importance of feminists challenging those who deny that "there are 'women' and 'men' " or that they enjoy "very different privileges and positions precisely because they have been tricked by gender variety and identity positions" that are intrinsically part of patriarchy. Roof asks us to not ignore "patriarchy and its adherent sexism, colonialism, and racism, or its model for capitalism" and reminds us of some of the legal realities, such as "women are accredited no constitutional protections by the Fourteenth Amendment, for example." Many of us would agree with her stating that, "sexism is as alive and thriving as always," while diverging from her position that

what has happened ... is the production of a larger binary—queer versus normative—that can never be politically efficacious because it ignores the cultural regimes and binary compensatory structurations that have produced the opposition in the first place, mistaking surface performance for deep structure, or mere symptoms for persistent discursive formations. In so doing, paradoxically, gender play supports the very thing it wishes were not there—oppression based on difference.

(*Roof*, 247–248)

The scholarship, activism, and multidisciplinary conversations and locations that tackle the notions of gender as play and performance as compared to gender as deeply influenced by a sexist, patriarchal system continue to be heated and fiercely debated.

19 The term *vanilla* is most often used by BDSM practitioners and allies to describe sex on the "normal," conventional sexual proclivities spectrum. Gender is irrelevant to the term's implications, although to many, "normal" sex is still regarded as only occurring between a male-born man and a female-born woman. Vanilla could also be described as sex without much variancy. Culturally, "regular/normal" sex involves a set standard of predetermined and assumed "best" practices, positions, and preferences. Vanilla sex also implies a certain sense of "purity": the purest form of vanilla sex would be sex not for pleasure but for reproductive, within marriage, purposes only. The Catholic Church's view on masturbation and sex would be good examples of vanilla. "Kinky" is often a word used to refer to non-vanilla sex. For example, a kinky, perverted or subversive reading of even the term *vanilla sex* might see the assumption of purity as an invitation to play with the opposite notions. More will be said on cultural norms when discussing Gayle Rubin's "wheel of sex hierarchy" later.

20 More will be said on sexual norms and deviance later.

21 BDSM can refer to any of the following activities and/or modes: bondage, dominance, sadism, and/or masochism. To engage in BDSM is always a consensual choice and can most broadly be described as involving, often intense, playing with power, roles, and sensations. I love Pat Califia's description: "S/M eroticism focuses on forbidden feelings or actions and searches for a way to obtain pleasure from them. It is the quintessence of non-reproductive sex" (*Public Sex*, 170).

22 The notion of "real" lesbians or dykes playing with and/or being attracted to men (pansexuality, for example) is still a subject of controversy for many gay folks. There is a degree of judgement and distain, if one steps outside of the norms of LGBTQ choices of same-sex attraction, even if the sex is "queered." For most, having an opposite sex attraction would be labelled, at best, queer or pansexual, and at worst, bi and/or a traitor to whatever component of the LGBTQ community the person may belong to. A person might be stripped of their LGBTQ identity, losing friends, chosen family, community, and perhaps professional alliances and work; whereas genderqueer women who may entertain engaging, playing, and/or switching with a man (most likely queer, gay, or variant himself) would most likely still regard herself as queer (or a dyke).

23 Some of them were friends and reading in the same communities and/or at the same events.

24 The words of critic and theorist Sagri Dhairyam are a good example of creating and reinforcing multiple oppressive binary structures that reinforce the systemic

pressure for people—educators and writers among them—to choose one politic and identity category over another. He wrote that readers of Audre Lorde's work must eventually choose between being "an agent for political reformation who emphasizes social and historical agendas for change *rather than* literary or aesthetic merit."

I wonder if he/we the public would subject Noam Chomsky or Michael Moore, Cornell West or Henry Louis Gates Jr., all similarly brilliant visionary agents for revolutionary social change as Audre Lorde and the list of women above, to such a confined box/choice? Certainly not, we say; we admire their literary merit *and* wordsmithing of activist ideas and theories, for which we give them wide berth (in subject matter, format, audience, and medium). Listening to the eloquent and smooth Cornell West voice his progressive ideas and political commentary harkens back to the recordings of Martin Luther King Jr. Both men brilliant agents for change whose compositions drip aesthetic merit and a better world. Certainly, even when pressed, we should not ever have to choose? But in what ways are we coerced (encouraged) into a box based on patriarchal standards that police and penalize variant identities?

While a few feminist women activists and scholars have quoted and look to Lee Maracle's wisdom that "the woman's movement is all about the liberation of humanity for the yoke of domination," they most often ignore the first part of Maracle's statement, which is just as important:

> for me, Audre Lorde most properly represents the women's movement in North America. The woman's movement is all about the liberation of humanity from the yoke of domination. It's all about the fight against racism and sexism and their effects on our consciousness, no matter what colour we are. It is about the struggle for unity between oppressed women and men.
>
> (*I am Woman*, 138)

While many of us work to keep the revolutionary ideas and dreams of Martin Luther King Jr. alive how many North Americans even know Audre Lorde's name? Surely the poetry, prose, essays, speeches, and life of women like Lee Maracle and Audre Lorde, the self-identified "black, lesbian, feminist, socialist mother of two, including one boy, and a member of an inter-racial couple" would be a worthy inclusion into the canon of North American literature, history, and education? Instead Lorde would write in her essay, titled "Age, Race, Class and Sex: Women Redefining Difference," that she found herself categorized or "a part of some group defined as other, deviant, inferior, or just plain wrong" (*Sister Outsider*, 114). In "My Words Will be There" Lorde relates her disjunctive experience between heritage/identity issues and gender/identity issues: "I looked around when I was a young woman and there was no one saying what I wanted and needed to hear. I felt totally alienated, disoriented, crazy" (Evans, 261). She continues:

> [M]y critics have always wanted to cast me in a particular role, from the time my first poem was published when I was fifteen years old … my critics have always wanted to cast me in a particular light. People do. It's easier to deal with a poet, certainly with a Black woman poet, when you categorize her, narrow her so that she can fulfill your expectations. But I have always felt that I cannot be categorized.
>
> (261)

Gerda Lerner would articulate what many other feminist scholars have advocated for, namely, that the "particular and general" of identity is important and must be kept in perspective with a larger context as what is key is "to understand that people do not define themselves by a single identity but by a number of interacting identities," and that "various aspects of people's identities which are being manipulated by the systems of dominance are interconnected and mutually constitutive."

2 Hidden spaces and the switch
Gertrude Stein does man-space and girl pink

Gertrude Stein said to Picasso: "Paint what is really there. Not what you can see, but what is really there." This chapter looks at how Gertrude Stein creates, displays and meditates on desire, how she and her subjects shift in roles and identities, and thereby how Stein subverts, reinvents, and births the language of desire and the erotic. My aim is to display the places where Stein's modernist experimentation with language and writing connect to her experimentation with gender and sexuality: where Stein is consumed with being in action around desire and her experimental writing as locations of gender, identity, and sexual *play*. Stein's writing, which "asks questions of everyone" (*A Stein Reader*, 3), creates and offers the reader many options of play for the switch, as she kneels "to be ... to be pleased and to please" (Idem as cited in *A Stein Reader*, 378). This chapter contributes to the feminist scholarship of Stein's juicy oeuvre and establishes a new and exciting reading of Gertrude Stein's work. I engage in this process by embracing the complexities of desire, switching, sexual difference, sexualities, identities, roles, and language play found in Stein's earlier and romantic work, primarily *Tender Buttons* (1911–1912), *Pink Melon Joy* (1914), *Lifting Belly* (1914/1915), *A Valentine to Sherwood Anderson* (1923), *A Book Concluding With A Wife Has A Cow: A Love Story* (1923), *An Elucidation* (1927), *Stanzas in Meditation* (1929–1933), *Before the Flowers of Friendship Faded Friendship Faded* (1931), and perhaps the most evocative of Stein's work, *Baby Precious Always Shines: Selected Love Notes Between Gertrude Stein and Alice B. Toklas.*

I would like to offer a little background on Gertrude Stein and her life-long partner Alice B. Toklas. Gertrude Stein was born on February 3, 1874 in Allegheny, Pennsylvania, near Pittsburgh, and passed on July 27, 1946 in Neuilly, France. Her family, of German-Jewish descent, moved from Baltimore to Allegheny, and then to Europe, where Stein spent her first five years, in Venice and Paris, after which her family moved to Oakland, California, where she would remain until the age of eighteen. Stein was one of five children. Her mother passed when she was only fourteen and her father when she was seventeen. Perhaps due to her parents' early passing, and also due to their common interest and love of the arts, the most familial mention is made of Stein's two brothers, Leo and Michael, as the three of them would move to both attend school and live in the same locations for a number of decades.

At eighteen, Stein attended the Harvard Annex (later renamed Radcliffe), where she studied Psychology until 1897. She then went to Johns Hopkins School of Medicine. In 1902 her brother, Leo, who had been simultaneously studying at Harvard, departed for London and then to Paris, and Stein followed. Stein and Leo lived together, with Michael nearby. All of the Steins resided in Paris for considerable durations: Michael and his wife, Sarah, for thirty years, Leo until 1910, and Stein for the remainder of her life. The three siblings were avid patrons to a number of the unknown artists of the time: Picasso, Matisse, Cézanne, Renoir, Gauguin, and Gris, to name a few.

Gertrude Stein and Alice B. Toklas, who would become life-long partners, first met in California prior to Stein leaving the United States. Toklas was born into a middle-class Jewish family in San Francisco, on April 30, 1877 and passed on March 7, 1967 in Paris. They met again on the first day Toklas arrived in Paris, in 1907. Toklas moved into the Stein's residence, and after a few years, Leo and Gertrude separated, divided the art, and Gertrude and Alice remained life-long companions and partners until Stein's passing in 1946. In addition to the multi-dimensional role of wife, Toklas acted as Stein's typist, editor, secretary, and muse. Toklas remained in Paris until her passing in 1967 and they are buried side by side at the Père Lachaise Cemetery in Paris.

Stein's writing was incredibly varied and eclectic. She was repetitive, lyrical, and playful; each work hermetic and her style without compare. Like the artist friends of her time, Picasso and Cezanne, Stein was a prolific modernist and avant-garde genius who reinvented what literature and language—as well as a lesbian's and writer's life—could be. Stein disregarded any and all confines of the English language and her poetry, fiction, plays, opera, and memoir, and letters demonstrate that she was one of the most experimental and creative authors of the twentieth century. Her first book, *Three Lives*, was a collection of stories, published in 1909, and it marked Stein's first literary success. *Tender Buttons* followed in 1914 and was well received by artists and writers who were appreciative of her reworking language. In his 1922 Introduction to *Geography and Plays*, Sherwood Anderson astutely claimed that Stein was producing "the most important pioneer work ... in the field of letters in my time," and urged other writers, "particularly young writers," to "come to understand a little of what she is trying to do" (6). Anderson would be astute enough to recognize that Stein's work constituted a "rebuilding, an entire new recasting *of life*, in the city of words" (8, italics mine). However, it was not until 1934 when "*The Autobiography of Alice B. Toklas*" was published, that Stein became a widely read, best-selling author. Stein, with Toklas, embarked on a successful lecture tour throughout the United States in 1934–1935 and from then on her stature was solidified as one of the leading modernist writers of her time.

Stein's opening lines in *Descriptions of Literature* share her interpretation of the drive behind all literature and writing: "a book ... shows that the next and best is to be found out when there is pleasure in the reason. For this reason. To be distinguished is what is desired" (cited in Dydo, *A Stein Reader: Gertrude Stein*, 471). With "pleasure in the reason" I will deconstruct "what is desired" and demonstrate that Gertrude Stein can (and really ought to) be considered one of the most brilliant, sexy, and evocative writers of the twentieth century.

Stein's work illustrates a deep commitment to writing the poetics of the body, pleasure, and lover-ship. Stein was writing subversively, perversely, yet "passing" as nonpornographic. Her writing is full of the nonconformity she was attracted to, leaving and critiquing her bourgeois American upbringing and life to favour an unconventional, avant-garde lifestyle. In *Poetry and Criticism*, Edith Sitwell would write that Gertrude Stein is

> bringing back life to our language by what appears, at first, to be an anarchic process. First she breaks down the predestined groups of words, their sleepy family habits; then she rebrightens them, examines their texture, and builds them into new and vital shapes.

Her writing centres on playful language, orgasm and sex metaphors, and her books are titled as such, yet the majority of Stein scholarship and reading has de-sexed and conservatized this playful modern genius.[1]

Perhaps it was Stein's way of speaking: a serious monotone when reading her work—her oh-so-proper woollen skirt suits and highly buttoned shirts, or how she and Toklas adopted very stoic and formal poses when photographed—that contributed to the bulk of scholarly discourse to limit Stein? Might her no-nonsense, yet jovial approach to life, her dedication to being a prolific writer, or her scholar-like, yet experimental and poetic, writing on topics like grammar and writing literature, take our gaze away from seeing her as simultaneously playful, sexy, and fetishistic? Could Stein's brilliance with language—by some she is considered intimidating and unreadable, childish and nonsensical—have distracted us? Or could it be the reader's discomfort or shyness with sex and intimacy? Or the unfamiliarity with lesbian sex?

Within the last twenty years, and since my writing this chapter—which I began in 2003, lectured and spoke extensively at conferences, and then first published and made available in 2013—further feminist and queer scholarship has helped to correct this error. First and foremost, in addition to her very informative archival and historical contextualization's of Stein's writing, Ulla E. Dydo has produced very welcome and needed scholarship of Stein's ouvre. See *Gertrude Stein: The Language That Rises: 1923–1934*, with William Rice, and Dydo's very comprehensive and thorough primer, *A Stein Reader*

(*ASR*), which stands as a must read for anyone interested in the history, process, and writing of Stein. Another scholar who does not shy away from the lesbian erotic nature of Stein's writing is Kay Turner, who has a long career of contributing to lesbian scholarship, writing, and thought, being known in both academia and subculture. Turner compiled and selected the previously unpublished love notes of *Baby Precious Always Shines* and provided a very thorough and excellent Introduction to them. Other writers of note include Karin Cope, especially her *Passionate Collaborations: Learning to Live with Gertrude Stein*; Catharine Stimpson, who has contributed a great deal of Stein scholarship, and articulately written that *Lifting Belly* concerned the "repeated, repeatable sexual act" ("The Somograms of Gertrude Stein," *Poetics Today* 6, No. 1–2 (1985), 74) and *Really Reading Gertrude Stein: A Selected Anthology with Essays* by Judy Grahn.[2]

In conversation with some of the other Stein scholars and admirers—who have long sought to read and share the lesbian erotic of Stein's brilliant writing with the world—that I submit and offer this chapter. I think a few of us have our own private love affair/crush with Stein. For me, it's been many decades of revelling in de-coding and reading the lesbian erotic in Gertrude Stein; it's time to bring the sexiness back into her letters and writing—back into her life-long partner Alice B. Toklas's *cookbooks*! This chapter generates awareness, makes present, and then deconstructs how Stein was writing lesbian desires in language and roles, driven by a freedom to "speak of *it*" (*Pink Melon Joy* as cited in *A Stein Reader*, 282, italics mine).

Vivant parmi les fleurus

Gertrude Stein's writing formed out of the relationship with Alice B. Toklas, rather than in isolation or something separate. Both Stein and Toklas were writers, intellects, artists, and art patrons. They were key members of the vibrant expatriate community of writers and artists in Paris. Their home was essentially a private art museum, and they hosted a salon at their home, 27 Rue de Fleurus, which served to create a space and community of mutual support for many of the best-known writers and artists of the 1910s through the 1920s and 1930s. During World War II they would move to 5 Rue Christine, on the Left Bank, where Toklas would live until she was evicted three years prior to her death.[3]

Many of these writers and artists dealt in lesbian and homoerotic art and writing. For example in 1925, Stein saw the work of Russian-born artist and set designer Pavel Tchelitchew. His bold, homoerotic work was controversial, but for Stein her appreciation led her to purchase the entire contents of his studio after seeing his work. He would go on to do portraits and sketches of both Stein and Toklas (Starr, *The Queer Encyclopedia of the Visual Arts*, 329–330). Similarly, Stein was one of the first Americans to befriend and support the work of bisexual painter Marie Laurencin. Stein endorsed homoerotic photographer and artist George Platt Lynes, who took one of the most stoic and familiar of Stein's later photographic portraits, titled "Bilignin" (*The Queer Encyclopedia of the Visual Arts*, 1931). And Stein was an early supporter of Picasso, with whom she was a dear friend, buying his pictures "when no one else in the world wanted any" (Lord, *Six Exceptional Women*, 16–17).

Paris, like most large cities that sexual and gender variants have always gravitated to, was a place of exploration, freedom, and self-expression for many of the modernists. Djuna Barnes's *Ladies Almanac* (*The Queer Encyclopedia of the Visual* Arts, 1928) is a bold, erotic lesbian satire of the "literary women of the Left Bank," or "the Academy of Women," which gathered at Natalie Barney's weekly Salon. These now famous women of letters included Stein, Toklas, Barnes, Barney, Mina Loy, Sylvia Beach, and Radclyffe Hall, among others. There is a naiveté in any assumption that the modernist women of the 1920s and 1930s lacked the sexual enlightenment of our own time; however, before the 1960s women's and sexual revolution, Barnes's *Ladies Almanac* is just one striking example of how pornography, erotica, and taboos were boldly at work in the writing *and* lives of the modernist lesbian and sexually fluid women.

Women were not the only ones exploring their sense of expatriate freedom, of course. Many experimentally focused male writers and artists gathered at Stein and Toklas's home as well, and much has been written on Stein's loving friendship with Picasso and shorter friendships with Matisse and Cezanne. Interestingly, the male producers of art and letters would often gather in one room with Stein, while the wives/women would often join Toklas in a separate room (Imhof, *The Queer Encyclopedia of the Visual Arts*, 278). That said, boxing Stein and Toklas into delineated, unshifting, heterosexually based wife and husband roles would be an unfair reduction. Rather, I will demonstrate that Stein and Toklas's switching between roles, genders, and identities—the couple switching and playing with dominance, submission, giver, and receiver—is frequent, organic, and authentic, even as some roles predominate both in their public presentations and in their letters. Stein as the dominant, bulldagger husband and Toklas as the supportive, submissive wife are not quite as solid in stature as their stoic photographic images might have us make meaning of; in fact, both women were absolutely committed to a very maternal caring and nurturing of the other in a marriage of reciprocal support and equality.

This chapter looks at Stein's writing that shares a sexual longing despite knowing "that there is politeness" (*Pink Melon Joy*, *A Stein Reader*, 282) when discussing sex, especially lesbian, same sex, desire and lust. Does politeness evoke propriety or shyness? Discomfort or awkwardness? Or possibly shame? Much of Stein's work spends at least a few sentences questioning the silence and unjust illegality around LGBT love and romantic union. Lest we neglect the obvious, Stein and Toklas lived together, as an out lesbian couple,[4] married unto themselves, for thirty-six years—starting in 1910, a time when homosexuality was illegal and punishable by law and with imprisonment. Much of Stein's work bravely constructs and shares the couple's wedding vows, lesbian love, and union. Stein's life was housed in her love and marriage with Toklas: her pronouncing, "it is to be certain that love is lord of all" (*How to Write*, 28) proves to be foundational to her life and work.

While most of the photographs of Stein and Toklas have them at a domestically familiar yet polite distance, Cecil Beaton's 1936 photograph stands out as the most familiar, loving, and comfortable; Stein is in a nightgown or housedress on the terrace at Bilignin while Toklas is standing very close and right behind her, with her hand on Stein's shoulder, almost holding her in place. A bouquet of roses is in Toklas's other hand as Toklas gazes down at Stein while Stein looks to the camera smiling. Both of them look a tad smug, and the roses, well, ever the flower of love, desire, and metaphor, the roses are very large and in full bloom. This couple's love existed outside the laws of marriage and the privileges legality affords, yet their commitment was apparent, visible, and shared with us. In her Introduction to *Baby Precious Always Shines: Selected Love Notes Between Gertrude Stein and Alice B. Toklas*, Kay Turner writes "in the happiness of being one, Gertrude and Alice created a unique blend of the conjugal, the erotic, the domestic, and the artistic ... while maintaining separate identities" (35). She further notes that "the alliance and affection—the marriage—between Gertrude and Alice was truly their religion" (35), which is a wonderful way of expressing the honouring, sometimes idolizing, rituals that these two women shared; the meditations on their love and each other are the content and foundation to much of Stein's writing.

Toklas's later poverty, her unfortunate legal and estate experiences after Stein's death, exemplify some of the unfairness around same-sex love that Stein would write about; the refusal for societies to fully and legally recognize same-sex love and marriage continues to be something same-sex couples experience as painful over seventy years later. So, while Stein would write and publish their vows, stating that their love and selves are complete without the permit of marriage: "I am not missing. / Who is a permit. / I love honor and obey I do love honor and obey I do" in *Sacred Emily* (*Geography and Plays,* 178), she would also write: "[T]hey will be felt not well / not as ours hours are polite. / Or they think well or violent or weeding / or maybe they be spared ... it is not ordinary standing or standard" (24). Making the point that disturbed sensibilities, judgement, or violence, the "weeding" out of unsuitables that are "not ordinary" are not in alignment with being "well." She continues to offer that, while people may experience fear, love is a gift and there is no difference between a heterosexual or homosexual union:

[N]ow I know everything of which it is that there is no difference / between then and now but very much the same / as of course then it was not only here. / There they came well / here they come well / often make it believed that they marry / it is not only that there was no doubt. / Indicated why they left in fear.

(24)

Stein grappled between the social climate of her time being somewhat liberated, acknowledging, "that they see this" (24) while also recognizing that modernity engaged in a backlash against the bolder Victorian times, to which Stein would ask: "[P]lease forgive a mess" (25). So, while Stein lived and wrote with a remarkable boldness and independence, she also could be affected by the world around her. She agreed for some of her more personal material to be published at least twenty years after her death, for example.

For the most part, however, Stein and Toklas both refused to be closeted and bound by imagined, perceived, or substantiated societal prudery. Thus, variations on the word *polite* occur six times in the first six pages of *Pink Melon Joy* to create a clearing for what is to come. Notifying the reader that this poem is "not polite" (*Pink Melon Joy, A Stein Reader*, 281), Stein created a space for forty-one variations on the words *to please* and *pleasure* to then be articulated. By acknowledging, "that there is a politeness" (282), Stein creates the tension and seduction of upcoming taboo desires while powerfully choosing to dwell in and describe pleasure, to smell the rose and, further, to invite us into the room where the rose lay open. She does this similarly throughout *Stanzas in Meditation*, in a tug and pull of silence and speaking, insisting that she is and is not polite, writing, "I refuse I I refuse or do / I do I do I refer to refuse / or what what do I do ... I feel the necessity to do it / partly from need / partly from pride / and partly from ambition" (Part IV, Stanza III) so that "they were not denied their pleasure," and to "say yes ... we will say yes" (Part II, Stanza IV 42–43).

In *Stanzas in Meditation*, Stein wrote:

> Let me listen to me and not to them
> May I be very well and happy
> May I be whichever they can thrive
> Or just may they not.
> (Original version from the original
>   manuscript as cited in "Notes,"
>   *Stanzas in Meditation*, 8)

I am addicted to this stanza because it holds agency, action and non-attachment in a ridiculously perfect and beautiful poetic form. To add, this stanza is Stein's ultimate "fuck you" to fear and constraint. This stanza succinctly epitomizes Stein's entire life: from her personal choices to her impressive oeuvre. This short passage perfectly expresses the foundation of Stein's philosophy and way of being in the world. Stein was a woman who (very early on) recognized what many human beings struggle a lifetime to comprehend: that it was *up to her* to listen to her inner guidance, *and from there* to create her life as happy, fulfilled, and powerful *regardless* of what other people think. Each poem she wrote, each book published, and each artist she supported was undertaken from this location of taking responsibility for her own self-acceptance, pleasing, and thriving, which resulted in her life and work being one of astounding generosity, inspiration, and aliveness. This stanza holds the gift of self-love and respect and serves as *an invitation* to live our lives from a position of responsibility and freedom over our thoughts, actions, and choices, to live by our own inner compass, regardless of any external circumstances. She gives us permission to thrive, to be well and happy, just as we are. Rather than acquiesce to what others may think or want, and thus be at the affect of life, Stein's philosophy was to look within, to "listen" and act from that internal place of knowing. Further, she lovingly undertook listening *for and to* others. She writes, "should there be a call there would be a voice" (*Tender Buttons, Selected Writings*, 504). The voice and this place of thriving exist where "anything is righteous" in "cadences, real cadences" where the diversity of "all accounts" (504) are intimately shared.

One of those internal places of knowing shows up where Stein worked to challenge defining "true" sexualities, desires, and practices that would have (perceived) societal norms, and binaries frame who and what any person may be: all women are ..., all men are ..., all butches are ..., all queers are ..., and so forth. For example the husband/wife, butch/femme, boi/girl, top/dominant and bottom/submissive roles or ways of being can lead to specific and predefined assumptions regarding behaviours, preferences, and modes of conduct. While these roles can be incredibly empowering, fun, and healing, they can also prove limiting, in affording people—regardless of their sexual or gender identity—much shift or play within their identity. As my Introduction demonstrates, mainstream North American society and culture put a great deal of emphasis on the consistency of identity and the ease of the familiar that it brings; yet, all the while, sexual and gender variants and theorists speak and live an identity and sexual politics, as Stein did, that voice dissent to many of these set expectations. While there are very real, tangible, and productive reasons for celebrating the characteristics that make up these roles and identities, this chapter and book work to *transgress* these boundaries *while still allowing* a strong sense of role or identity. To be as "we may thrive" becomes the chosen performance of gender, sexual, and identity freedom advocates.

When looking at the letters between Stein and Toklas we can thus begin to ask fun and opening questions such as: How did Stein's role of being a husband benefit and work for her? How freeing was it for her to then switch and play with being the "wife" who would go on her knees for her lover? How did Toklas's being a wife contribute to her sense of being a top? How did the marriage and love-ship of these two women allow for a body of work that lays open the switching, sexualized, and loved body and domestic life? If we allow some room to challenge the fixation our culture has with policing roles and identities (as outlined in my Introduction) we could choose to feel safe, rather than disoriented, as we dwell in the incredible galaxy of *not* knowing, where *multiple* truths and possibilities exist by embracing the complexities of their play with the language of sex, sexuality, identities, and roles. Consider this playful gender switching, and the room it leaves for choice, from *Tender Buttons*:

> [T]he sister was not a mister. Was this a surprise. It was. The conclusion came when there was no arrangement. All the time that there was a question there was a decision. Replacing a casual acquaintance with an ordinary daughter does not make a son.
>
> (500)

For creating space to play and share identities really is at issue here. Amber Hollibaugh, in her book *My Dangerous Desires: A Queer Girl Dreaming Her Way Home*, asserts

> erotic identities are not just behaviors or individual sexual actions; they reflect a much broader fabric that is the weave and crux of our very personhood; a way of mediating and measuring all that we experience, all that we can interpret through the language of our bodies … erotic identity is not simply a specific activity or "lifestyle.
>
> (258)

For many, their identities as dominants or submissives, switches or egalitarian lovers, carry over into the realms *outside* of the sexual. And so it is with this chapter: I am fascinated with the crossover of the personal/memoir with/in the textual as Stein and all my authors in this book reveal. According to Hollibaugh, "[Q]ueerness, our desire, our otherness, *cannot be removed from place and context*. We are queer at the tables we eat at and at the tables we serve. Queer: femme, butch, transsexual, bisexual, wanting. Needed. Necessary." (268, italics mine).

How pink is your melon, Joy?

Ulla E. Dydo, Stein scholar and editor of the selected works collection, *A Stein Reader: Gertrude Stein* writes that *Pink Melon Joy* is "the most lighthearted, humorous, and erotic work" of the early World War I period; further, she invites the reader to consider how *Pink Melon Joy* "absorbs events and objects into its verbal process" and that "Stein's verbal games are not fictions *but always start from facts*" (*A Stein Reader*, 280, italics mine). Similarly, Stein's *Stanzas in Mediation* (written in 1932 and published after her death) is also an erotic set of meditations on perceptions of facts. Stein would say the long poem was an "exactitude of abstract thought" achieved in a disembodied form (cited in Dydo, *A Stein Reader*, 569). The work actually reads as a meditation or prayer. It should not come as a surprise that the book's title was also written to be *Meditations in Stanzas* (568). The stanzas exist as meditations on the body, desire, lesbian sex, and love. The first part of much of Stein's erotic work, and these texts are no exceptions, is almost entirely made up of answering questions, thus inviting a new understanding of sexually fluid, switching, variant sex: she explains that which *seems* different really isn't.

To add some complication to the erotic narrative, Toklas, in her editing process, removed almost every word "may" from the stanzas, replacing *may* with *can*, which is hardly as evocative. The reason? In the same year of typing the *Stanzas in Meditation* manuscript Toklas read Stein's first autobiographical novel, from 1903, *Q. E. D.* Therein, Toklas discovered Stein's triangular love affair with a woman named May Bookstaver (and Mabel Haynes), which Stein had failed to mention to Toklas. While *Q. E. D.* wasn't published until after Stein's death, the manuscript shows Stein's revisions of replacing all of the "mays" with "can," and a second manuscript drafted by Toklas. Dydo's research adds that in addition to Toklas's "purge" of the stanzas, she also "destroyed or made Stein destroy May Bookstaver's letters" (568–569). The word *may* thus evokes the lesbian love triangle, the name of a woman, and Stein's previous lover as well as the season and last month of spring, named after the Greek Goddess Maia (a Goddess of fertility), which begins with the holiday of May Day and the tradition of dancing around the maypole. May can also refer to a distinguishing feature of Stein's work—"one's bloom or prime" (*New Oxford American Dictionary*)—and the notion of conceivability, possibility, permission, and a wish or hope for something; whereas the word *can*, while similar in evoking possibility and opportunity, denotes capability more than a permission.

The underlying themes of pleasure and desire and the erotic nature of the stanzas, despite or due to, abstract language choices comparable to *Tender Buttons* and other works of Stein, stand out powerfully. So while Douglas Messerli's reading concludes that the *Stanzas* are not "primarily about her personal relationships" (Notes on the Text, *Stanzas in Meditation*, 10), it is the author herself who *tells us* in Part IV that "this is an autobiography in two instances" (Stanza XIII). Stein also cautions that you / "they are very likely not to be / reminded that it is more than ever necessary" additionally, "they should never be surprised at any one time / at just what they have been given ... they can easily indulge in the fragrance" (Part II, Stanza I, 38). Are you ready to be surprised, yet not surprised, by what you are being given: a sexing of Stein? According to Stein, the reader consensually accepts something as they pick up the text: "pleasure" (Part II, Stanza II, 38).

Beginning with the title of the work, *Pink Melon Joy*, Stein invites us to participate, voyeuristically, in just how joyful the act of making the melon pink is. The melon: round, soft, fleshy and like one of the pleasure centres of a woman's body: the clitoris. The outer skin of the labia, which house and hold the clitoris safely so its delicate skin does not bruise, protects the clitoris. The g-spot is Stein's other melon, with the walls of the vagina, the pelvis, and layer of skin the protective shell that can be easily bruised, yet keeps the sweet, fleshy inside so safe until one is given permission to open and penetrate through the outer shell. Stein's melon is a woman's sexual pleasure zone, which Stein is absolutely fascinated with making, witnessing, and describing how they are made pink. To be made pink, they must be touched, pleased, and brought into a state of in-joy.

As with all of Stein's writing the reader can easily switch the pronouns and play with the gender of the narrator and subject. Gender switching is recurrent, with subjects inhabiting both female and male identities and roles: Stein was both husband *and* wife to Alice, so there is no reason to confine oneself to a gynocentric reading of Stein's work. Stein was a lesbian *and* her writing demonstrates a gender and sexual switching and fluidity that was highly exploratory; she uses both receptive and feminine as well as phallic and penetrative imagery often, for example. Thus, one could easily say that her *pink melon* is variant: the delicate pink head of her "can be can be men" (Part IV, Stanza VII, 107) male/masculine gendered, a mental or affixed penis, protected by the shaft, which grows more pink and redder with each joyful touch, and the tender prostate gland, which is similar to the g-spot in that one has to "hunt" to find in order to please, protected by the walls of the anus. Pink melons equate to joy in this text, and are no doubt for many feminine, while also we can gender and queer them any way we wish!

A further switching occurs, and it's a switching that occurs in all of Stein's work that I will be discussing, between the role of the narrator and subject. The "I," "you," "they," and "me" are not always clear and switch often, causing an ambiguity and haziness to exist between the speaking voices. Cyrena N. Pondrom notes, "[I]nformation is withheld for clear attribution of speaking parts to be made, and the resulting imprecision mimics both shifting roles and a dissolution of ego boundaries between the two lovers" ("Introduction," *Geography and Plays*, xlvii). This shifting and dissolution of subject positions is key in allowing for the switching of roles to be articulated and explored. Switching within roles, identities, and sexual top/bottoming is very much about the melting of the ego; not only is intimacy birthed, but the pleasures reaped from switching are allowed space to be in action when any protective ego stands back. Similar switching occurs within the texts of other authors I explore in Chapters 3 and 4, particularly Jeanette Winterson and Anne Carson.

Stein's *Pink Melon Joy* is a long poem that is divided into three parts and consists of many small segments that have subheadings. I would like to note the poetic flow and evocative content of the subheadings, which read like a poem in themselves. Citing just a few: "Exchange in Bicycles," "Fourteen Days," and "Pillow" are followed by "That's Right," "Very Likely," "I don't care what she mentions," "I did do it then," "Oh dear," "That's a picture." She continues with the peaceful "All recovering" making way for "This is it mentioning," "Feeling Mounting," "What is the matter with it," and, of course, the act of being "Willing" to the invitation to "Come in." "Polite," "Absolutely," "I Come to Say," "Come in," "I meant to stay" and "put in in," which are followed by the BDSM-esque "Not any more begging" "please be dark," "Anything," "Harnessing on or another. Harnessing another." The lover then shares "I went Faster" with "Two hands." The last subheading of the poem "I cannot count" can reference the number of orgasms throughout the entire poem or the number and myriad of ways she loves her lover; "I cannot count" is ever so sweetly followed by the last lines "Would you have another. What. Kiss." These last lines evoke a depth of longing, and intimacy. A commitment, happiness, connection, and communication between the lovers complete the poem.

Stein writes early on that for "fourteen days" she "was aching" (*Pink Melon Joy* in *A Stein Reader*, 282). This Stein, who was seemingly "meant to be closeted," boldly uses the first person "I" to describe her hunger: "I was aching," she writes, when "I saw all the rose." The botanist defin-ition of "Labium" refers to "the lower lip of the flower of a plant" (*New Oxford American Dictionary*). Flowers are the reproductive/sex organs of a flowering plant, and so a woman's sex and sexuality have often been represented as a flower in literature, art, and song. Such is the case with Stein's poem: in a flower, the sex organs are contained *within* the flower and so too the *rose* of *Pink Melon Joy* has labia petals, which can be spread open, those inner and outer folds of the vulva opening and closing around the clitoris and vaginal opening. Apply this image to where the rose and other flowers appear throughout Stein's work and gardens of colourful sen-suality and pleasure explode all over the page.

Metaphors of the rose—used for a woman's name as well as the flower—come into play as Stein sees "all the rose": love is a red, red rose after all and it was Stein who wrote "Rose is a rose is a rose is a rose," in the 1913 erotic poem *Sacred Emily* (later published in *Geography and Plays*, 187; the line repeating in homogeneous forms in *Operas and Plays* and in many other works). Stein's rose is a "loveliness extreme … sweeter than peaches and pears and cream" (187). Stein is so enamoured with the gorgeousness of her created turn of phrase that the wax seal she used to seal the back of her letters bore the saying "A rose is a rose …" (*Correspondence: Pablo Picasso Gertrude Stein*, 308). To add, she had the phrase written on china, on her ceiling, and on linens. Embossed printed, and embroidered sex. Sex, a woman's genitals, desire: all over the home, integrated into a life and the sharing of that life.

In her Introductory essay to the 1993 edition of *Geography and Plays,* Pondrom does a beautiful job of deconstructing the sexual and intimate layerings of Stein's *Sacred Emily*.[5] Pondrom supports the sexual unmasking and deconstruction of Stein's work. She notes, for example that previous

Stein scholars have drawn attention to the fact that when reading "a rose is a rose is a rose" quickly, the repetition can read and sound like the word *eros*, so "a Rose = eros = eros = eros" ("Introduction," *Geography and Plays*, xlv); thus, a rose becomes equated to sexual love and desire.[6]

On Stein's narrative strategy, and what is underneath it, Pondrom writes that

> extreme hermeticism ... provided Stein with the opportunity to write of very private matters without public outcry, and several of these poems celebrate lesbian erotic joy ... Critics ... have argued that the hermetic style is motivated by the desire to code lesbian erotic experience ... [Stein's work] is a sustained effort to speak female experience, finding methods that lie beyond or outside the male-centered symbolic order, the order of traditional language ... her effort is not to recuperate herself to the (patriarchal) world, but to reconstitute and revalue that world—to "act," as she commanded in *Tender Buttons*, "so that there is no use in a centre."
>
> (xliii)

Coded or not, the majority of Stein's poetic narratives weave together female identity, lesbian-love making, and female love relationships (xlvi). In *Stanza in Meditation* the exploratory garden is diverse, and flowers appear repeatedly: "only one dahlia" and "she has been very kind about pansies," while of course, "a rose which grows" is the dominant flower, "after all it astonishes even me" (Part IV, Stanza XXIV, 133). How the rose becomes redder than red is what *Pink Melon Joy* dwells in. The intimacy that comes when a woman's pleasure is unfolding, each petal a layer of pleasure, unfolding to its own rhythm, becoming the entire rose: the lover fully open, receptive, each petal soft, delicate, vulnerable. The rose reveals its beauty and unique scent ever so slowly as it opens. Stein's "aching" holds suspense and craving—it is the kind of yearning for pleasure that makes any lover anticipate the layers that intimacy and sex bring, as the rose eventually opens and flowers, wave upon wave of opening of pleasure.

Stein instructs us how and where we are to behold the rose: "all of it on leather" (*Pink Melon Joy*, ASR, 282). We can now see skin on skin, the rose being sweet smelling, the leather being both a luxurious animal product, soft and subtle, and ... an important accoutrement in BDSM. Those who have gravitated toward using leather for sensual pleasure date back centuries; leather objects and textures can be seen from the earliest erotic photography and published pornography to contemporary 21st-century haute couture fashion and marketing strategies that allude to locations for queer and/or sexually deviancy to be celebrated via BDSM play. In fact, the language and art of BDSM and taboo pornography, such as flagellation and role-play, were most pronounced in Victorian times. Pornographic books such as *My Secret Life* and *The Pearl* would be good examples of sexual deviancy. And so the bold, determined Stein takes on what many of us are inclined to do, yet perhaps unable:

> She can think the thought that they will wish
> And they will hold that they will spell anguish
> And they will not be thought perverse
> If they angle and the will or which they wish as verse
> And so may be they can be asked
> That they will answer this.
> Let me see let me go let me be not only determined
> But for which they will mind
> That they are often as inclined
> To have them add more than they could ...
> They will be left to be determined
> As much as if they pleased they pleased
>   (*Stanzas in Meditation,* Part II, Stanza XIX, 62*)*

This is an autobiography in two instances.

(Stanzas in Meditation, Part IV, Stanza XII, 114)

And so variations on perversity and verse, which leave us empowered, "determined," and "pleased," look like the words *present, horses, harnessing, resist, surprise, astonishment, satisfaction, believe, miracle, toys,* and *spread* that are repeated throughout *Pink Melon Joy,* while in *Stanzas in Meditation* we have variations on the words *pleasure, please, I do, like it, pink, satisfy, cows, fasten, will, willing, would, wish, may* (changed to *can* in the revised text), and *accept.* It is no coincidence that Stein's word choices occurred equally as often in modern erotica and subculture conversations and writing[7]: discussing sex with an openness, freedom, and honestly that plays with taboos and experimentation is something Stein was very adept at. This is a Stein who wants the lover of her narrative to "please be restless" (*Pink Melon Joy, ASR,* 305); a Stein "willing for needing" (*Stanzas in Meditation,* Part I, Stanza XV, 35); a Stein who writes of "harnessing on ... harnessing another. Harnessing on or another is a great success." Toys are harnessed, lovemaking is harnessed, and lesbian sex is harnessed. Stein alludes to a dominant and submissive BDSM context when she writes: "I offer. I offer. I offer. I do need it" (*Pink Melon Joy, ASR,* 301). A distinctive pleasure seeking is echoed, rhythmically, as is submission and the giving over to a dominant lover. Stein writes, "I meant to be told," which illustrates an engagement in verbal dominant/submissive play (301). She is "beautifully rich" as "harnessing is a great success ... a result. A repetition ... an offspring" has been produced (301). The lover proves just how much she "needs it" when she shares: "I knew I wanted four hundred" (301).

Stein asserts that she *will* "speak of it ... in the retracting glory" (282). Few women writers have written so intently on the sexually giving *and* receiving self. What is the *it* she is speaking? Might *it* refer to the rose or the pink melon? Or might *it* have something to do with one of Stein's most written of subjects: Toklas producing a cow? In Stein's writing, endings and completions repeatedly look like a wife having a cow (more on "having a cow" will be discussed later when looking at *Baby Precious Always Shines* and *A Book Concluding With As A Wife Has A Cow: A Love Story*). What is retracting? Retracting means to pull in, to draw back, to withdraw. The Latin origin of the word *retract* means "drawn back" and derives from the verb "retrahere" from "re" (meaning "back") and "trahere" (meaning "drag") (*New Oxford American Dictionary*). Therefore, to retract is to drag back. What is dragging back from the rose on leather? That which brings the rose and pink melon joy? Stein's phallus? Alice's? The poem narrates that whatever is retracting *brings joy*.

Stein asserts that in the retracting glory "there is more choice" than that which is proscribed: "there is what is threaded." Leather culture is very much grounded in play, choice, and variation. To thread is for something to run through, or "on the inside of a cylindrical hole, to allow to parts to be screwed together." To thread is to "pass through something into the required position for use" and to "move carefully or skilfully in and out of obstacles" (*New Oxford American Dictionary*). To thread in and out is to switch. To thread implies a running through the centre. A body is threaded through the centre in many sexual acts, when receiving penetration being one. And yet Stein also counsels us to "act so that there is no use in a centre," which implies that any threading "spread" and be felt through and into the entire body to bring us into a space of "nothing" (*Tender Buttons, Selected Writings,* 498).[8] A switch "acts as if there is no use in a centre." To thread can evoke pushing, poking, weaving, to inch, to pass through and into. The switch weaves and threads what is threaded. No coincidence, similar wording echoes through Stein's work: in *Tender Buttons'* "Objects" she writes: "I hope she has her cow. Bidding a wedding, widening received threading, little leading mention nothing" (474). Treading, threading, widening, having her cow. Stein's switchy narratives continually weave and thread to create a new, unpredictable way of being; what is threaded is woven, complicated by choice, and is a glory to be present to, to speak of and share. In *Stanzas in Meditation*, she writes:

There has been a beginning of begun.
They can be caused.
They can be caused to share.
Or they can be caused to share ...
It gave me pleasure and fear
But we are here
And so far further

It has just come to me now to mention this
And I do it
(Part V, Stanza LII, 190–191)

Penetration and describing the genitals can also take on a poetic language that carries a pornographic boldness. She writes that when "they were alone ... little pleasures are seeking after not exactly a box then comes the time for drilling" (*Pink Melon Joy, ASR*, 281). The statement "little pleasures are seeking" offers a welcome invitation to the reader for it allows desire to be pleased and room to be made for it. We are left seeking after something with Stein. Is she seeking "not exactly a box," or does the "drilling" occur "after" the boxing? Is "box" a verb, and action here? A penetrative one unto the box itself? The predisposition to vulgarize the word "box" can be offset here: boxes are containers, they have sides, and their contents are safe, enclosed, protected. Boxes hold secrets and hidden spaces. The term *box* can also refer to "any of a number of trees that have similar wood or foliage" (*New Oxford American Dictionary*), and, seeing as both women have similar foliage to their trees of life, this could work nicely with the sentence that follows "not up Really believe me it is sheltered oaks that matter;" a woman's genitals sheltered, boxed, her genitals not up, roots nestled inward, foliage on top, the box, the oak tree, has its acorn (the clitoris) sweetly hanging, but protected. Or might Stein's narrator be voyeuristically witnessing a drilling and be left to relish in her own "sheltered oak"? The familiar proverb "mighty oaks from little acorns grow" alludes to the overall impressiveness of the human body, desire, love, sex, and intimacy over time: the little acorn a "little pleasure seeking." Sweetly, she ends with describing the subject and the subject's subject, as "it is they who are sighing it really is." A pause is then followed by "not when I hear it," which can be read as an ironic playfulness because, really, "it really is." Further readings could have the difference allude to the meanings we add that support different points of view: the same sex sounds sounding and resonating very differently to different people.

In a room with the smells, touch, and instruments of leather Stein adds that in this choice, in this threading, "I don't mean permitting" (*Pink Melon Joy, ASR*, 282). There is a taking of her lover, a dominance and submission; a fetishizing to her taking and watching *all the rose*, lush, open, and blooming, on the sweet, robust-smelling, soft skin of an animal. Stein's romantic and adoring self drips sexiness from every unpredictable turn of phrase as she (re)creates, writes, and switches in her roles, genders, sexual identities, and desires. Stein's seeking "harnessing" and "kneeling" actions may seem benign: they are not; we are a witness to their sex, time and time again. We are a voyeur to both women in the active "to be" state of being pleased and pleasing (*Idem the Same, ASR*, 378). Stein is fixated on desire, roles, sex, orgasm, fetish objects, and various modes of pleasure.

The language of BDSM is further evident in Stein's repetition around begging and asking: submission and dominance play out with the lover saying she is "Willing. Willing, willing. Willing willing ... it was deepened" (286). Willing to do what her lover wants, these lovers are willing to take what is deep to a point of it being "deepened." Being "willing" pulls for the notion of pleasing her lover by being "willing," of pleasing her Master, Mistress, wife, or dominant, or of pleasing the submissive, making sure she is taken care of and enjoys the deepening. Later she will instruct, "leave it in there for me. Leave it in an especial place." She tells her lover not to "make that face. Show it by the indication." For, she writes, she means to put a "spell" on her lover, asking/telling her: "believe me." (288). When she writes, "I am not pleased. I am not satisfied and pleased. I am not pleased and certainly I am not more pleased," she answers with: "I am so repressed and I can state it. I can say" (286). And she does say, and this communication allows for different actions to produce different results. The "I" subject (lover? writer?) becomes "satisfied" even as the "we" neglect their life by "not resting" (288). In a lovely turn of phrase, Stein asks "shall it be continuous the liberty of sobriety ... little tremors ... with a wide piano. Come. Neglecting cherishing says shall I mistake pleases. In mistakes there is a salutary secretion. What. I said it" (288). With a clear-headedness the "little tremors ... with a wide piano" of penetration are felt, the beneficial orgasm and release of fluids are made, and the subject shares: "I shook." The we and I playful here, the mistakes not mistakes but pleasures brought about by a spell that has one believe in love and trust.

I seek, as Stein did, to be reminded that sex and sexuality can be unconstrained and open: "She reminded me that I was as ready as not and I said I will not say that I preferred service to opposition. I will not say what or what is not a pleasure" (from "To Remind," in *A Book Concluding With As A Wife Has A Cow: A Love Story*, cited in *A Stein Reader*, 459). Stein explores "service to opposition," submission to dominance, being open to what will be pleasurable, switching on a pleasure spectrum. A switch does not have to choose between service and resistance, service and defiance, servicing and topping. The loving act of allowing and reminding the other to engage in the fluidity of choice and of switching—in the present moment of desire rather than acting out a scripted role or scene—is clear in this passage. "She reminded me" is such a loving holding onto the unknown: you are ready, as ready as you ever will be. This is a loving act of expressing that there is no need for perfection or waiting; there is no need for postponing pleasure and play. There is no need to know anything for certain: who is going to do what, or who is going to be pleased, how.

"Anything can astonish a citizen ... I believe in the best"

(*Pink Melon Joy, A Stein Reader*, 303)

The subheading "Feeling Mounting" describes more of the doing: "[S]he was standing filling with a pepper thing and she had a collar not on her head but because she was shining. She was shining with gloves." The retracting of earlier might be any kind of instrument inserted for pleasure, a "pepper thing," and also, a hand or hands. The fetishization of objects and BDSM themes reverberate throughout Stein's work. Here it is a "pepper thing" filling her lover and the "collar" around her neck (not *on* her head, but nearby, on her neck) and heightening the sensory pleasure that contributes to her shining. The gloves are shining from pleasing her, she is shining from being pleased, and here Stein openly and honestly shares: "this is a new destination ... I never was surprised before" (286).

Lesbian sex makes especial use of the hands, and when practicing safe sex, gloves are used. Leather gloves are often an accessible BDSM tool to utilize. Gloves appear later in the poem when an attentive, caring lover, post orgasm, details the post sex scene:

> [L]ittle dove little love I am loving you with much more love ... I saw an extraordinary mixture. By nearly leaving out gloves and washing them ... and towels, by nearly leaving out towels and all of it by way of reminding every one of every time, by leaving out invitations ... Not with the carelessness ... I meant to do it.
>
> (297)

Not only do we have description of orgasm and ejaculation as "an extraordinary mixture," but we have the detailing of what was used to bring it about (gloved hands) and catch it (towels). Visitors to the home are "nearly" invited to be exhibitionists, with one of them leaving the accessories of their sex "out." This invitation by way of seeing the room almost littered, carelessness not difficult in the post orgasmic state, but, possibly with intention as she "meant to do it."

Later, "two hands" (303) are used after "harnessing on or another is a great success" (301). Harnessed up, the lovers and their hands are compared to horses. Stein writes, "I believe in two horses ... it was a surprise then I said I would stand. It was pleasant. It was not gentle. It was black and hopeful." We watch the lover standing and being filled with two hands the size of horses, or is it what is harnessed that is the size of a horse? Are the lovers the two horses or are there two "horses" being harnessed? The description reads that it is "principally very shapely." Might a dildo be the harness? Instruments of pleasure recur thematically in Stein's work and are always worded in code, allowing for us to imagine *all* the possibilities that would "surprise" both her and us as readers. Is she standing for comfort while being penetrated, or is she alluding to the surprise of being able to stand after such a successful session of being harnessed? Lest disbelief or prudery step in, she writes, "anything can astonish" but "I believe in the best" (303). The best equates to whatever makes these lovers happy, pleased, and surprised. The "best" is having had a "great success" after "harnessing;" the best is when a lover tops from the bottom, speaking "I offer. I offer. I offer" myself to your harnessing because "I do need it" (301).

The lover is instructed to "go slowly and carefully and love your dearest" and also "to place a cloth ... where I have hotter water, to place paper where I have hotter water" to catch the orgasm and ejaculate that is sure to come (289). She then asks, "shall I be splendid." The answer is a resounding yes as the lover brought to a place of uttering "Baby mine baby mine I am learning ... to be sent baby mine baby mine" (289). The lover is the baby, the ejaculate is the baby, and the lover is learning to explore and birth her baby; to add, there is a possessive ownership over baby, baby is "mine," which illustrates a giving, a receiving, a holding of that which a lover can give to her lover: her body, her ejaculate, her orgasm. The narrative then moves to more horse and BDSM imagery and language as Stein describes: "this is a place to water horses" (289). The horses thirsty, the paper or cloth laid down, the lover can then relax into "I like to be excellently seized" whereupon they switch in their giving and receiving so that she now says, "I like to be excellently seizing / north north I went around and went in that minute" (289), and so we have the tender button in the north, which likes to be touched round and round, and then, within a minute, the penetration. The lover begins to "like to be excellently searching" then (290).

In *Stanzas in Meditation* Stein shares "that is why a like in it with it / Which they gay which they gay / But not only just the same" (Part III, Stanza VIII, 77). The substitution of "a" for "I" a clever way to offset the "gay" and the bold liking "in it" and "it in," but hardly convincing to her audience who reads her erotic coding. The remainder of the stanza explains her use of subtleties and language, her choice to not name in an effort to create an expansiveness that a more specific referent could not offer; they are, after all "not only" gay—our sexualities being just *one part* of an identity and lifestyle, many switches dwelling in varied and various complex identities and preferences that fuel other aspects of an identity—while at the same time, the poem goes on to celebrate their touching, noting they are not the first to utter tender-hearted sentiments and commitments such as: "tell me darling tell me true / Am I all the world to you" (Part III, Stanza VII, 77).

Which returns us to a narrative of talking, darkly, dirtily, with her lover, the entire poem filled with word play. The black and beautiful could also be the dark beautiful recesses the hand or dildo enters, which could be the vagina or the anus as Stein writes of "the description of mud" (*Pink Melon Joy*, ASR, 303) as well as the mental, physical, and emotional space that opens up in the body and mind when sexuality is pushed beyond any limit previously known. In *Stanzas in Meditation* she asks us to "remember this once they knew that the way to give / was to go more than they went / for which they meant immediately faster / it is always what they will out loud" (Part II, Stanza VII, 49). Stein is asking us to meditate on stasis, on going further in how they love, in what they will, to go faster and to say it out loud, to remember how to give. Giving and receiving pleasure, and remembering to give, repeat over and over again in the *Stanzas in Meditation,* as this passage illustrates:

And if they offer you something and you accept
Will they give it to you and will it give you pleasure
And if after a while they give you more
Will you be pleased to have more
Which in a way is not even a question
Because after all they like it very much
(Part II, Stanza II, 39)

The best would include "rubbers" bought with mindfulness: "the mischief lies in getting the wrong ones. They are remarkable in many shapes and when you ask for hurrying see that you get it" (*Pink Melon Joy, ASR,* 304). Unhurried, these lovers have not only chosen each other with great consideration—Stein was thirty-six and Toklas was thirty-three when they moved in together—but they also chose their sexual aides and accouterments without hurry, making sure to get the right shapes. Stein expands into diversity when she writes, "there are plenty of rubber wheels of a kind," implying that there are diverse degree of variancies on the spectrum; adding that the "many shapes" of "a kind" are to be considered fully, lest mischief result. A more specific reading would have this passage acknowledging the many variancies *within subcultures* (such as theirs), which might include varying switch and sex practices and preferences among lesbians and homosexual men, for example. As Stein so often wrote in perverse verse, there is no doubt she would turn a nod of inclusion *while at the same time* writing of the full, complete, and sexy nature and composition within the circle of deviance that she and others of her time revelled in.

This new destination is variant, switching sex that surprises and delights Stein's narrator with each new turn of joy-seeking. So while much of *Pink Melon Joy* occurs without a clear referent as to who is pleasing whom, consider one instance of the writer speaking Alice's name and the gender switch that happens in this flow of subheadings (noted in italics) with first lines:

I cannot mention what I have. I have. Guess it. I have a real sight. This is so critical. Alice. *Put it in.* Put it in … I wish I was a flower … *That is.* That is astonishing. *Mother.* I meant it … I said whisper. *Anyway pink melon or joy.* Is that the same. Pink melon and enjoy. Pink melon by joy. Is that in him. Is that in. Positive.

(293–294)

Not only do we have Stein asking Alice to "guess" what she has (a phallus, a "pepper thing," a pink melon?), which is a "real sight," which implies a largeness, we witness her asking to "put it in" in repeating, submissive, begging-like intonations. The penetration, the wanting, the *begging* to "put it in" proves so astonishing that she calls out "Mother." If we read just the subheadings we read: "Put it in. That is. Mother. Brutes. Anyway pink melon or joy" (294). Mother resonates a call out to mercy, and comes directly after "that is astonishing" (294). Mother attunes the sacred Mother, a Mother who tends to and nourishes her "baby" in an endless giving, a Mother who gives birth to babies. *Baby* being code for Stein and Toklas's orgasms, *Mother* evokes the bringer of pleasure here. The pleasure has the lover encouragingly say, "pink melon and enjoy / pink melon by joy," and then a gender switch occurs when the pleaser, Alice, asks "is that in him. Is that in" (294), which not only allows Stein to dwell in her he but also to dwell in being submissive while being pleased. The lover being asked provides a space for dialogue and communication for their pleasure and pleasing. Stein concludes the stanza by answering yes, "positive," it's in (294).

Stein continues to tease out the dominance and submission between the two lovers. While not content to have "any more begging" she simply asks— or is she instructing—to "please have it ready" (295)? The *Stanzas* see that "all can be glory can be can be glory" in a kneeling, after which they were "fortunate ... after it is all given away ... and so it is ... come" (*Stanzas in Meditation,* Part I, Stanza VI, 21). Orgasm is a gift, possible ejaculation something fortunate to give to her lover, something that is glorious: magnificent, praise-worthy, holy. Pleasure through multiple orgasms is "theirs to undo/ getting it better more than once alike / for which fortune favours me" (Part I, Stanza VI, 21). She continues with "all who come will will come or come to be / come to be coming that is in and see / see elegantly not without enjoin ... shall we be there I wonder now" (Part I, Stanza VI, 22). To dwell in enjoining, wonder, the repetition of the action *to come,* the *glory* of the being and doing follows with the remarkable pondering and switching occurrence of if "every one knowing this could know then of this pleased / she can be thought in when in which it is in mine a pleasure" (Part I, Stanza VII, 23).

In the sub-headed section "Hymns," a recurring object appears: the table. She writes, "I have forgotten the height of the table" (*Pink Melon Joy, ASR,* 283), perhaps she forgets due to arresting thoughts or is it that her lover away from the table, now lying on leather in this poem. Stein writing about forgetting the height of the table serves to bring attention to the height. What does it evoke? Why would it be important? The height of a table is only as important as it is used for harnessing and birthing a cow or baby. Hymns sound like "we were right. We meant pale. We were wonderfully shattered. Why are we shattered. Only be an arrest of thought." And yet, she claims, "I don't make it out," suggesting, toying with, reflecting, and perhaps singing: "Hope there. Hope not." (283).

The most evocative reference to the table as a facilitator of pleasure occurs in *Tender Buttons*'s "Objects":

[A] table means does it not my dear it means a whole steadiness. Is it likely that a change ... a table means necessary places and a revision a revision of a little thing it means it does mean that there has been a stand, a stand where it did shake.

(474)

The table is shaking from their revisionary lovemaking, a stand for their romance, "harnessing," and lovemaking, whereas the state will not take a stand for them having marriage. The revision of the word *stand* to evoke standing with and for someone or something is interesting here. A revision of a little thing, the meaning of a table, the angle of penetration, the necessary places broached, the steadiness of a table not only needed, reliable, and trustworthy, but also an erotic piece of furniture once employed in the service of pleasure opens worlds of possible interpretations. The notion that the table will always be looked at as a place to make shake, a place of their lovemaking and sex, turns their room, that table, into a sexual mnemonic.

Act so that there is no use in a centre. A wide action is not a width

(Tender Buttons, Selected Writings, 498)

The Rue de Fleurus contains "Objects," "Food," and "Rooms" that are made up of the tenderness of buttons being looked at, eaten, explored, written, lived in; the rooms of these two lovers are the boxes, the containers for purses that are "hardly seen," tables that shake, and tender buttons that show "shudders" and "spread into nothing" (469, 472–74). For Stein, "the difference is spreading" as she wills and manifests that "she has her cow" through a "widening received threading, little leading mention nothing" (461, 474). Her lover, and we as voyeuristic readers, are led with "little leading" along threaded paths that spread *into nothing*. With tenderness, we are ushered to sit in an open field of mindfulness where we are to "act so that there is no use in a centre" (498). And like every enlightened master teacher, Stein offers us line after line of reasons and riddles as to *why and how* we might want to do this: because "a wide action is not a width" (498). Stein creates this mantra, a mantra of switching, as a way of knowing the serenity of living without a centre that binds us. To "act so that there is no use in a center," knows "the hope," which "necessarily" will "spread into nothing. Spread into nothing" (474, 498). The subject, and we as readers, are asked to give up our centre, what we think we know, to allow "width," and yet "spread into nothing."

Stein's philosophy of action: to "act so that there is no use in a centre. A wide action is not a width" (498) is an essential tenet of my theory and of switching. "To act so that there is no use in a centre," knows that action, not belief, creates a new realm of being and of what's possible. To know, to allow, and then to act as if "there is no use in a centre" creates the decentring necessary to create a space where gender and sexual variancy and fluidity can breathe; it creates the space where a victory in identity and self can be experienced and breathed. Stein continues to write that "the hope" of this action is that, "necessarily," there will be the experience to "spread into nothing. Spread into nothing" (474). By acting as if "there is no use in a centre," by *giving up* her centre, a new hope springs forth: a hope, which is so free it "spreads into nothing." Nothing is not a scary, isolating place, it is the location of everything and freedom, it is the nothing by which anything can be created, free from constraining past-based frameworks or imagining. Creating out of something "is not a width." Creating out of and from nothing is the space of transformation. Nothing is the space of freedom and pure creation. Contrast is absent in the space of nothing. This is why the mantra "a wide action is not a width" comes after the teaching to "act as if there is no use in a centre," because it is a new, creation-based future she is pulling the reader into.

Do not think that "a wide action is a width," she writes. A wide action is a wide action; a width is a width. The clarity of this teaching and practice occurs as a singular action: do the action, practice the action, and do not get muddy with it. The action is: "act so that there is no use in a centre." Just do that, she seems to tell us. Practice that: *acting as if* there is no use in a centre. In this space, everything opens up into connected nothingness. Stein offers a way to know this expansion when she instructs that "the difference is spreading" (461). A spiritual transcendence seems possible; no overthinking or analysis is needed. The difference between thriving and surviving, between happiness and unhappiness, is in the spreading; creating outside of a centre, out of nothing and in the present, rather than attempting to create within a centre of past-based concepts, thoughts, or actions, creates something new and life-giving. The difference in getting Stein as a transformative writer is in allowing the spread into nothing. Spread wide, she says, that is the difference, that is the access to freedom.

Like her *Stanzas in Meditation* and much of her work, these lines can be read as meditations: thoughts meant for contemplation, deliberation, rumination, study, healing, and prayer. They are sutras: threads by which teachers can then extrapolate and expand in the effort of furthering the initial teachings and practice. The practice of meditating on the idea and the action of "acting so that there is no use in a center" involves acting so that there is no use in any structure that might bind the heart or mind. This is her practice and offering to us as teacher. One only has to listen to the recordings of Stein reading her work to understand that meditation and mantra are at work and play.

The queer temporality of Stein evokes a present-tense narrative rendering of "the continuous present," and any meaning we may make of it, to "spread into nothing" (From "A Little Bit of a Tumbler," *Tender Buttons, Selected Writings*, 472). In the section sub-headed "Pauline," Stein shares that "a little called anything shows shudders" (473). Any movement, any "difference," any "spreading," any action, any practice of "acting so that there is no use in a center" "shows shudders." The wording of "a little called anything" in showing "shudders" resonates the language and conversational dialogue that Stein writes as happening in sex: the naming, the speaking of that which shudders. The invitation to name is itself a generous and courageous act. Calling it "anything" leaves the naming up to the individual or the lovers. Calling it "little" evokes a delicacy, tenderness and even a safety and enclosed place. Calling it "little" also evokes the contrast: What is filling up little to make it shudder? Something big? This is the dialogue of little and of baby, of husband and wifie, of "Aunt Pauline" ending the erotic poem *Lifting Belly* with the song of orgasm. Showing shudders anew, the shudders of orgasm or thought, the shudders of releasing past patterns and ways of being, the shudders of words that resonate aliveness and spark, the shudders of *each movement toward a decentred* way of walking and being in the world, the spreading into the nothingness of the universe, the tenderness of each unbuttoning is Stein's orgasm.

The shuddering, spreading, freedom-loving place that Stein speaks and writes about contains urgency. At the individual and collective level, there is no time to waste: sooner rather than later is when action is required. Do not postpone freedom, love, joy, she writes:

> [T]he sooner there is jerking, the sooner freshness is tender, the sooner the round it is not round the sooner it is withdrawn in cutting, the sooner the measure means service, the sooner there is chinking ... the sooner there is none do her, the sooner there is no choice, the sooner there is a gloom freer, the same sooner and more sooner, there is no error in hurry and in pressure and in opposition to consideration.
>
> (481)

Stein carves out a large space, a large field, with each of her texts wherein we can examine the roads that lead to happiness. Her invitation is one that involves a great deal of open-mindedness, willingness, and trust.

Stein's questing after a "sooner" pleasure and freedom finds expression in "top and bottom" living to explore "much heating" as "all the pliable succession of surrendering makes an ingenious joy" (484). Surrender to the lover, surrender to joy, surrender to not knowing or being attached to a centre, Stein seems to say. Surrender. Top and bottom live to make joy and poems of telling tenderness that take "care with which there is incredible justice and likeness" and which, in all their likeness they make a "magnificent ... fountain" (509). Outside of centre, the fountain of orgasm reappears.

Stein's work is filled with much pink and pleasure-making as orgasm after orgasm takes on a striking language. She explains in *Stanzas in Meditation*, "it did it a great deal of good to rub it" (Part IV, Stanza I, 101). In giving up politeness and choosing to "pilot it ... not polite" (*Pink Melon*

Joy, ASR, 282) the pleasure seeking, request to "do satisfy me" is granted. The "Hymns" of sex contain "words of praise" alluding to a vocal, word-play component to their sex as she "rushed in" (283). Stein writes, "the reason I mention what is happening is not by way of concealing that I have babies. I don't mean to leave so and I shall speak in silence. What is a baby." (289). She now knows "what to say": she will not conceal that she has babies and what a baby is: the pleasure of orgasm and ejaculation (289). The process of baby making leaves Stein to write, "[W]e were wonderfully shattered" (283). Words like "shattered" and "shutters" occur throughout Stein's writing. I love the use of the word *shattered* here: it's unexpected and evokes an experience of total exhaustion after the rush of sex. She writes, "an arrest of thought" is what shatters, implying seizing and attracting that which serves as pleasurable, as well as stopping any thoughts that might come from politeness or interfere in the uninhibited acts of sex. In "Pillow" Stein then very tenderly writes of either Toklas, whom she often called *baby*, or orgasm experiences, because *baby* is also a term Stein and Toklas used to describe having an orgasm: "[T]his is to say that baby is all well. That baby is baby. That baby is all well ... this is to say that baby is all well. This is to say that baby is all well" (283). The repetition of soothing, tender, comforting, and sexy words holding the lover in a perfect, loved completion.

In the *Meditations*, completion sometimes looks like sharing the intimacy of food: "[I]t is well known that they eat again ... nearly often after there is a pleasure" (*Stanzas in Meditation,* Part I, Stanza II, 15). Other times, completion comes as the narrative ends by acknowledging that "there has been a beginning of begun. / they can be caused ... we are here / and so far further (Part V, Stanza LII, 190–191). And so the narrative of their love and lovemaking as told in the *Stanzas of Meditation* affirms: "I wish once more to mention / that I like what I see" (Part V, Stanza LXI, 201), the lover's only regret being "I wish that I had spoken only all of it" (Part V, Stanza LXIII, 203). Witness how in one meditation Stein's stanza can be seductively subtle, philosophically questioning, and open-ended while at the same time sexually aggressive, evocative, and explanatory:

> Which they tell which they fill
> Could they make might it be right
> Or could they would they will
> If they might as if they will
> Not only with a will but will it
> Indeed it will who can be caught
> And sought
> For which they will in once
> Will they they will ...
> It is of every ready pleasure
> To add treasure to a treasure ...
> Shove

Shove is a proof of love …
And now they add this which
In which and well they wish
They add a little pink…
We had been as well
And we do.
        (Part V, Stanza LXVI,
           204–206)

Summoning the courage to speak it all, she boldly shares that "shove is a proof of love" (Part V, Stanza LXVI, 205), shoving into love "they add a little pink" which could be the colour changes to her lover's "treasure" or the colour of the item being shoved into her treasure. "We had been as well / and we do" affirms the living "proof of love" (Part V, Stanza LXVI, 206). "I need not hope to sing a wish" Stein affirms, "there is no hesitation" (Part V, Stanza LXVIII, 207). The last lines follow as an empowering, choice-and-pleasure-driven completion: "[E]verybody knows that I chose … I will be well welcome when I come. / Because I am coming. / Certainly I come having come. / These stanzas are done" (Part V, Stanza LXXXIII, 218).

Precious, precious baby

In *Stanzas in Meditation* Stein wrote, "can we call ours a whole. Out from the whole wide world I *choose* thee" (Part I, Stanza VIII, 25). Stein and Toklas choose to dwell in a vast, complete, world-size love that found expression in one of the most exciting publications of Stein's writing: *Baby Precious Always Shines: Selected Love Notes Between Gertrude Stein and Alice B. Toklas*. I would affirm that because of the long time span that the love notes cover—from 1935 to 1946—the emotive, uncensored, and courageous intimacy, and the historical quality of these love notes, they are the most stirring and telling of any published in the genre of romantic letters / correspondence and writing. They are letters that reveal a partnership of humour and decades of loved-filled years where "every New Year is a happy new year for the Cuddlewuddles" (*Baby Precious Always Shines*, 146). They are letters that speak of a love that has our author "just cry when I think how tenderly / you are me and I am thee" (134).

Like most intimate love letters and correspondence, the notes between Stein and Toklas were never meant to be published; Toklas gave them to the Beinecke Library at Yale, which houses the manuscripts, notebooks, photos, correspondence, and entire written archive of Stein's work and life, by mistake. When Toklas was made aware of her gift, she asked that the notes be destroyed; thankfully, she was convinced to have them kept in safekeeping with the agreement that they never be made publicly available. However, fourteen years after Toklas's death, in 1981, archivists at the library chose to make the notes accessible for research and in 1995 they were officially added to the catalogue of the Stein/Toklas archive. There now exist "a little over three hundred notes—two hundred ninety-five from Gertrude and seventeen from Alice" that we can revel in (6).

There can be no doubt as to why Toklas wanted the notes to be destroyed, or, at the very least to stay forever private and never made public: the love notes are of a very deeply personal, open, and revealing nature. In fact, the notes are dripping ripe with desire and sensuality; an intimate language of the heart, role-playing, gender bending, and switching is exposed. We can begin with noticing that Stein completes every note with the closure "YD.": Your Darling. This is not only a loving and endearing closure, but also a chosen, consensual offering of herself to her partner and lover. Stein's repeated *I am yours* is powerful and not to be glossed over as we read the notes. Stein never deviating from ending a note with *I am your darling* illustrates her unwavering commitment to Toklas.

The love notes allow us to witness two women choosing dynamic, flowing, effortless expressions of love, pleasure, identity, and role-playing with each letter. One such expression, which is also found in Stein's epic, erotic poem *Lifting Belly* and in *As A Wife Has A Cow A Love Story*, is the well-used metaphor of one of them having what the two women playfully term as *having a cow* or *baby*. Speculating on the meaning of the phrase *having a cow* has occupied some time of Stein scholarship. The term remains ambiguous regardless of interpretations; there are contradictions to any solitary meaning and charting-to-prove the code-word meaning *one thing* can produce no certainty. That said, there are two main interpretations and I propose to add a variant third.

The first interpretation is held by the majority of scholars,[9] who view Stein's linguistic creation of *having a cow* as code for "making love" or orgasm. It's important to note the terminology used by scholars: *making love*. The foundation of the act is created as soft; Stein's erotica and pornography are constructed as a sharing and expressing of love. And while Stein's erotica *is* soft, loving, and tender, the act of having sex for release as well as the rawness that can accompany sex is also present, and so I move to include those aspects in my reading of Stein's erotica. The pleasures derived from sex are many and multiple, so having an orgasm is sometimes added to the *having a cow* expression of love, especially by feminist, gender and sexuality studies scholars. This addition is a welcome one and connected to my third interpretation of what it may mean to have a cow.

Kay Turner has offered a recent, second reading in her introductory essay to *Baby Precious Always Shines*. Turner notes that her reading may be disconcerting to some as she understands *having a cow* as code for having a bowel movement (25). She reveals that Stein's notes with Toklas explicitly write cows as stools: "[W]hat is a stool. That was / the elegant name for a cow" (79). Turner further notes that this interpretation is based on Stein's concern for Toklas's digestive and expulsion issues. She writes that this fact supports "the degree to which Stein was Toklas's caretaker as much as Toklas was Stein's" (27), which is refreshing to read as it seems so obvious in Stein's writing and their correspondence.

While the two interpretations above certainly work, with Turner's being quite exciting, a third reading would add another layer: ejaculation. Ejaculate or ejaculation holds a slight degree of difference from having an orgasm: it accompanies orgasm and has its own referent. That no one has broached ejaculation as Stein's cow is not that surprising; while female ejaculation is an accepted medical and biological fact as the physical effect of orgasm and pleasure for many women seen in an ejaculate of clear fluid from the urethra, the term is most often defined and reserved for a male's orgasm and the ejaculation of semen. A dictionary definition makes no mention of the fact the female body ejaculates; female ejaculation is most often regarded as a mysterious, freak happening. Applying this reading to Stein's *having a cow* opens up the spectrums of switching, of larger gender and sexual possibilities and variancies, that women can experience.

In one love note Stein congratulates Toklas on having an "extremely promising husband" who "promises everything / and he means it too. He did not not / mean it. He means it. The darling. This ejaculation refers to Mrs. not to Mr. / as might be erroneously supposed" (75), clearly linking promising happiness and "everything" with the speaking of Toklas experiencing female ejaculation. Stein continues, "Mrs is the fountain of all good / all beauty and all sweetness. Mrs. / is a graceful fountain" (75), which allows for Toklas's ejaculate to be regarded most highly, as beautiful and sweet, fountains being places of centrality, art, and celebration in any city. She continues to say that the grace of Toklas's fountain is that "she plays over Mr. who is certain that / Mrs. Is a grateful fountain which / means that it is grateful to / Mr. to have Mrs. Play over him" and yet Stein too is a "Mr. ... so grateful" (75). We witness Toklas playing over Stein, playing with Stein, ejaculating over Stein. We also witness both lovers experiencing the gratitude that comes with intimacy and pleasure.

In another erotic poem, Stein shares that the lover experiences and emits a "thunder" when the belly is lifted (*Lifting Belly*, 20); thunder and lightning become another lovely metaphor for an ejaculation that effortlessly fits into many of the readings where cows happen. As noted earlier, Stein writes of having cows with the rose's full opening and blossoming, after the belly has been lifted. Stein or Toklas having a cow is a *result*. As discussed above in *Pink Melon Joy*, the result looks like extraordinary mixtures of fluids all over the table that will serve as evidence to their visitors of an afternoon of sex and splash like fountains (*Baby Precious Always Shines*, 65) unless they clean up. Kay Turner writes that "orgasms are not 'smelly,' nor do they go 'splash' (27), and certainly those adjectives might apply when comparing orgasms to defecation. However, my experience as a sex educator has found that in fact orgasms can be just that! Stein's describing Toklas as a "fountain," during and in sex and intimacy supports that ejaculations can go "splash." The fluids may be female ejaculation or urination, both of which can occur when orgasm takes place. Once alert to this notion, one can quite easily read female ejaculations and/or urination happening all over Stein's pages.

Having a cow is a type of completion to her poems, one in which a post-orgasmic body emptied of its contents, with exhaustion setting in afterward. A consistent holding, sweet talk, and comforting, usually by Stein, often immediately follows having a cow; Stein's writing shows her attentively following the post-bliss exhaustion of orgasm, ejaculation, and vulnerability that accompanies intense sexual fulfilment and release. Toklas is a "graceful fountain" to which "this ejaculation refers to Mrs. And not to Mr. As might be erroneously supposed" (75); while both lovers are babies to each other the cow is "to be found. Close inside Mr," which comes from "filling," idolizing, and adoring (149) with the result of a "baby achieved by Mr. And Mrs" (75). The couple switches often between, roles, gender, identity, dominance, submission, giver and receiver and so occur as organic and authentic, even as some roles predominate in their love notes and public presentations.

For a professionally driven, upper-class, traditional yet unconventional, modernist woman such as Stein to own and write the private acts of lesbian sex, the body, and female ejaculation a great courage was summoned; even as she writes of society being "polite" and heteronormative, any fears she may have had concerning public scorn, refusals of publication, loss of reputation, and/or friendships never appear in Stein's work. Her narratives consistently remain free of any disempowering, external social context or mapping, which makes them even more powerful; Stein's writing is not a response to what is missing: it is purely creation-based. Like any great and influential writer or artist, Stein creates from a space of a blank canvas, from a clearing where anything is possible: *this* love, *these expressions* of love and desire, are real, beautiful, and possible. In her unfailing, relentless, and consistent presentations of variant lesbian sex and identity, Stein presents us as readers with a space to *live into* the possibility of owing and freely creating our bodies, genders, identities, variant sex acts, pleasures, and creative, erotic language. I would thus assert that the variant spaces and renderings Stein provides us with are actually incomplete without reading the ejaculate.

Stein's penetrating and shoving, producing cows and babies, open up many possible interpretations to the variant ways female pleasure, ejaculation, and orgasm can be experienced; these openings allow the giver of pleasure (Stein or Toklas), and us as readers, to witness a queering and switching of gender, sexual, and identity variances: they are birthed and have visibility with ejaculation.

Another example where gender and identity variancies are allowed space is evident when Stein takes on a "he" role and pronoun in the letters. The "he" role allows Stein to inhabit a switch in gender: it is an identity that complicates and expands what being a she or woman is. The change in pronoun also complicates and expands the reading of sexual identity. One way Stein's "he" can appear is with the he'ing of the penetrative, pleasing—metaphoric, material, mental—dildo or penis.[10] In one note Stein writes that her baby "will smoke / me instead of cigarettes and that / will do" (100). The love notes illustrate very clearly that Stein embodied aspects of the he, and that Toklas provided space and support for this aspect of Stein's identity to be seen and celebrated.

Stein's birthday note to Toklas begins with the sex act of Toklas sitting on Stein's "bough": "my baby is a birdie sitting on a / bough, and the bough is hubby ... my baby is a treasure sitting on / its pleasure, and its pleasure is / its hubby" (134). Sexual taboos and variances are allowed space by the very nature of these acts not being written in a mainstream, heteronormative, and cultural context. So while many scholars have noted orgasm as a probable meaning for cow, and Turner has noted the passing of feces, I offer adding the tangible ejaculate of female fluids and orgasm to the list of possible meanings as we read the cows, ejaculate, and fountains of Stein. I propose that all these interpretations can co-exist as possibilities, that we don't need to pick one definitive interpretation to the exclusion of the others; concurrent readings respect and pay tribute to her playfulness with language and honour how effervescently Stein sought to create an abstract, ambiguous, playful, and fun world.

Reading the pornographic and BDSM playfulness of their notes, we can look at some additional contexts and spaces where these lovers transgress and shift in their sexual and identity roles. When Toklas writes to Stein, she describes her as "good baby," a "baby boy" who is "better behavioured every second" (158–159). Behaviour, good or bad, alludes to playing with power dynamics. In another note Toklas tells Stein that "no more naughty's be endured" when the "husband is an instantaneous obediencer," which brings the submissive/dominant dynamic into view for us. Toklas's word choice of "instantaneous" in describing Stein's obedience positions Toklas quite solidly in the dominant, top role, which she takes on with exacting standards and firmness. The repetition of the word "obey," in various forms, is a constant in their love notes. To command, instruct, direct, submit, follow, and behave are underlying themes of the Toklas/Stein relationship; and while they are mostly seen in the love notes, the land of obeying is in nearly all of Stein's published work. Their relationship writes what it is to obey. Both lovers occupy a space of flux and switch in her role depending on who wants to be in control of what.

Stein is described as "he likes to be well / and be hers," which presents us readers with an unsure sense of who the he is: [I]s the he Stein herself, Stein's dildo or mental member? Toklas writes, "Mrs. Speaks he ups & obeys her" (160), which again adds ambiguity: is Stein's member "up," to enter Toklas, does she rise or get "up" physically, or is she opening "up" to allow Toklas to enter her? What is clear is the two lovers dancing with role-playing and Dominance/Submission. The words "Mrs. Speaks" and he "obeys" are just one point of role-play; the tone of the line also illustrates how Toklas tops

Stein from the bottom; topping from the bottom occurs for both partners, switching between dominance and submission, quite often. She says that Stein is "no toy" and both a "baby boy" *and* "a strong-strong husband" to Toklas (158). With topping and bottoming comes a reciprocity and coexistence of equals, the switch nature of them both, Toklas tells Stein: "I don't obey / do this you say / well do it together and / that's the way we obey" (158). She chooses not to want to "obey" her Wife, yet, what is alluded to in the language of the notes indicates play with dominance and submission. "Do this you say" is consensually played with in some locations, whereas other instances have an equal doing "it together."

Toklas writes that her loving and sexing Stein is Stein's "constant food" as she seeks "to delight with all my might / hubby is my pleasure" (158). She delights in affirming that they are always near and that "wifie's good / hides it under a thick hood" (158). The *it* repeating is ambiguous: *it* is hidden "under a thick hood" and "*it*" is Stein's "constant food." Stein's—or is it Toklas's?—hood could very well be her clitoris; the *it* could also be what is inserted and penetrated just underneath the hood: that which is penetrated becomes hidden when inserted. Fingers, a hand, or the head of her penis/dildo could be the *it*. Toklas may be switching herself or her lover in this note as gender switching happens throughout.

Toklas is very intentional in feeding Stein: from taking care of the food purchases and meals in their household to taking care of Stein's sex appetite. This is Toklas's Christmas note to Stein, so written in a time of culinary decadence. Toklas writes that "it" will be Stein's constant craving, her constant hunger. The content of Stein's oeuvre, which is heavily layered with lesbian erotica, might allow us to conclude that Stein had an active obsession with love, intimacy, and sex. Toklas alludes to this when she writes to Stein that their lovemaking or sex is *a hunger*: these lovers are each other's "daily food" (91).

She then evolves her love note to the second stanza, which takes a turn toward possession and S/M ownership: "good baby / is all me / to delight / with all my might / hubby is my pleasure." The words *all* and *my* echo here and throughout the notes; it is Toklas's role to please *all* of Stein: no part of her reserved or left for anyone else. The present of Stein is *all* Toklas's pleasure. Toklas's gift is to please with all she has, all she can give. We can almost here her say *mine mine mine* here. Stein is coaxed and stroked with the affectionate "good baby" who Toklas wants to "delight" her "with all" her "might," implying some effort or force here.

Talk of rough sex is endearingly in the notes (as with other Stein writing). One love note has Stein entering their bed where "love is sleeping sweetly" to "shove the hotties too near," and another note has the using of "her / big finger and her whole hand ... and the two little apples inside her" (62–63). Other notes write of the lover having "nothing but sweet breath" as she is "coming softly" (55).

The Christmas note/poem moves to end with a third stanza wherein Toklas affirms that her lover is "no toy / but a strong-strong husband" whom she invites to "do it together" (158). Stein declares herself to be a "good obedient hubby" (98), which is a term often used to describe Stein's relationship to Toklas in the notes. Stein describes herself as being "devoted" to Toklas (90). What does this look like? In another note, which is actually a poem Stein wrote to Toklas, titled, "A Command Poem," Stein is "commanded by wifie ... who is always commanded ... loves to be commanded" (109). Stein is "commanded by wifie to be wifey's / hubby and he is, would be even if he wasn't / commanded cause *he just is* but loves to be commanded" (109, italics mine). Stein *just is* submissive to Toklas; she *just loves* "to be commanded" (109). Don't question it, revel, *and be* in it, Stein seems to tell herself, and Toklas, in this poem.

Stein creates her *self* with her writing to Toklas. These letters can be seen as acting as a memoir at its finest: each lover sharing, discovering, and creating herself through a love note and poem to her partner. Stein genders herself he and hubby and dwells in being submissive and submitting as she longs to be commanded, and yet even without command *she creates the space* to be submissive to her wife. The intense pleasure of submitting consensually, by one's own crafting and invention, allow commanding to grant a beautiful, big space of self-expression and love. Stein carves out this sexy identity and location for herself; she gives herself this space! And she is asking Toklas to step into her role by extension: *please, please command me* she is asking. Stein's love notes and poems cannot be underestimated: they are extraordinary switch moves of gender and sexual variancy and of dominance and submission. They are also bold and unconventional acts of self-love and actualization *while being at the same time* acts of generosity and vulnerability within a partnership.

In the same poem s/he asks Toklas to listen to her, to "feel it to see ... inside in me" and tells her to make sure "they are tight" the plural of which is interesting here (109). Stein speaks of countless kisses, of not missing anything in their kisses, of hitting the mark, and how blessed they are. With Stein asking to be commanded, we witness a Stein topping from the bottom here. And at the end of this confessional, asking-to-be-commanded poem where she has been filled, tightly Stein is a "blessed baby ... tired ... sleepy" (110). Her last words are her biggest offering, which occurs in other poems and notes as well: "I am all yoursy" (110). The offering of the self, I am *yours*, repeat and repeat with this couple and, truly, is this not the biggest offering a lover can make? The "I am yours," relates back and into Stein's ending each love note with "your darling." We can look at related words to "darling" to expand Stein's offering to Toklas: "precious, adored, loved, beloved, cherished, treasured, esteemed, worshiped" are all adjectives that relate, which allows Stein's closing term to really speak to not only her, but the couple's, unwavering commitment (*New Oxford American Dictionary*).

One expression to *darling* that stands out is *worshipped,* which allows us to see yet another angle in the switching that occurs in their relationship. An implicit reverence, devotion, and adoration exists in Stein's offering herself up to and for Toklas *to* adore *and* a similar worship/idolizing reverence, devotion, adoration through her consistent, full, and giving submission of herself to the belonging and care of Toklas. And this exaltation switches as when Stein writes: "I adored my wifey, I just completely / and entirely *idolized* my wifey" (*Baby Precious Always Shines*, 149, italics mine). In another letter Stein writes to Toklas that she is "my adored one," continuing to express that she loves Toklas "here / here in my heart in me all through / and I am in she" (148). The *you are in me and I am in you, you are mine and I am yours* is a felt connection echoed throughout the love letters. This particular letter ends with lines of repetition declaring their both offering themselves up to the other: "I am all her treat and she / is all mine and together we shine brightly" (148).

There is a dominant/submissive context to the word choices that speak to the rationality of belonging to each other; Stein's ending of *your darling* allows a context that holds the specific taste and flavour of dominant/ submissive switching sexiness that only happens when one offers oneself to someone. To be treasured to the point of being owned and possessed, to give oneself over to be someone's, to give oneself to be in *their* care, to be *their darling* is a submission that is untouchable. No offering can match the humility, generosity, and trust that comes with the giving of one's self *over to the care* of another as it implies the surrendering of one's will, one's being. And so, for Stein, this offering is a total surrender of herself to her lover, to the love-ship, to the "whole" of what they are together as partners.

This submission and giving over exist as switch moments for both lovers. Toklas writes to Stein, most probably from another room in the house, that she is "quietly waiting" for Stein to "call your dove," adding that she, Toklas is Stein's "own" (157). Toklas speaks in the third person as she offers herself to be Stein's. This particular letter has a reassuring tone to it as Toklas tells Stein to "know always" that "she's mating / with her dored own boy" (157). Despite being Stein's typist, Toklas also plays with words or typing mistakes: "dored" can read adored or, more playfully, as affixing her boy Stein with the aspects of a door; considering the content of mating and waiting in the note, I might suggest she is referring to Stein's door handle here: the metaphoric and tangible handle to grab onto, an adornment to open the door and room beyond. This note constructs Toklas as waiting to mate, being in constant, "always" state of wanting to mate with her partner. It also constructs Toklas as belonging to Stein with "she's your own" and Stein as Toklas's with "her dored own boy." The speaking of possession, ownership, dominance/submission, and giving of oneself is very much a reciprocal part of the couple's switching in their role-playing.

A fluidity of switching roles surfaces in all of Stein's erotic literature. However, we can begin to distinguish that sexual switching actions exists most especially in the love notes between her and Toklas. Stein identifies as a needing husband, a boy, and a submissive *as well as* a care-giving husband, daddy, and dominant: she switches to take on the role or identity of a man and a he *as well as* that of a woman and a she. Toklas, for her part, keeps up with an often (but not always) easy going, accepting, and rarely seen switch nature of her own. Toklas is a "happy queen for her little King" (113) and is most often referred to as "wifey," "baby," and "baby precious." Revealing, teasing out, and unpacking the gender and sexually fluid and variant identities of the letters exemplify Stein and Toklas's deep love as well as how both women played with non-normative/variant sexual identities, practices, roles and desires.

This kind of possessional giving and owning may be seen as dysfunctional outside an S/M context. General and psychological standards of best feminist/humanist practice suggest that our relationships be formed from distinct, independent individuals who form a union of equals joined for a common purpose, with little possessiveness or ownership present. The dominant/submissive context of *yours and mine* in the letters between Stein and Toklas is informed by lesbian sexual variance (rather than heteronormativity) and is a consensual choice to play with owning, possessing, taking, and offering. Perhaps because to own a person is such a taboo, and to give up one's self also something of a risk, this type of consensual role-play is an allowing like no other. It thus produces results that are incredibly freeing rather than confining: the entire being of the lover is in the hands and care of her lover: it is a complete and utter surrender of one's will. Stein's submission speaks to a foundation of BDSM: to explore *all* the senses beyond that which we know in an effort to enable, activate, and reach new heights of sensory pleasure, experience, and connection, with oneself via another.

We witness a Stein who is asking to be controlled, dominated, and restrained. She is intent on "filling" her "baby precious" who "needs filling with love / every second and she is she is / she is filled up full every / second" and "nicely every day" (98). Producing a cow "not every second but nicely every / day" (98). Turner's reading of a cow applies here along with mine: the daily cow, the filling every day: and it is Stein who fills, repeating verbal play with Toklas with "she is she is she is filled up." Stein writes about talking of the sexual act *while in the act*, which resonates the sexiness they have when Stein is not writing and Toklas not sleeping or typing. Plainly put, these notes reveal that when not living and attending to life, these lovers were engaged in states of passion, sex, and lovemaking. Obsessive wishing and fantasy, dreamscapes of love connection, are evident and rather than being hidden, the letters reveal a refreshing openness of both quality and quantity. In one note, Stein laments not being able to be with Toklas, writing, "not yet but to-morrow you / bet he will be as stimulating as a / cigarette for his pet and in that / way will after the light of day he / will give the blessed sweetness a cow" (96).

Of course, Stein cannot stop there and must give either herself or Toklas the verbal foreplay towards "tomorrow" or "later" that these notes are so ripe with. Stein continues to share that "here he is being a cigarette / to his pet, an anything be more contentful / to blessed baby than a nice fat cigarette / you bet and he is it, for his pet ... a big cow / now, I am your cigarette blessed pet" (96).

Stein's tender, *Tender Buttons* of elucidation and teaching

Stein and Toklas were both masterful at the art of clarification and illumination, especially when it came to elucidating their love, relationship, and connection. Stein will thus begin her poem "An Elucidation" by encouraging one to "elucidate the problem of halve. Halve and have" (2). Stein shines a light on a problem, rather than solve it: something only a master teacher would do. "An Elucidation" is actually a manifesto, a call to action, wherein Stein explains that no problem is really a problem at all, rather, they exist to shine a light on what can be unpacked ideas, concepts, and ways of being toward a new understanding: an elucidation. The subject: "halve and have," plays on the words *half* and *to have*. Stein is playing with multiple dualities here: two halves (individuals) co-existing as part of a whole (in relationship and/or union), the switching that occurs between the two lovers of the poem as well as the occupying a "having" of the lover, a possession, or an occurring of what there is to have and elucidate: pleasure and the space of poetic exploration.[11]

One can read two individuals outside of a romantic union; pleasure and lover-ships are merely one location or route Stein uses to exemplify what she is asking us to consider. "An Elucidation" lays out an introduction to understanding and unveiling, by various points or "examples," the abstraction, relativism, and construction of shifting pleasure sites, identities and community, which in turn gives rise to identity (at the personal and communal level) as inherently self (or community) defined, self-created and self-constructed, and thus switchable, changeable, and always up for creation and recreation.

Stein begins switching and considering the places between and betwixt in the very beginning of this poem. Her first heading is "Madrigal and Mardigras" (2). The poem is a madrigal: a song made of parts for several voices and strongly influenced by text. The poem is also the ritual of Mardi Gras, a time of carnival and celebration, costumes, masks, overturning social conventions, and parading; Mardi Gras is bookmarked by devotion as it begins on or after the feasts in celebrating the Epiphany and before the day of confession, fasting, morning, and repenting of Ash Wednesday/ Shrove Tuesday. Stein sets up the subject of the ritual with the lines "she is in and out" (2): neither displaced, both in and out at the same time. We are welcomed into a world where Stein "happily ... gives examples" and is "very communicative / on pleasure" (3), switching in identity and actions, between in and out, celebration and devotion, overturning social conventions and adhering to social conventions, between traditional ritual and language and playful experimentation with ritual and language, between masculine and feminine, top and bottom, submission and dominance, between the pleasure and elation of sacrifice and confession and the pain and suffering of sacrifice and confession.

Stein's focus is, once again, on the interiority of what is happy-making. She writes, "I will give other examples to you … in a place, / a place for everything and everything in its place. / In place in place of everything, in a place. / Again search for me. / She looked for me at me" (3). The placing and what is to be placed are explored later with the notion of the "stall," and so one reading can locate the placement of pleasure within the body, the notion of the body's containers, or stalls, as a place of pleasure, searching, and looking. The looking for self, the lover looking, the creating of self through another's gaze, the creating of self (and couple) through placing (and gaze) becomes clear. A few pages later, a powerful line resonates another looking: "do you all understand why she sees me" (8). The direct questioning of "[D]o you?" as in, do you get it, she seems to be asking, and the "why" allows room to question. Yet the why and how are implicit even as the sentence is a statement of invitation to query and look at the how behind the "why" of seeing and knowing of a lover, partner, or another.

She affirms their pleasures as "our fancy pleases" (4) allowing for the fancy and the pleasure of the fancy to have space. *Fancy* seems such an old-fashioned word that resonates with dandyism, the highly decorated, and the imagination. The term stems from the Middle English word *fantasy*, possibly allowing Stein to explore how fantasy pleases her and Toklas: the "our" revealing here. And so Stein enables fantasy to be made visible: they will indulge their fancies and pleasures and, by extension, permit us as readers to do the same. Stein affirms: "so we may be fancy as we please, we may fancy what we please" (4).

Stein addresses the reader and audience, and perhaps Toklas more covertly, when confirming that they "do understand … yes you do," yet, Stein will take the time to "completely introduce" her "explanation" and not leave any aspect out (4). The reader will "come at the end," declares Stein, who is "dealing in accelerated authority … dealing in their delight" (5). We understand how and why this love is seen, how fancy pleases, all that involves an exploration on love: we understand Stein's commitment and confidence when she declares: "I know how to please her" (5). Stein's "authority" has "regularly arranged decision" and deals with a masochistic giving over that plays with that which is "to diminish" yet has "no fear" (5).

The poem continues to write and repeat the pleasures of placing pleasure and switches voices and point of view as it does. The happiness the lover experiences when receiving the intentionality behind pleasure: the *placing* and active, clear communication of roles figures prominently in their pleasure. The poem has switch voicing: moving from one woman's voice and point of view in asking the lover to "happily say so" to recreating the lovers' communication: "too happily say so / very communicative" (3). The switch in voice and perspective joins the lovers in a dance of speaking desire. For these lovers, no happiness with placing pleasure exists without communication, and it is constantly praised when and as "it is placed in there" (3). Stein repeats the language of placing and to place, echoing the rhythmic movements of sex as "everything" is "in its place," which permits a begging lover to have space to say "again search for me" (3). The "do you understand why she sees me" is answered repeatedly throughout the poem, early on with response to searching and placing it in again: "She looked for me at me" (3). The looking for and at the self, as the lover looks at and through her, creates her in her gaze; Stein presents a self-searching both within the self and outside, in the social world of mirrored recognition and oneness. "A fourth example shows more plainly what it does show, what does it show, I see you and you see me, I see that you see and you see that I see. A fourth example shows a tendency to declaration" (5).

Stein's elucidation is, like much of her writing, full of declarations. The power of the action of declaring what is, what is shown and what is seen, who is shown and who is seen, cannot be overestimated in Stein. To declare something makes it real in the world, it allows the subject to carry a personal and social accountability through the presence of word and language; our words creates our world and through our words and our speaking, others are invited and allowed to witness, support, and participate in what is being declared. Stein thus declares the liberation that comes with declaring through words: a new seeing and understanding:

> [W]hen we see that they are not as we understood they would be when we see, when we say we see we hear, and when we say we hear we feel and when we say we feel we see and when we say we see we hear. In this we declare we declare all of us declare what do you declare, declare to me. Declarations rapidly reunited.
>
> (15)

A new creating of self, community, and world can occur through declarations. Might we be able to use such an idea when exploring and trying on switching as a lived and experienced gender and sexual identity?

Stein immediately follows with the statement that

> action and reaction are equal and opposite. Astonishment means list of persons and places and if she were to be represented there if she were to be represented there. Call me a smiler and fit the fifth exactly. I fit the fifth exactly.
>
> (15)

I am particularly taken with Stein calling for action rather than reaction. Stein evokes the larger community and collective of representing and seeing of "she" and of an "us." She also draws attention to the notion of fitting into a structured system and, by extension, her revision and creation of a newly numbered system—this poem—where self-representation counts. Stein continues in a conversational back and forth on the conscious construction of what, how, and who one wants to be, how one wants to be seen, and what the "astonishment" can look like: an exact fitting into what she declares, even as shifting, *to be seen and known as*. Through this creation, worlds open.

Stein opens these worlds as she explains that "this is not an instance," this location is not fixed, it is not isolated, it is not a passing now, rather it is a creation-based place to come from, be in, and return to: "this way makes rounding out rounder" (15). "This way makes rounding out rounder" is one of those meditation-worthy sentences that Stein so poetically and masterfully offered. In the roundness opening, it's like the sky just opened up and we can now see the vastness of the stars and universe with a pronounced clarity. Similar to her declaring that "a wide action is not a width," "this way makes rounding out rounder" allows the reader to dwell in a new switch location of being, choosing to be expansive and open, round, *and rounder still*, rather than confined, rigid, closed and … *square*. She continues to expand her point: "it is round around and rounder if it is around and we tell all we know let me explain directly and indirectly. In the fifth instance there *was no coincidence*" (15, italics mine). The rounding, cylindrical forms of the body, the rounding of the thoughts, the fitting of the roundness, no coincidence in and to any of it; the telling is a liberated existence and being in the world: a fifth instance of gender and sex, and pleasure and desire, are an access to examine and declare ourselves freely round in the world.

Stein writes that she will "lead" us to "yes": that saying yes, and the willingness that lives there, is a location to birth the roundness. Further, she asks us to lead—and be led—to say "yes." She includes the individual reader directly as well as the larger "we": ever the life-long patron of the arts, Stein includes the small, collective communities and larger world of something bigger that we form as individuals, which are important aspects to the activism within Stein's work. She tells us: "you lead to yes you do, we lead to yes you do they lead to yes you do" (16). Stein ends "An Elucidation" by explaining what is necessary for the "yes": honouring our humanness while at the same time stepping beyond what we have known and are familiar with. She writes that we must understand differently, that we must "undertake to overthrow our undertaking" (16), or put another way, consider overthrowing that which we thought we understood. She says "we understand you do understand that we will understand it correctly": do not concern yourself about being understood, do not get obsessed with getting it right and looking good because "correctly and incorrectly, prepare and prepared" will all be present. She asks us to thus move forward, "patiently and to prepare, to be prepared and to be particularly and not particularly prepared" (16). Stein then brings her manifesto home with calling us forth into action:

Do prepare to say Portraits and Prayers, do prepare to say that you
  have prepared
Portraits and prayers and that you prepare and that I prepare.
Yes you do.
Organisers.
Yes you do.
Yes you do and you, you do.
To portraits and to prayers.
Yes you do.

(16)

Stein is creating us as creators and leaders of our own evolution here. She is asking us to construct our own portraits, both as individuals and as communities, which are likened to prayers; she is asking us to pray, and to accept the ritual and humility of prayer. With the head and chin bowed, the heart can lead and prayers offered. The song, the elucidation, has many voices heard, seen, offered. Ian Hacking writes that "if new modes of description come into being, new possibilities for action come into being in consequence" ("Making up People" in *Forms of Desire*, Ed. Stein, 78, as cited in *Sexuality*, Ed. Robert Nye, 8). Stein's oeuvre gives us just that: new modes of description and new possibilities for action. Stein's work is a call to take responsibility for our own portraits and to take new, prayerful actions that prepare and illuminate our happiness.

Stein's experimental, modernist writing, and I hope some of my new deconstruction and readings, could serve to mean something in the direction language, gender and sexuality studies is taking: a more experimental, liberating, and sexy language, theory, and practice of gender, sexuality and identity. The letters between Stein and Toklas demonstrate beautiful switch moments with gender, identity, sexual desire, roles, and practice. A metamorphosis of loving transactions and intimacy is continually birthed through their switching: a "spreading into nothing" and giving up of the centre (through language and intimate actions) allows switch moments that range from lesbian desires and BDSM practices to being nurtured and pleased through many avenues of surrender and love-making. The decentring of identity through Stein's use of experimental language and writing allows the reader to give up our own centre. Toklas, who valued being thorough, methodical, accurate, and slow in her cooking, would evocatively write in *Aromas and Flavors of Past and Present*: "[V]ery few people are indifferent to either the aroma or the flavor ... there is a harmony and a suitable progression ... there should be a climax and a culmination. Come to it gently. One will suffice" (xxv–xxvi). For Toklas and Stein, these were the ingredients and the method that fed their lives.

Gender, queer and sexuality studies must continue to take such bold, decentring steps of steady, climaxing progress. They are essential for our full self-expression. Daring, open-minded readings and scholarship of variant, experimental texts and writers like Stein are needed so that they might transfer into the mainstream body politic and contribute to the inclusion and celebration of variant, multidimensional gender identities and sex practices. For creation from nothing and transformation at the level of gender and sexual identity to take place, in true Steinian form, subverting what it is to not be a width could serve us very well.

Notes

1 Prior to sexuality and gender studies entering academia as a distinct discipline, the majority of the discussion and teaching on Stein was heavily influenced by formalist critical theory, which focused on the modern art connections (Picasso especially), and/or Stein's political and geographical affiliations, especially during the time of war. Some theorists noted that Stein was a lesbian, and may have given a polite nod to her relationship with Toklas (which may occur as too personal, irrelevant, and/ or subversive enough to a conservative reader or scholar); however, the brushing over of lesbian/same-sex love, sex, the body, and eroticism can be, at times, quite confounding considering how consumed and overt Stein was with the topics.

   Many of us would be incensed to read the *New York Times* obituary of Alice B Toklas, which devalued and silenced one of the most rich and loving public lesbian couples of the century by referring to Alice as "the lifelong friend of Gertrude Stein." Further examples would include the work of Harold Bloom, Julian Sawyer (who, in *Gertrude Stein, A Bibliography*, would write that Stein's writing from 1912 to 1936 was "essentially concerned with geography," page 13), Peter Quartermain, who downplays Stein's sexuality by saying it is "insignificant" (*Disjunctive Poetics: From Gertrude Stein and Louis Zukofsky to Susan Howe.* Cambridge: Cambridge University Press, 1982, 32), and Richard Bridgman, who talks about her sexuality in a tame fashion (see *Gertrude Stein in Pieces.* New York: Oxford University Press, 1970).

2 Wayne Koestenbaum, Cyrena N. Pondrom, Judy Grahn, and Jean Mills are a handful of other scholars who have brought thoughtful new teachings and reading to the lesbian erotic in Stein's work. No doubt, there are many others, especially in the last ten years since I originally published this chapter.

3 Despite Stein providing for Toklas via her estate, with the paintings and other personal property (such as royalties for all published and future published writing) deemed for her upkeep, Stein's heirs would impound Toklas's inheritance. The odious legalities of the estate would prove so problematic that Toklas would not be provided for via Stein's wishes. In her last years, she was in poverty, and it was fellow writers and friends who would support Toklas. Stein bequeathed her published and unpublished literary remains to Yale University, where it has undergone decades of discussion and debate around public/private rights, and much like the Stein/Toklas collection of art, held, dispersed, sold, resold, etc.

4 While they may have been understated in their being a couple they were "out" in the way we term married couples now.

5 Pondrom's thorough and unabashed work is why I do not need to undertake the book to any large degree, even as Stein echoes many of the same themes in *Sacred Emily* as she does in *Pink Melon Joy, Stanzas in Mediation, Tender Buttons, Lifting Belly,* and *Baby Precious Always Shines.*

6 Stein was not the only influential artist playing with the word *eros*. Marcel Duchamp's female alter ego, *eros* persona, Rrose Sélavy. Man Ray's stunning 1920s photographs of Duchamp as Rrose Sélavy reveal an alluring femme *and* dandy, who is playing with switch notions of gender, sexuality, and desire.

7 And it still continues today: erotic language as well as leather, BDSM, and LGBTQ subculture uses coded words just as Stein did.

8 Further readings of this passage occur later in this chapter.

9 See: Ulla E. Dydo, *Gertrude Stein: The Language That Rises, 1923–1934* Evanston: Northwestern University Press, 2002; Jane Goldman, *Modernism 1910–1945: Image to Apocalypse* New York: Palgrave, 2004 (where she states that cow is "slang" for orgasm, p. 192); Janet Malcolm, *Two Lives: Gertrude and Alice.* Yale University Press, 2007; other writers who have referred to Stein's cow as an orgasm include Jeanette Winterson ("All I Know About Gertrude Stein," Granta 115; Summer 2011).

10 This genderqueer, transgendered, or transsexual identity location—of knowing, feeling, and thinking from and with a mentally formed penetrative genital—is very real for some genderqueers and gender variants, as well as for some lesbian, butch women and trans folks; it is worth noting that this is an aspect of switching sexual and gender identity that is not often spoken of or seen in LGBTQ dialogues. This notion can best be seen in the subcultural art, photography, erotica, and pornography of gender-variant LGBTQ folks. More on this will be discussed later with Jeanette Winterson's work.

11 "An Elucidation" was first delivered as a lecture at Oxford and entitled "Composition as Explanation." It was later printed in the April 1927 issue of the Hogarth essays titled *Transition*.

3 Theory must be doing

Jeanette Winterson, Eileen Myles, and Kathy Acker switch in the spaces and language of non-normative identities and desires

This chapter focuses on how three gender and/or sexually variant writers—Jeanette Winterson, Eileen Myles, and Kathy Acker—switch to practice, evoke, and play with concepts of desire that encapsulate subversive identity practices. Winterson, Myles, and Acker all actively employ switching in gendered bodies, gendered identities, sexual practices, identities, and/or roles to such an elevated degree that stable notions of identity are continually, and very wonderfully, destabilized. Dwelling in these experimental locations, I specifically look at where and how gender, sexual, and/or identity switching allows for characters, and us as readers, to rework and play with gender and sexual identities so as to create an access to aliveness, authenticity, and freedom.

This chapter asks to what degree these queer and/or gender and sexually variant writers are practicing, evoking, and playing with desires that elicit exciting and subversive sexual and identity practices. Further, to what extent can private desires become public celebrations of freedom from identity and exploring variancy?[1] Looking at the variant gender- and sexual-switching moments and identifications of the lovers alongside the characters' love quest contributes to an opening of what's possible. Within this context, all of my chosen authors make incremental, degree-like movements towards both love and pain; I will deconstruct the BDSM translation of those degrees—the slow gradual movement without any certainty, foreseen finality, or exit—as well as the masochistic or surrendering practice. Subversive and perverse desires can be seen in the gender slippages throughout these authors' textual performances. This chapter deconstructs and demonstrates how the non-normative genders, sexualities, identities, and desires of these daring authors map out *circumference*, a term Emily Dickinson used anew as she turned her poems in and around desire and the love-quest, specifically the masochistic.

You can change the story. You are the story.

(Jeanette Winterson, *The Powerbook*, 288)

Jeanette Winterson was born in Manchester, England in 1959 and currently lives in the Cotswolds in England. She was born into a very poor family that could not support her and was adopted by humble, Pentecostal evangelical Christian folk and raised in Accrington, North England. At sixteen she fell in love with a girl, an act that was deemed unacceptable to her adopted parents and thus prompted Winterson to leave home shortly thereafter. Her first book, a semi-autobiographical novel, *Oranges Are Not the Only Fruit*, was published in 1985 when she was just twenty-three. The book gained wide success and critical acclaim and won literary prizes, which encouraged many successive printings. The novel was made into a three-part BBC drama in 1990. By the time she wrote *The Passion*, in 1989, she was able to support herself as a full-time writer.

Winterson is a prolific and accomplished writer who, at last count, had published twenty-three books, not including poems that she publishes on her website. She is a very active and astute literary and cultural figure who writes fiction, children's books, poems, essays, memoir, as well as articles for *The Guardian* (and other newspapers) on current world events as well as about her life. Winterson has won numerous book prizes and awards, is published in over eighteen countries, and has taught writing at the University of Manchester. Despite worldwide acclaim and success, her writing and interviews offer and reflect a modesty, humility, truth, and caring that is refreshing; she allows for a real sense of inclusivity and connection with the reader/public and the larger world in which we live. Winterson's writing demonstrates a deep courage and steadfast resiliency in linking the personal with the political. She has consistently offered a very rare, raw, and authentic voice in the world of literature and letters and, indeed, is a beautiful example of what it is to be a caring, evolving human who is committed to exploring and sharing one's own intimate life and making a difference in the larger world via the process.

Winterson's *The Powerbook* (2000) and *Written on the Body* (1992) offer a joyous, refreshing, and unfamiliar place to begin to gather with the variant and non-gendered. The driving promise of both lyrical, romantic, love-driven books is bold: desire and freedom with identity. Winterson thus locates gender and sexual variancy as a real possibility for living. In both novels Winterson's main characters are gender and sexual variants who are in love with women and have rich fantasy and role-playing lives. In choosing to switch and alter a gendered or non-gendered body, and to switch gender and sexual identities and roles, Winterson designs unimagined possibilities for her characters and for us as readers.

In an interview for *The Paris Review* Winterson attributes her characters to having something of the

> hero archetype about them in that they are largely stripped of context. But they offer a kind of operatic salvation, for themselves and for the reader in that through their lives one's own struggles can be experienced without being overly definitive, without pinning them down too much, which I wouldn't want to do. Obviously I have been able to escape that

by setting something in an imagined past or in an imagined present, tinkering with place and time so that the reader can't quite say, Oh yes, I know where this is, I can identify here. I want them rather to identify with a being, with a state of consciousness, with a particular kind of imaginative value rather than some sort of TV character.

(The Paris Review, Spring 1999)

And it is this "imaginative value," this inability to know, conclude, pin down, or fix her characters that is so appealing in Winterson's work. To "identify with a *being, with a state of consciousness, with a particular kind of imaginative value*" is indeed the fundamental intoxication of Winterson's work. Operatic? Yes, most definitely.

Similar to Myles and Acker, as I illustrate later in this chapter, Winterson must create a suffusive world, a kingdom, where her characters can play with transgressing roles and identities, and where she can offer up the possibilities she sees and seeks. Her characters straddle the worlds of role and identity. While Winterson takes time to explore occupying the male and female body, roles, and desire, she also lyrically ventures into who and how one variant gender and sexual mind frames are inhabited. What is most exciting is how her narratives and characters take up the challenging inquiry of what it can look like to traverse the spaces of being a switch.

Winterson thus broaches where and how it occurs to occupy locations outside of the norm or the expected. In *The Powerbook* Winterson's playfulness with sexual switching, dominance, and submission is located in occupying a narrative core that destabilizes her character's roles and place in society. She writes of the places betwixt and between, two worlds, those switch locations and ways of being traversed by many variants, yet still remaining out of reach, high above dominant discourse, like a tightrope. "I keep telling this story," she writes, "different people, different places, different times ... because a story is a tightrope between two worlds" (141).

Choosing to walk the tightrope of variancy, where multiple worlds and characters coexist and are drawn together by the commonality of sexual and gender variancy, Winterson creates her kingdoms, one of which illustrates a castle housing a lover's body, who under falcon hands finds the pleasure to be "as shocking as the thought of pleasure" and then marries its brother (148). The writing unravels, and discovery of a cohesive narrative, even among vignettes that stand alone as short stories, is like "the partition between real and invented" and as "thin as a wall in a cheap hotel room" (108). Her main characters are in an "exile," longing for a "narrative" of their own in a "kingdom she could control" (166).

The Powerbook begins with the gorgeously titled chapter "Language costumier." This very short chapter begins with a non-gendered character telling their mother that s/he/they are going to do volunteer work for the poor when instead they enter an empty costume shop asking, with quest-like urgency, for "freedom, just for one night" (3). She continues to ask to buy "the freedom to be somebody else" (3). The character seeks to be fashioned and "transformed" into and through an "invented world" (4), one of her/his/their making where freedom is self-created and lived. A transformation is a creative and intentional act of metamorphosis, a "process by which one figure, expression, or function is converted into another that is equivalent in some important respect but is differently expressed or represented" (*New Oxford American Dictionary*).

Switching is a transformative act. As different identities are tried on, the worlds that allow for gender and identity exploration expand. As in other Winterson novels, the characters of *The Powerbook* time travel to experience their transformation. The multiple worlds where transforming switch locations exist in *The Powerbook* range from the sixteenth century to the present contemporary world. And while the secondary character asks for the freedom to be someone else, it is the narrator of *The Powerbook* who takes this freedom into the realms of gender and sexual identity. Gender switching begins soon after the request to be transformed into somebody else and, as early as 1591, where the mother of a girl child argues to save her life (the father wanting to drown her) by disguising the girl as a boy child who can thus work to improve the family's economic situation. The main narrating character thereby begins her gender-bending adventures, which include being charged with transporting tulips by ship. With the help of her mother s/he hides the species of tulips, named "Key of Pleasure" and "Lover's Dream," in her pants. The mother constructs a leather harness, sewing and fastening a narrow leather strap, which is affixed around her hips to hide the bulbs.

A dialogue of intimate fixing and constructing the character's gender identity with the aid of hidden embalmed tulips ensues. The tulips are shaped and hidden but the mother realizes there is "something missing" (12). After the mother compares the character's package to the father's "the bit in the middle" is the "something missing" and is deemed necessary to complete the gender modification (12). The character then journeys into nature to find a tulip with "a well-formed fat stem supporting a good-sized red head with rounded tips" (12). Her created member is "about eight inches long, plump, with a nice weight to it" (11–12). Once her gendered piece is attached and the switch complete, mother and child inspect the gender-variant youth to realize that no legend can compare to her; she is a unique genius, an original. What's more, she is self-created and handcrafted, designed and made from organic materials. The character is now given a gender: she is now a he.

There exists a potential perversity in the mother's next action, when she smells the character's genital area; a closeness that seems unfamiliar and uncomfortable to our modern time takes place as the "mother knelt down and put her nose close." The familial scene ends with the mother saying, "you smell like a garden" (12). This shared, consensual intimacy: both the close proximity and the awakened sense of smell breathing through the text speak a sensuality, yet we are left with no more, and no less, as the passage above is followed by an ellipsis after which the character is on a ship, bound to deliver the bulbs. Likening a self-made, gendered anatomy to a garden, one that is constructed of flowers, is a remarkable way to begin to build a foundation for switching: new beginnings and the freedom to rewrite the story are a cornerstone to this foundation. The seed was planted, and now is the time for the flower to burst open.

Kidnapped by pirates, the character is chosen to initiate and educate a princess in the art of sex; they are chosen precisely because he is perceived as just a boy who can do her "neither hurt not insult" (23). The princess has never seen a man before, so seeing the tulip, which the character tells her is called "my Stem of Spring" and the bulbs, which he shares, are named "Key of Pleasure" and "Lover's Dream" (25), elicits laughter and a playfulness. The princess "kissed the red flower" and the flower comes to life: "its petals fastened tight into a head" (25). The character then morphs into their trans creation:

> [A] strange thing began to happen. As the princess kissed and petted my tulip, my own sensations grew exquisite, but as yet no stronger than my astonishment, as I felt my disguise come to life. The tulip began to stand.
> (25)

This type of enlivened embodiment, where the affixed and revised genital becomes one with its wearer's body and psyche, is important for some genderqueer switches who, in multiple ways, occupy multiple genders and have deeply known and felt associations with the phallus of their genderqueer/trans mind: the desire and standing, the coming to life of the tulip/penis, can be experienced in the mind and body and in sexual desire. There is a s/witchy magical realism to this scene wherein Winterson gives the genderqueer, switch space to exist and, what's more, to be in sexual relation and discovery.

As the harness is hidden, and the members attached securely, all the princess is said to see and feel "was the eagerness of my bulbs and stem" (26). When the character looks down, he comments, "[T]here it was, making a bridge from my body to hers" (25–26). The "tulip waving" the character *feels* "the firm red head and pale shaft plant itself in her body" (26). The character *knows* what it is to have and feel a penetrative object attached to the body, to want to use it, to want to insert it. The character is genderqueered in body and mind, and with an ownership in dwelling in her created gender. The next line details "a delicate green-tinted sap dribbled down her brown thighs" as an offering to the reader, locating us in the virtual world of sex, of the fluids and the body, and is followed by "all afternoon I fucked her" (26).

And here a very direct switch in the language of desire, of desire itself, occurs. Within a breath of a sentence, there exists a switch in the action and perception of the moment. A rapturous act and uninhibited language enter the scene and are used to describe this moment of consummation and connection between princess and prisoner. Reading the passage together magnifies how organically gender and sexual switching can happen: "[A] delicate green-tinted sap dribbled down her brown thighs. All afternoon I fucked her" (26). Switching can be abrupt in its transgressiveness. In these lines Winterson triggers the switch: the reader moves from the erotic, descriptively feminine and flowery language to the vulgar and pornographic.

This hard switch of "I fucked her" not only ends the scene, it ends the chapter and this particular vignette. What occurs next is a switch from the previous time, location and experience of identity, gender, and sexual play to a new, yet connected, location and experience. The narrative that follows moves us into the contemporary time, where the two lovers—who have previously been the shopkeeper and customer and then prisoner and princess— are now in an Internet email exchange discussing what will come next. The main character is weaving yet another story of fantasy so that the secondary character can have the "freedom to be somebody else—just for one night" (32). The writer of this new narrative creates a romantic/sexed encounter of multiple infidelities, the game of the chase and conquest, vulnerability, and abandon.

An unquestioned effortlessness is present in the character's genderqueer switch nature. For example, Winterson slips into the narrative that the tulip-wearing lover of many women has breasts to accompany her mind-made phallus (67–68). The lover has breasts and a phallus of the mind, a phallus that is conjured in a switchy magical realism space of fantasy and wish-fulfilment. This character is a remarkable example of a gender switch. The mind birthing a self-created, gender and sexual switch body and self that functions to support the roles that desire seeks. While the tulip does not surface in the chapter, "New Document," the hotel room sexual encounter with the married woman has the narrator instructing: "[G]et on top of me. Ease yourself, just there, just there … push … harder" (68). We are exposed to a phallus *and* breasts, which serve to genderqueer the character. For some readers who revel in the genderqueer narrative, what is evoked in the character having breasts followed by her instructing her lover to sit on her dildo, provide an affirming visibility that is rare and delicious.

The directive, topping sentences that follow: "[M]ake me come. Make me" illustrate our narrator luxuriating in topping from the bottom. S/he also enjoys verbal play: language and words are a turn on. The repetition is especially delicious and a cue. Notice the switch: the Dominant/Submissive aspect of "making" someone do something, telling the lover to make her have an orgasm, the instruction to the lover to "make her" and yet in a supplicating, repeating way. A beseeching tone can be read here, and the line serves to unmask the receptive nature of the narrator. There is a real vulnerability to her verbalizing what s/he wants, to her seeking connection as well as satisfaction. This, too, is a switch: from confident, strong, take-charge lover to vulnerable, open, and receptive lover. S/he is in action position with the phallus, while also on her back, so they are rather passive even as they control the scene by way of instruction. Another switch then occurs through language as s/he tops from the bottom: they move from "make me come. Make me" to the last lines of the scene, "Just fuck me ... fuck me" (68). The language of desire indicates a subtle switch here: from "make me," which is a seeking of dominance, to "just fuck me," which is a telling of what to do; additionally, and this is a key switch of language that repeats throughout Winterson's work, the character once again moves into a switch that is a trigger to orgasm. The language switch, the repeated words, the subtle, but very deliberate, switch to a more crass and vulgar "fuck" marks the sexual switch to orgasm.

What is soon made apparent is that Winterson has constructed each chapter to serve a narrative that is concerned with switching temporality, surroundings, circumstances, and identity through an ever-present, larger thread. This larger thread constructs the fantasies, roles, and desires from what seems a consistent yet gender-bending, genderless first-person narrator. While the narratives occur in different time and space continuums, there is a similar, overarching first-person narrator in every vignette: so, while each chapter stands alone, they are deeply interconnected.

At the same time, Winterson complicates any knowing or wanting to assign a overarching, genderless main character, indeed, any of her characters, with certain characteristics or genders. The most surprising uprooting occurs when the main character assigns the colour of what was perceived as his (her) tulip to the princess/lover of the previous chapter! When Winterson constructed this next episode, one of *The Powerbook*'s foundational tropes in switching occurs: the secondary character's urgency to experience the "freedom to be anyone else" allows a totally unpredictable switch to occur when the main character asks her accomplice what colour hair she wants. The conversation that follows ushers in this confusing switch as the lover replies with: " 'Red. I've always wanted red hair.' To which the main character asks: 'The same colour as *your tulip*?' 'Look what happened to that.' 'Don't panic' the weaver of the stories states, 'this is a different disguise' " (italics mine, 31).

While the "your" of this dialogue is easily glossed over, it unpredictably acts to bring forth the previous chapter and a dramatic switch: in the preceding sentences, as well as in the previous chapters, the character who is the "your" is the secondary character and not the tulip wearer. The roles are thus switched here; with the simplicity of owning a tulip, a gender, sexual, and identity switch has occurred. Later the narrator will write: "[Y]our hair like a bonfire ... red, spread out, sparks flying ... I want to climb through the fire until *I am* the fire" (204).

As Winterson links her vignettes to the whole of a powerful book, we think we know who is who in the journey: the "I" writing and weaving each vignette of fantasy is the gender-variant switch to whom gender nor identity are to be made and unmade. They are a character who responds to the question, "[A]re you "male or female?" with "[D]oes it matter?" (30). This main character's gender moves and is (re)constructed to suit their wants and needs.

We may have begun to think we have some clarity as to knowing who is who in this novel: who is seeking to assign a gender, who is the gender variant, who is wanting "freedom for one night," and who is providing that freedom. Further, we may begin to understand which character is led into stories of freedom and disguise, and which character is writing their script? The reader may come to think that we know who donned the tulip phallus and switched her gender to a he as a child. We think we know who is the princess and who is the slave, who is being penetrated and who is doing the penetrating and, yet—with the simple question of hair colour, of matching the carpets to the drapes—Winterson twists and turns the gender-variant character inside out, complicating and switching any sense of knowing for us as readers. There is an uncertainty to this narrative, and that too is an important aspect of the topology of the switch.

A further daring reading could allow for the switching and morphing of the characters, not simply within the fictional whole, but with each character being a switched facet of the narrator. Might there not be multiple characters after all? Could this character be in the conversation of created romantic, failed but requited love, fantasy worlds with her/his self? A single character playing all the roles of the erotic, fantasy screenplay she has written, directed, and starred in? Isn't this what it is to dwell in the grey matter of a fantasy? It's interesting to consider the notion of creating, and seeking out, others to act and play supporting roles in one's life narrative. This character is a transgressive outsider who, "like other exiles," experiences that her "longing grew a narrative of its own. Her desire told itself as memory" (166). Common, but not exactly reliable. She continues, "[H]er past was ... the only kingdom she could control" (166). And so, while it's common to resist the responsibility involved, Winterson asks us to consider what kingdoms we as readers control. The thoughts that create our past-based narratives, which inform the present, are one. *The Powerbook* begs us to consider that we conjure, write, star in, and direct the narrative kingdoms of our life. We are in control to choose the actions, behaviours, characters, and script that authentically serves and inspires us, or we can choose to survive within a script and narrative not of our own making. Winterson illustrates choice.

Unpacking the switching moments of Winterson's work opens up endless opportunities for our aliveness through choice and risk. Winterson's character *is* the story, we *are* the story (288): all of it, and "the stories are maps. Maps of journeys that have been made and might have been made. A Marco Polo route through territory real and imagined" (63). We create the story, chart the map, and are at the source of our journey: "real *and* imagined." The narrator is not a writer, crisscrossing countries and centuries by coincidence—no, this time and situational traveling mirror a life of switching and directing one's crafting, editing, and choosing a life's script. She is out to find the treasure of her life, which as a child she is told that as she ages, "[Y]ou'll be looking in the wrong place ... people don't know where to look" (168). However, the child is prone to see other worlds and experience the reverie of them (170).

Thus, we can read *The Powerbook*'s character to be powerful, effective, and aware at playing the game of creating her life and kingdom with illustrating the variancies of gender, sexuality, and identity, *having switch conversations of choosing and allowing* in each moment of doing so. She is a narrator who is her "own hero," winning at what matters to her by her own strength, in her own way (183). This may go undetected by any reader unfamiliar with the rapid-fire quickness of authentic switching that can occur for a switch s/hero. Winterson leads the way by having her character ask what colour her alter ego's hair would like to be; this is our first covert access to a reading of the strategy of oneness. With this question the character may be asking a basic question: might s/he like the same passionate colour as the phallic tulip or something unfamiliar and not yet foreseen?

A close, gender- and sexually variant reading demonstrates that we are invited into the performance and pleasure of creating a character to penetrate and switch within their own switchiness. Winterson crafts and offers us the most private of internal dialogues of the mind: those secret longings and fantasies, those unspoken wants and desires, those unasked questions and wonderings, which are "real enough" (30). The most secret of longings see her occupying the locations of desire and sex as a permanent country of anarchistic citizenship. No "rights or territories" would be sought, no "frontiers or controls," and as such it is "a model of government for the world" (205). This present-day kingdom of the bed is a "country without ruler" where she is "free to come and go as I please." It is ... Utopia," and she laments that "it could never happen beyond bed" (205).

You need a label. But I'm not a piece of furniture with the price on the back.

(Jeanette Winterson, *The Powerbook*, 65)

Another facet at the heart of *The Powerbook* is the freedom that comes when no identity is present, when identity is not something to construct, but something to release and be free from. Third-wave gender and identity variants have both demanded and clung to identity labels, politics, and lifestyle as a way to validate the self (which society often fails to do); current forms might include the overly polite and discretionary questioning—and pre-emptive revealing—of which pronoun or gender to use when addressing or referring to a person, regardless of their being genderqueer, non-binary, or trans. The later has become so mainstream that many people who regard themselves as progressive allies now announce which gender pronoun they prefer before or at the beginning of a communication. Examples include pronouncing one's preferred pronoun at the beginning of a conference or roundtable or adding a line to their email contact tagline which specifies their preferred pronoun. I think it's important to ask how might these clearly demarcated pronouns confine and limit switches and genderqueers? Choosing a preferred pronoun can serve to make those who switch, and revel in a more complex and multiply gendered identity, invisible.

Small communities and subcultures that support variant identities give many gender and sexual variants the support, safety, and acceptance of a chosen family and, while absolutely imperative, notions of "home" can also become constraining and limiting if and when switching is an identity that is sought. Identity is a living, breathing, and (sometimes) changing experience: it is deeply personal, confrontationally political, and tenderly profound.

Without identity we are able to "see through the disguise" because the armour of an externally constructed identity is taken off (74). Winterson writes, "I've been looking for us both all my life" (74), implying a search for much more than a singular, external, separate other: a seeking of unity and supportive coexistence within the switch self. Without fixations on a singular identity, authentic connection becomes increasingly real and attainable. We can stop looking; we can start being.

And so, Winterson invites us to consider the freedom that comes in a world of choosing freedom from identity. She writes:

> [T]here are nights when I'd prefer nothing at all. A structure without cladding. As you get older, the open spaces start to close up ... you keep the form and the habit of what you have, but gradually you empty it of meaning.
>
> (44–45)

Rather than base the present and future on an already existing inherited, unyielding, or fixed cladding by clearing the space, emptying meaning, and coming from nothing, one can choose to create a new, inspiring be-ing. To get to no-thing, what is must be stripped down to a "structure without cladding;" the outworn, ragged layers, and the significance and meaning attached to them, removed. The concepts of beginner's mind and impermanence can guide such a freedom: being empty of meaning becomes a place to stand in, and from there, choosing that which serves to inspire and feed grounds and leads, rather than any set dogma, point of view, affiliation, social conditioning, and/or structure. Winterson takes a page from mystic texts and spiritual traditions when she refers to this location as the "middle ground" (47).

Winterson constructs characters who are "happy ... with the lightness of being in a foreign city and the relief from identity it brings," thereby guiding us to the freedom, lightness, peace of mind that we as readers can both give and receive *if* we release ourselves and others of *fixed ways* of thinking and being with identity construction (gender, sexual, racial, social, etc.). But it takes something—and that something is often much more than the geographical shift that affords one the freedom to step out of those past narratives that limit who one knows and constructs themselves to be. It takes both the choice and action to *rewrite* the narrative, asserts Winterson, and "sometimes a letter at a time is all we can do" (90).

Our versions of identity—as reality—occur as *real* and *fixed*. Our narrative and point of view, our mind's thoughts and the stories we construct as "truth," could be questioned rather than unconditionally believed; the switching and/or fluid morphing in and out of roles and identities can experience new heights of freedom when we release our attachment to those stories and beliefs. Winterson's world weaves her story, "trying to collide the real and the imaginary worlds, trying to be sure which is which." We may think we are in reality when, really,

> the more I write, the more I discover that the partition between real and invented is as thin as a wall in a cheap hotel room … as soon as I reckon I know the geography of what isn't and what is, a chair scrapes in the room beyond the wall and a woman's voice says, "You don't understand do you?"
>
> (108)

Winterson's narratives empower the reader to question our scripts and self-created narratives. While our mind is often juggling survival-based dialogues (assessments, judgements, and evaluations) with our and others' identity, Winterson creates safe places to let go and begin a new creating process; "[T]he world is a mirror of the mind's abundance," Winterson writes near the end of the novel (263). She sandwiches the large landscape of a whirling mind of abundance with her seeker character realizing that she can "really quit" the drama because "everything I had sought had been under my feet from the beginning" (261). This is an empowering switch action and realization, after which a new chapter, titled "restart," begins with the opening lines, "The map. The treasure" (267).

Before we reach the end of the novel, however, we witness that the majority of conversations with others in the novel (mimicking life) take place with individuals who are distracted by their own internal stories and dialogue; what is going on in the present moment and the possibilities of freedom are mostly missed. Instead, a juggling of survival-based identities controls the conversations. Like the unanswerable question that the woman in the hotel room asks, which speaks to her mind's roaring internal dialogue, Winterson's variant narrator is asked such a pseudo question by her lover: Is her name "real?" They respond that her name is "real enough" (30). Here, again, the switch appears as we glimpse into perceived reality versus point-of-view; any answer is irrelevant. What is real, what is false, is already decided. Yet this character's realness and name are "real enough:" hers to create, anew, at any time. These scenes allow us access to what is being intentionally created with present-based verse and what is being unintentionally created through past-based verse. We are then given some choice with where freedom with identity can live.

Worlds upon worlds of experiences that feed into this narrator's life, as is the case with all my writers, point to seeking a switchable and free identity life. Winterson's character writes of her own overarching narrative:

> I talk to people whose identity I cannot prove. I disappear into a web of co-ordinates that we say will change the world. What world? Which world? It used to be that the real and the invented were parallel lines that never met. Then we discovered that space is curved, and in curved space parallel lines always meet. The mind is a curved space. What we experience, what we invent, track by track running together, then running into one, the brake lever released.
>
> (108–109)

Readers will begin to notice where the mind collapses story and reality, where this character disappears and feels an outsider, where she creates like an exile, ever seeking to be part of, yet staying, "on the run" (185). She is in a constant state of being open to redrawing, revision, and rewriting. Switching to free up their identity and allow for multiple points of view, ways of being, and existences to occupy the narrator's journey drive this novel; indeed, they can serve to mirror our own.

We come to know multiple roles coexisting within fluid characters, with shifting, ever-malleable identities, sexualities, and genders throughout the novel, throughout a life, perhaps experiencing and playing with many s/witchy magical realism spaces in a day. Each variancy, each switch, is authentic and worthy of celebration and acceptance rather than occurring as mutinous transgressions to question, compare, stifle, or doubt. Switching gender and sexual identities, desires and roles are able to be created in a present now phenomenon, existing in a space of play and s/witchy magic. This play, this ability to dwell *and* switch between *multiple variancies, while having them each be authentic* is, most especially, what the switch excels at, seeks to embody, and celebrate.

Accepting herself as that which is not solid or fixed, but mutable and open to switchability, the character affirms: "Nothing is fixed. These are images that time changes and that change time, just as the sun and the rain play on the surface of things" (52). How simple to create oneself as effortlessly and changeable as raindrops! Raindrops *playing*! Seeking, exploring, finding solace in comparable forces of nature, like the sun and rain, which radiate unpredictable and complex beauty at the micro and macro level, like the human body, the narrator stretches her mind in order to free it: "My mind reached forward into the unlimited space it can occupy when I loose it from its kennel" (52). A willingness *and* wilfulness exist here, and so a new possibility is unleashed: an unconfined and unlimited space she wants, and chooses, to occupy (not one that is given up easily by her surrounding environment, perhaps). One's environment (social, familial, etc.), like the mind, can be prison-like, a "kennel," keeping us confined in roles and identities never agreed to or actively/consciously created.

For this narrator, to be free from the prison of the mind involves many moves, one of which is moving to another location, somewhere *foreign*. This geographical hift away from the familiar and known allows the narrator to take steps on a new path, one with more openings, more possibilities, and more play. The escape, switch, or "geographical cure" constitute a current running through *The Powerbook*; its narrator echoes the lives of many gender variants who, in switching their identity many times, allow for "another life" (59).

Past lives and identities can seem distant and removed "until I remember it was my life, like a letter you turn up in your own handwriting, hardly believing what it says" (59). Winterson's metaphor of rain is again resonant: as rain is formed from recycling the Earth's rivers, lakes, oceans, and seas, human beings are likewise called to reform ourselves by way of recycling and transforming the old. As the play of the raindrop that emerges from a cloud as a droplet is enlarged by moisture from the surrounding air and then coalesces with other raindrops as it descends to take form, this gender-fluid narrator needs a new surrounding community with which to coalesce and form a transformed self. Winterson explains that

> in those other worlds[,] events may track our own, but the ending will be different. Sometimes we need a different ending. I can't take my body through space and time, but I can send my mind, and use the stories, written and unwritten, to tumble me out in a place not yet existing—my future.
>
> (63)

And it's the invented choice of futures that Winterson concerns us with. The stories are simply "maps. Maps of journeys that have been made and might have been made" (63).

The invented boxes, beliefs, and familiar stories, fed over years, add layers weight and burden to a life; the "story on story, map on map ... warns me of the weight of accumulation," cautions Winterson's narrator (64). "The other worlds I can reach need to keep their lightness and their speed of light," she writes, for "what I carry back from those worlds to my world is another chance" (64). Lightness, *another chance*, increased possibilities free from a confining past or identity are sought. Those who want to limit or box in the narrator are confronted with an unstoppable urgency in being free: "You want to explain me to yourself," the narrator says to her lover. "You're not sure, so you need a label. But I'm not a piece of furniture with the price on the back" (65). As with my other authors, Winterson's writing is concerned with the existential questing of "more life into a time without boundaries" (53).

A life, a time, without boundaries—a book, a life, rewritten with each turn of the wheel, is adventurous and courageous. It is also filled with uncertainty. Winterson shows that trust in love, romantic for some, unachievable for others, global for all, is at the heart of her character's life of exploration and success, and it is by this searching and seeking that her character is led.

> Only the impossible is worth the effort. What we seek is love itself, revealed now and again in human form, but pushing us beyond our humanity into animal instinct and god-like success. The love ... has a wildness in it ... human love ... is an encampment on the edge of the wilderness ... the wilderness is not tamed. It waits—beautiful and terrible—beyond the reach of the campfire. Now and again someone gets up to leave, forced to read the map of themselves, hoping that the treasure is really there ... I do not know if what I hear is an answer or an echo. Perhaps I will hear nothing. It doesn't matter. The journey must be made.
>
> (91)

While there are many readings and shifts in the speaking of *The Powerbook*'s narrator, what is consistent is the overarching theme given to each vignette, chapter, and story weaver. In a fluctuating time and space narrative we are invited into the worlds and voices of characters who write stories that are predominantly centred around complex and shifting boundaries and desire (40), switch moments and identities that inform love and the journey of a variant's life. The raw vulnerability that comes from the tender openness of revealing oneself through one's surroundings is what gives an extraordinary context and *power* to switches and *The Powerbook*.

Revising the map

At its heart, *Written on the Body* is a romantic novel. It is a novel that comes early on in Winterson's career and, like all her work, is extremely bold in presenting a gender-free/variant narrator, bringing awareness to the variant possibilities of queer lives and queer love, and a work that gives us powerful, lyrical poetic lines to roll around in. Overarching the top layer of the novel is a flowery, tragedy-lurking, romantic innocence. The language and writing style that predominates the novel is almost love-sick. While much has been said about *Written on the Body*, it is still a benchmark for writing a gender-neutral character who falls in love and has intimate relations with a woman. Digging deeper, we have an obsessive character who confronts identity and the self and who switches to do so.

Written on the Body has attained critical acclaim for being a romance/love questing novel wherein the narrator's gender remains anonymous. To preclude an opportunity for gender assignment throughout a novel that is highly attuned to the body, sex, and love is quite a feat. Winterson rejects even opting for a gender and invents a gender-neutral, nameless character with an undefined body. The character is a self-described bottom (*Written on the Body*, 10) who, like the character creations of Acker and Myles, is playful: she anamorphosizes her lover, a married woman named Louise, who is likened to butterflies and trees (29), a cat, a filly, and a sea anemone (73). The mythical Pegasus is also called forth as the narrator seeks to ride and tame the God who "would not be saddled" (131).

Winterson's novel has the highest level of integrity in that she is consistent in never allowing or permitting a gender to be revealed; further, she has kept this silence in every interview since the publication of the work, refusing all those who desperately want her to gender her narrator. *Written on the Body* is thus a work that can be hailed as an example of how genderqueers and gender variants can experience the freedom in choosing to live without fixed gender assignments. The value of this aspect of the novel is both profound and revolutionary. The novel is an example of how we can write our bodies, our identities, and our love interests in any manner that serves us, whatever that looks like! Her novel is an example of how anyone can live identity- and gender-free while still writing and experiencing the body, sex, making love, falling in and out of love in beautiful, heart-rending, connecting, tender, and meaningful ways.

No matter how hard readers and critics may try to distinguish or identify the character's gender or sexual identity, it is all for naught; any reader who is tempted to match socially constructed behaviours, language, actions, and assumptions of gender is stymied: Winterson refuses any knowing or disclosure. We experience a who rather than a what: a romantically driven character who begins and ends "alone on a rock hewn out of my own body" (9). This body is never described or gendered, the author and narrator maintaining full control and ownership over the body.

The degree to which Winterson controls our experience with gender variancy allows her to ask us as readers to suspend how, when, and where we gender behaviour, actions, and thoughts. Rather, we are urged to consider the redundancy of a gendered body. For a novel that is centred on sex, love, obsession, and the mental landscape of negotiating the terrain of falling in love, it is a remarkable feat to maintain a consistency of abstract and undefined gender and identity. The fact that Winterson has successfully accomplished this task is perhaps enough of a statement of purpose: a gender-variant and identity-free life—even in momentary interactions and happenings—*is* available.

Winterson creates what some of us will come to love and appreciate in her fiction: another sassy narrator who takes lyrical, dramatic, and metaphorical turns inward. This s/hero, like many of Winterson's main characters, seems to ache for the release of love and leans into the hope, and ultimate pain, of a happy ending that never comes. Hope without faith, trust, and action don't often make for results, however, and such is the case in this fictional work. More than her other novels, *Written on the Body* is obsessively focused on the love interest and the interior tickings of the mind as they specifically pertain to the lament of the love quest. Other Winterson novels bear similar internal dialogues, but they involve the outer world more: landscape, colour, interpretations of the outer world; in this novel, another person, the lover, is the sole obsession. Anything surrounding the married lover and the love triangle becomes superfluous.

One of the rare locations of Winterson linking the character's obsession with her love interest within a larger context occurs with mapping, which is a lovely metaphor that I addressed above in *The Powerbook*. In *Written on the Body*, mapping occurs when she is leaving her lover, Jacqueline, for her new lover, Louise. Winterson writes, "[N]ow, standing here in this in this familiar unviolated space, I have already altered my world and Jacqueline's world forever. She doesn't know this yet. She doesn't know that there is today a revision of the map" (38). What is so refreshing is Winterson's calling on the character to take ownership and design of her life through revision. A revised topology of the map of one's life, and to another's life by extension, is hers to draw and create. Here, the character is coming to terms with the fact that her choices in revising the map of her life have an effect on others—in this case the lover she is about to leave. She creates the space of their home as unviolated, which she is now going to alter. It will become a violated home, a violated space, with the introduction of the new lover. The ownership of her life is what is striking with this narrator: she is ready to bear the consequences as she revises the map of her life, in full control of which bodies of water she will swim in, which continents she will travel over. These are all characteristics of the switch.

Written on the Body allows the reader to get lost in chapter after chapter of love-seeking, unravelling desire. and the quest for love and pleasure through sex, while dwelling in both discomfort and serenity: each reader has the choice of uncertainty. There is the uncertainty of love being reciprocated, the uncertainty of the affair moving into a relationship of its own, the uncertainty of consequences, and the uncertainty of the two staying together despite the obstacles. Something the novel thus broaches, while also avoiding it, is the fallacy of a happy ending, of any certainty, of even the most committed of promises being honoured. *Written on the Body* constitutes a triumph of inquiry into love and pain, gender and identity, love and loss.

Don't be rehearsing, be doing it for the first time.

(Eileen Myles, *Skies*, 82)

Eileen Myles, similar to Kathy Acker, unearths how the interior self's non-acceptance and resistance (as well as society's) pose many rapturous dangers. Like Winterson (and Carson, who follows in Chapter 4), Myles explores gender switching: magical realism informs the body morphing and switching into a new version of the self, often animalistic and/or anthropic, that serves desires being fulfilled.

Eileen Myles was born in Cambridge, Massachusetts in 1949. Having moved to New York to become a poet in 1977, Myles continues to be known foremost as a New York school poet. Myles has published over twenty books of poetry, fiction, non-fiction, plays, and performance pieces, regularly reads their work and attends poetry conferences and such, and has won numerous awards and prizes. For decades, they have been recognized and appreciated in various poetry and writing circles, as well as experimental, subcultural, artistic, lesbian, and underground writing and poetry scenes.

While previously using female pronouns, in recent years Myles prefers to use the gender-neutral pronoun, "they," and to use the identity descriptors lesbian and trans. I will refer to Myles as "Myles," "they," or "their."[2] For some readers, this may elicit some confusion when determining if "their" or "they" refer to the author or the subject; others may find reading "their" instead of "she" or "he" awkward or unfamiliar. Considering the dominance of hetero-normative, binary pronoun use and language, this is very normal: the alterations of pronoun use can be challenging and similar to learning a new language. That said, I would like to invite readers to be open to noticing gendered language and to look at expanding their default pronoun use as an opportunity.

In choosing to re-feminize the male-dominant and influenced vocabulary I grew up with, I first began with noticing that my and other's language was patriarchally influenced. I then began altering all the "he's" to "she's" (please see footnote 3 in Chapter 1 for a comprehensive discussion on this subject). In the last ten or so years, I have found the increase of "they" to be a further opportunity to expand and decolonize my language use: to reflect, question, think about, and alter my habitual word choices and gendered language use; this serves to keep me present, awake, and attentive to the different gendered experiences and needs of others *and* create the space for variant identities to exist beyond "he" and "she."

Myles reveals a vulnerable truth when they write: "how I see / is in constant / danger" (*Skies*, 37). Of all their work, Myles's 2001 book of poetry, *Skies*, brings an ethereal and expansive openness to gender ambiguity and variancy: the "sky's the limit," as Myles titled a panel discussion that is presented as an Introduction to *Skies*. *Skies* is similar in presentation to Myles's previous books of poetry: lines are short, there is very little punctuation, and there is an economy of language; however, *Skies* differs from Myles's previous work in that, like its title, it is ethereal. *Skies* contains little anger or hostility; rather, it is a book of poems that bespeaks a deep maturity of awareness and observance.

Dwelling on the queerly sexed body and mindset, the infinite sky truly *is* the limit for my chosen writers. While there is an infinite sky and infinite possibilities for gender and sexual expression, my authors portray their characters' *seeing, feeling, living,* and *being* in a world that switches between both a location of danger and a location within which their ways of walking the world are dangerous. A complicated, differently gendered and sexed-self is the distinction here; it is the variant switch state of identity awareness and existence that is precariously hinged.

In *Skies*, Myles explores the island or cloud in the sky-like mental communities that humans create to thrive and exist in, be we poets, writers, artists, teachers, food growers, builders, crafters, and so forth. They offer us solace to create, and that solace can easily move into rooms and landscapes of isolation and made-up, constructed difference; rooms where our colour-filled, ritually led, art-inspired, safe environments form a "culture of one" (*Not Me*, 202). In their 1987 postscript to *Not Me*, an early book of poems written between 1986 and 1989, Myles relates to what many professionals who work alone may experience: while the "culture of one" is very satisfying, there is a need to be a part of the larger, outside culture to which a person seeks to belong (the basics of human tribalism). Myles writes that they begin this process "by making work which violates the hermetic nature of my own museum" and shares this action "as a friendly gesture towards the people who might recognize me" (202).

And so it is that each word, each poem, each shared creative crafting *is* a gesture to recognition. Some of us may recognize ourselves in these writers. We gravitate towards authors who we can associate with: the way they think, view and/or experience the world, the way they write feelings. Readers feel "got" or understood when we read familiar experiences on the page; what's more, we feel "gotten" when we read a familiar *way* of linking those innermost personal thoughts, turning our world turning into words. It's the speaking of the world that we associate with the most, perhaps, the world that recreates and remakes us over and over with each passing page.

There is an unlatched quality to Myles's articulations and writing. Myles creates the process as almost violent when describing the making and releasing of their work: sharing their poetry "violates the hermetic seal of" their "own museum." There is a rupturing, a forcing, an almost wilful, necessary destruction. *Skies* is noted for beautifully portraying "the sweet metaphysical tragedy of having to bear lonely witness to one's own experiences" (Scharf, 85); the sharing of this lonely experience, the breaking of the hermetic seal, is necessary because if Myles (and we) do not speak, if Myles (and we) are not recognized and seen, who are they? Who are we? How is anyone constituted if they are not seen? We are formed by the communities and worlds around us, forging our lives through connection, even if there can also be a sense of "all alone," the isolated islands are located in a chaotic sea. Truly, these are key components to switching and, for all my writers there exists a ripe space of journey and navigation to deconstruct, one that carries many cresting waves of switching in identity, gender, sexuality, place, community, connection, what it is to seek, explore and dwell, to watch and ride, this tidal sea of connecting rivers and streams.

There is always the community of being human waiting. For Myles's characters occur as introverted, the gift of extending must trump the familiar and safe holding in and onto: rather, the opening up of the museums of life becomes imperative to survival. Like any modern museum, Myles has constructed a written catalogue of sorts, so that those interested in what is offered as a show-and-tell can quickly locate ideas and choose either the vulnerable or the butch toughness. The beauty in *Skies* is that the readers can show up as casually as they might a craft fair or public lecture.

Myles's notes that the writing and sharing of the self is "exhibitionist work" to which they add the quip "really," and it is, of course, yet the action is often unspoken. We might propose a provocative question here: Are we not all either exhibitionists or voyeurs? All the while, pretending otherwise. Many would not be self-referential, or refer to other writers, artists, or anyone who creates and shares their work as *exhibitionists*; when this word is used it is most often not complimentary or something to admire and emulate. The word *masochist,* like the word *exhibitionist,* is used in a similar, colloquial way: a referent of what one *does not* want to be, or wishes to avoid. Yet, isn't this what novelists, poets, and memoirists, who are most often concerned with interiority, engaged with: *"the desire to expose parts"*? Are not most creative sharings a revealing, and simultaneously an invitation to watch and observe intimacy (*in to me see*) at some level? Could we read Myles's "exhibitionist work" as an invitation to (re)consider where and how we can engage on a sexual continuum of variancy as readers?

In "The Guest," Myles's exhibitionist character is not quite "good enough," not quite masculine or handsome enough, and so is posed as a guest: "I truly have/given up/on handsome" (*Skies*, 194), they confess. The giving up on one or another aspect of the self to fit into a way of being, is what the switch will challenge. As my own personal experience shared in Chapter 1, the sense of having to choose certain gendered aspects (to fit in), give up others, or resign oneself to social/cultural norms is a key factor that many variant gendered people experience and wrestle with. Where in the range between beautiful and handsome does a gender switch, lesbian, queer, or trans person fit and find locations of home? Having admitted this, perhaps even accepted it, the narrator is, at least, "animal pleased" as they remember "rumpled sheets" and face the hardened reality that they have "never loved anyone" (194). As I will later demonstrate with Acker and then Carson, the guest in Myles's narrative body resorts to identification with an animal: satisfaction with one's complex and variant sexual and/or gender roles and identifications give rise to animalistic behaviour; that is, within or without, a foreign species is used to explain the occupying deviancy. In a culture that dictates impossible-to-match beauty standards—and suggests surgery and treatments to "fit in,"—to not feel "good enough" is a common trope. To not see where or how to accept and love the variant self leaves little room for love of the self or other: the animal resides here now. A switching from unloving and not handsome enough to a sexed animal is a method to express deviancy and transgressive desire.

Later in the poem, Myles will switch to introduce tropes of gendered femininity—lavender, scents, baskets: women's work, and female healing herbs are situated in stark contrast to a masculinity and an inability to feel feminine: women's "laughing/and healing" are witnessed via photographs sent in the mail, and we witness a character who sits steeped in a gendered discomfort. Being/feeling handsome *while also* feminine in their facial features, the figure in the poem stands between and betwixt a place of gender variancy and genderqueerness in both body and mind. These places can be wonderfully affirming for lesbian, genderqueer, and queer folks, as *we see* our gender variancy in another and experience a familiarity and safety in our numbers. Physical features of the face, chest, and bone structure can sometimes reveal one's birth gender, and sometimes give away gender-variant and trans folks. In the heteronormative world, there can seem nowhere to hide in gender variant, trans masculine, androgyny or butchness when the eyes look down and caress the soft curves of the chest or shoulders, the interior identity shape-shifting disappearing as the viewer attempts to makes sense of and orient the person before them by fixing a birth gender identity.

A queer, feminist reading would allow for Myles making small, incremental movements towards looking at the complexity of passing on the traits and mannerisms of women's voices as well as female and male relatives; these locations of voice, mothering, and the feminine are something many genderqueers, butches, transgendered, and gender-variant folk often wrestle with when locating and recreating new agency with the self and body. It would thus be remiss to not note that for some, difficult choices of switching exist and are, indeed, part of the terrain. Choices between honouring the desire to self-create one's identity, body, and life *and* honouring the inherited, ancestral line, complete with "gifts," such as voice or breast size that don't always match one's chosen or changing gender identity.[3] The links between gender identity, the body, and shape-shifting can be experienced and move like a storm at sea, rapturous. This is perhaps why Myles and, as I will show later, Carson, morph and shape-shift into having either animalistic qualities and features or inhabiting an animal. Not only is bestiality a sexual taboo, which is a variant and transgressive sexual desire, but also animal identification can be a location to safely experiment and explore switching and one's internal switch nature.

In an interview published in *The Paris Review*, Jeanette Winterson speaks to the notion of tradition and which ones we may, or may not, carry forth into a newly created gender and/or sexual identity. She comes to the discussion by way of her relationship to the Bible and her Christian upbringing. She writes that her journey is actually a very typical one, and that

> if you have been immersed in something, there will come a point when you have to rebel against it. It was necessary for me to leave behind my entire early background—physically, emotionally and intellectually ... to have nothing to do with it. *Oranges [are not the only Fruit]* was a way of cleansing myself from all that, of saying, No, this is what I am. Not this other thing, this made thing. Now I am going to make myself, I'll be self-invented. Over the years ... I have continued to think long and deeply about those issues that I suppose I have thought about since I was a very small child. Now I feel comfortable again to use the Bible as one source book amongst many others, but as a very important one. It is

something that I know so very well that it would be ridiculous for me to try to do without it. And there's no point. I don't accept the God myth of the church. I think it's hogwash. But that doesn't mean that I don't accept the essential mystery of the scriptures and of the religious faith.

(*The Paris Review*, Spring 1999)

Winterson discovered a newfound comfort with scripture, something that was at one time so uncomfortable and restrictive and in need of a rebellion, now contributes to her self-generated identity. She points to looking for what is of value in traditions (such as spiritual and mystical books passed down) what can be appreciated, accepted, and used, even if they are not completely a match with one's choices. The interviewer then asks her if she feels the need to fight against that which she does not accept. Winterson's reply is candid, astute, and wise: "Absolutely not," she says, and explains:

It's of much more use to me as an ally. But that's only because of this relationship whereby it was everything, then it had to be nothing, and now I have come back to a point where it is as though a friend walks beside you, neither in front nor behind.

(*The Paris Review*, Spring 1999)

Myles, Carson, and Winterson all broach the topic of reconciling the past and tradition with the present and variant identities in different ways. Almost identical in wording to Acker, Myles tells us that how they see "is in constant danger" with a whistled voice "the desperate/sound/of a storm/ at sea" (*Skies*, 196–197). The variant's ways of seeing, in the stormy seas of the world, are a dangerous terrain for one who has a map that deviates from the gender and sexual normative navigational system. So, again, Myles will associate human and animal and asks, "don't you/know/that/you're the/ horse? Rearing/through your life" (199). The horse (and, really, all Equidae) is a beautiful metaphor for the switch, as it indicates immediate, powerful actions within safe, familial, social environments *and* new, sometimes lonely, hostile environments; a horse will constantly switch between meeting their internal, individualistic driven needs *and coexisting* with external, social, herd group ones. Instinctual, survival-based actions and behaviours switch quickly in a horse's life, and rearing is one of the most powerful actions a horse can exhibit. A horse lifting off, or rearing, from its powerful hindquarters is most often an expression of play, confusion, pain, or being scared: you don't have to be an equestrian, Pegasus, or Sagittarian lover to appreciate Myles's metaphor and ask: Which feeling is the movement driving your life? What locations are calling for you to "rear up?" (201).

While animalization can bring a freedom through a life and evoke a larger landscape, Myles will later lament, "I was your/landscape/Here I am a cold chunk/of marble" (199). The question of what the "I" can become when choice seems limited is cold stone marble—and that cold stone is a body that "has no friend" (201). For Myles, and later Acker, there is a desensitization that is conveyed. From the coldness of stone to the insecurity of living in rented rooms with non-functioning, broken toilets, the hardness of city living *as well as* the freedom to be anonymous, and so be able to more freely recreate one's identity, is written into the gender and/or sexually variant's narrative life. Hard and soft, confining and opening, tradition and revision, the past and the present, visibility and invisibility are all juxtaposed.

Myles may put the "final/touches on/your handsewn/manuscript/made out of/your mother's/old clothes" but the character is clearly a guest in the feminine mother's clothes that they do not wear (198). Who wears a "woman's/hat … an Easter bonnet … a band" with "little purple flowers" is the narrative's friend Tim. Tim is unable to pass outside of his male gender however, as he brings an obvious and clumsy drag to his trying on the feminine: Myles describes the accessory as "an old lady's/hat like a rug/with a muscle" (198).

Myles's narrator wears shirts, not blouses. These are stuffed in nooks: housed in rented rooms, cheapened: the interior selves, the gendered aspects of a self not seen or wanted are no longer visible. As noted above, identity is likened to cold marble; tragically, a person turned off. The stone coldness turns in, as the character will self-deprecatingly write, "I hate my/autonomy/cold knuckles" (196). This poem ends with "my body/ has no friend" (201) a bleak reminder of what happens when we run and do not create space for all the variant or fluid aspects of our identity: masculine, feminine, and everything in between to be befriended. The conflict that Myles writes their characters as living with demonstrates a very clear pathway to switching: their poems illustrate the importance of not stuffing the many different aspects and parts of a self into nooks—to gather dust, to be forgotten—the importance of not cutting off, silencing, or closeting that which is gendered or sexually complicated. Silently resting/retiring the desires of a life, in dusty nooks, draws attention to all the rest of the living space, where switching might be freely expressed and experienced.

In "Writing," Myles addresses not wanting to look at one's reflection, or "face in/the mirror," confessing a resistance to clearly look at, see, and accept what is (81). They "can't/bear" their "thoughts" (81). There is a discomfort and shame in not being able to be with the reflection, a location that many trans, queer, gender and/or sexual variants know very well. A disempowering conversation and context with the body is present; there exists a self-loathing and resistance. The body and mind seem out of one's control, one is a victim, a puppet, masterminded by an outside force of hands. Yet this writer is powerful, like a "god," and "can/connect/any two/things" (80). Perhaps the cathartic action of writing and speaking the unbearable may begin a more empowering connection and conversation? Surely God is that merciful?

Another poem, "Nameless," begins to encourage authenticity with one of the best lines in the book: "don't be rehearsing/be doing/it for the first/ time" (82), an apt and empowering mantra for switching and being free in one's gender and sexual identity if ever there was one. Myles writing that "language/takes/the size/of your/life" (96) surely allows the reader to consider the freedom we can have in creating our life through words and the language we choose: How else are we created if not through our words? Language being and becoming one's life complicates yet informs what we *can do* through switching. In *Skies*, names, performance, presentation, and identity take on both the ugly and the handsome: our internal narratives and stories, the daily activities and observances of daily living and writing, and variant creative expressions wrestle acceptance and then breaking free. For Myles offers the reader an okay-ness with difference, a navigating of what is, what is wished for, and what isn't; *Skies* is a living demonstration of how poetically one can navigate "the way everything moves in/my head (189).

Myles has the speaker switch through confronting and revealing both patterns and intersections. In a poem titled the symbol of a black dot they confess, "I don't know ... I'm trying/to read/the world/a smoky/criss/cross in the sky/paths/intersect/ occasionally" (161). These lines encourage the reader to pause and witness intersectional, criss-cross paths of identity and ways of being and, further, *embrace* how switching is a location of crisscross, smoky ambiguity. A newly empowered, higher self responds with: "[W]e were/a miracle/once," as if to remind themselves (and us as readers) that they *are still* walking miracles (161). The resigned self seems defeated, the fight ended, as Myles gives over to their top with the short, non-committal answer of "I'll try" (161). Myles has their characters enjoy dwelling in the not knowing and in the ambiguous, and it can seem a masochistic pain with the self, lovers, and love.

Little miracles of acceptance run through *Skies* while, at the same time, looping insanities of non-acceptance also coexist. There is relief when Myles switches and criss-crosses and a celebration and appreciation in those moments when her narratives relax into self-acceptance. Such moments are truly glorious and epic. The variant switch seems victorious when Myles writes, "My mind's/pretty/juicy/pretty crayon-/y/" (87). One may wish for the poems that resonate self-criticism to cosy up to those that write such a lushness: this mind is juicy, crayony, and akin to a "full moon" (87).

And this is the switch we can celebrate: a juicy one, a layered one, a loved one, a full, juicy moon of a mind! *Skies* evokes the never-ending vastness of the miraculous as Myles's speakers switch and morph with time, gender, subversive same-sex desire, and the play that exists along the continuum of the masculine and feminine, the body and role, want and need. As the sky is unlimited and never-ending, so too are we. We are just as full of promise as Myles's *Skies*.

What you risk reveals what you value.

(Jeanette Winterson, *The Passion*, 91)

Kathy Acker, like Gertrude Stein, was a determined, courageous, and bold pioneer of avant-garde, experimental writing. For Acker, switching is perverse and is located in language, relationships, the body, sex, and the unpredictable; more subtly, Acker's perversity and switchness can be seen as a movement, a fetish, a masochistic performance, and a feminist statement, which is most explicit when talking about ecstasy or pain.

Kathy Acker was born in New York City on April 18, 1947, and grew up there. Her life and contributions were tragically cut short by cancer at the age of fifty. Acker wrote prolifically for twenty-five years and is hailed by some as one of the most influential, transgressive, and experimental writers of her generation; others would propose of the latter half of the century.

Her first books were submitted under pseudonyms (*The Childlike Life of the Black Tarantula*, by The Black Tarantula, and *The Adult Life of Toulouse Lautrec, by Henri Toulouse Lautrec*, illustrated by William Wegman). They came out as chapbooks, published by Sol LeWitt. Like Gertrude Stein and so many other experimental modern and post-modern writers of the twentieth century, Acker was living and creating side-by-side with those translating their lives into art. In *The Transformation of the Avant-Garde*, a book that deals with the New York art world from 1940 to 1985, Diana Crane makes the connection between the differences in commercial success of experimental artists and writers. Without the successful artists helping the writers to achieve an audience, many of the most precious experimental literary works and figures would be even more marginalized than they were/are.

Like the hardness that existed in the 1970s and 1980s in New York's Lower East Side streets that she walked, lived, and created in, there is a certain drama to her life and her fiction. A rich world of avant-garde visual art, poetry, literature, philosophy, culture, politics, sex, music, drugs: it was all both conceptual and very alive and filled the spaces of her life and pages. Later, like so many of the messy, brilliant, confrontational, and sexual writers of her time, Acker was published by Grove Press, Barney Rosset's alternative press, located in Greenwich Village. Picador would publish her work in London, packaging *Blood and Guts in High School*, *Great Expectations*, and *My Death My Life by Pier Paolo Pasolini* in a single volume that sold out in three weeks. Pandora would later do the same, publishing her early 1970s work in 1989.

At age thirty, while working in a cookie shop, she would write in a notebook:

> [T]here was absolutely nothing in the society that in any way made it seem possible for me to earn my living as a writer. I was, & still am, the most non-commercial of writers. I said, if X doesn't exist you have to make it exist. You just imagine it.
>
> ("Cancer Became My Whole Brain": Kathy Acker's Final Year, *The New Yorker*, August 11, 2017, Chris Kraus)

Acker was a sub- and countercultural hero, a woman with a punk-rock aesthetic and "fuck you" personality who challenged conventions. Her writing, like her life, was unpredictable, disorientating, and untamed. She worked jobs in many fields and was a prolific writer, university instructor, and cultural influencer who, despite seeming to have anti-bourgeois and scarcity conversations around money, was able to buy property of her own (in London, no less) and travel quite extensively between New York, California, and Europe. Acker would adorn herself with high-priced, classic, current collection Gaultier, Vivienne Westwood, and Comme des Garcons haute couture pieces or a torn up tee-shirt and punk-influenced motorcycle jacket—enough of a collection that Dodie Bellamy would curate an exhibit of her clothes called "Kathy Forest" in 2006. Her friends ranged from accomplished writers and artists to astrologers and healers. Subculture legends Robert Mapplethorpe and Del LaGrace photographed her. William Burroughs—whose cut-up, conceptual methods of writing would influence Acker's subversive and experimental writing style and methodology—would assert in 1983: "Acker gives her work the power to mirror the reader's soul."

Acker was given the diagnosis of cancer in April 1996 and pursued various treatments until her passing in Mexico on November 30, 1997. In dealing with cancer, Acker found herself drawn to many alternative healing and spiritual practices. For Acker, there was a degree of suffering, a questing and a seeking, up until the end of her life. One of the healers she would work with was Stephen Russell (a Taoist-based teacher) whom she quoted as saying to her: "[E]very person has two selves: a local and a transcendental. The transcendental self is the one who watches. I help a person get there, for if he can, he can see or find how to heal himself." Sadly, what seemed missing until far too late was Acker giving this generosity to herself. Her last work, a novel, was aptly titled "Eurydice in the Underworld."

In "The Gift of Disease," which shares her dealing with the journey of fighting, and living with, cancer was an essay published in *The Guardian* in January 1997, Acker seems to realize one of the most poignant truths that resonated in every one of her fictional characters and literary works: "I am the one who must heal in order to be healed." She shares that she has now been given an opportunity to heal; she has now

> entered the school of the self. I thought I was, unwillingly, confronting cancer, instead, I was confronting myself. I no longer have cancer. To heal in oneself is to begin to heal the self, which is always whole. I have written down some of what happened to me in the past nine months, though I as yet understand little.
>
> (Duke Library Archive)

Similar to the characters in her fiction, Acker seemed to have had messy and complicated blind spots to her happiness and healing: releasing all resistance to access and allow the light of healing, with understanding being a bonus.

Looking at one of Acker's first published works, *The Childlike Life of the Black Tarantula by the Black Tarantula* (1973) alongside one of her last, *Pussy, King of the Pirates* (1996), illustrates bookmarked ends to an oeuvre of perverse switching and an explicit pornography of identity and sexuality; her characters are constantly moving, celebrating and struggling simultaneously between locations of sexual being and sexual objectification, becoming an animal and then either rejecting or embracing one's humanity, occupying multiple genders at the same time while struggling to maintain, create, or be free from a singular identity or self. Acker's work courageously and rigorously demonstrates the discomfort and anxiety of these sometimes conflicting and simultaneous processes; at the same time, Acker consistently exhibits her commitment to writing a "complete sexuality" as it "occurs within" even as "the ground pulls out from under my body" (*The Childlike Life of the Black Tarantula*, 49).

In the thorough, yet brief, "Introduction" to the book *Essential Acker: The Selected Writings of Kathy Acker*, Jeanette Winterson, who was a good friend of Acker's, writes,

> Acker believed that desire is the only honest part of us, and she believed that art is authentic desire. She never expected that art itself could transform the world, but she knew art could awaken in us the authentic desire buried under the meaninglessness of modern life. The responsibility to act on that desire is up to us.
>
> (ix)

And, thus, in the effort to awaken the authentic and dispense with the "meaningless of modern life," Acker writes, "I'm trying to figure out what reality is" (*The Childlike Life of the Black Tarantula*, 25).

Acker's writing discloses the tenuous and fragile intersections between what is natural and unnatural, what constitutes normality and the abnormal. As with Stein and my other writers, this writing of intersection constitutes all of Acker's work and takes the form of a deep, first-person inquiry wherein the personal is and/or becomes the political. Ambiguous, switching spaces of relationship, family, connection, love, order and disorder, subcultures, sex practices, and the body weave continually through the written texts and bodies of this blazoning author. These spaces and themes function as axes, where Acker provides a viewing of identity switching:

> [T]he relationship between erotic acts and erotic identities ... the status accorded to the genitals in defining sexual acts ... the fine line between virtue and transgression, orderly and disorderly homoeroticism ... the relationship of eroticism to gender deviance and conformity ... the relevance of age, class/status, and ethic/racial hierarchies to erotic relations ... the division between public and private sexualities ... the differences between concepts of erotic identity, predisposition, and habitual behaviors ... the dynamic of secrecy and disclosure, including covert signs, coding, and open secrets.
>
> (Traub, 133–134)

Acker's writing is a graphic, hard-edged, explicit pornography of all of these themes, with identity and sexuality constantly at switching crossroads. Acker's switches wrestle with the private and public identity, with the abnormal and normal. Acker and her characters move between being sexual beings and objects, where the character's sexuality and sex practices are at once her everything, to locations of nothingness, her sexuality becoming "impersonal," and a disconnection that leads to a dead-end road of confessing, "I'm rapidly losing my identity" (*The Childlike Life of the Black Tarantula*, 51).

Acker confesses in *The Childlike Life of the Black Tarantula*, "I've always feared most that someone will destroy my mind" (41). She engages her own confusion with the unpredictable with a daring courageousness; the results are narratives of continual slippages of gender, identity, and perversity. Her characters can occupy multiple genders at the same time, have the anatomy of a woman and that of many animals simultaneously, and exist in a drug-like, experimental world of poetic self-discovery, reflection, incest, fantasy, sex, BDSM, exhibitionism and voyeurism, bestiality, personal authorship and creation. Non-normative sexualities, genders, bodies, desires, and expressions are the waters Acker swims in. She is slippery and loves slippage—it is both the access to her sanity and her insanity—and while some may avoid it for fear of falling into an unknown pain, Acker explores to a dark, scary depth.

Acker provides such an utter subversion of predictable or socially acceptable content, language, narrator, and characters. She is a writer whose actions and behaviours switch in and around gender, identity, sexual practice, desires, and what normativity and perversity may be and look like. One chapter begins, "I'm two people and the two people are making love to each other" (29). Later, "[T]he big toe of my left foot is making love to the toe of my right foot. The toes become two people" (33). One of Acker's gifts is to speak a literature of pornography and fantasy: the subversive and perverse have her switch roles, desires, personas, and identities in a dreamscape.

Like Winterson, Acker takes a geographical cure to open herself to other worlds, to allow for her dreamscape to pop in Technicolor. Moving to San Francisco has her "begin to copy my favourite pornography books and become the main person in each of them" (29). And so, she is attending a girls' school while also unable to "decide whether I'm a woman giving birth to a brat or a five-year-old girl" (29). After having sex in the bathroom with a female classmate, the character will confess to her lover, "I want to blow my identity outward away, until I'm always running in a black ocean under a black sky and I can control my emotions" (33). Uncontrollable emotions, and the desire to have them manageable and controlled, the dark, limitless sky above and sea below, foreboding in their darkness yet big enough to hold a character who wants the freedom to run and create her identity anew. These are all actions and metaphors that accompany the switch and the desires behind switching, imagined, premeditated, or fulfilled; nature and its expansiveness, action, force, energy, movement, colours, heightened feelings/emotions.

Like my other authors, Acker makes use of an animal character, the black tarantula, to demonstrate existence in a hazy world of poetic self-discovery, agency, reflection, and sex. In it, Acker creates a character riddled with switching: she is both "helen seferis, and then, alexander trocchi" (41). She is in a perpetual state of switching: becoming and/or possessing the anatomy of a man, a woman, animals, and even the Divine Virgin Mary, Mother of God in *The Childlike Life of the Black Tarantula*. A few examples have the reader witness the main character get "rid of myself as a woman" to become "king" of a gang (25). A page later she will switch to "want to be the Virgin Mary" (26). The sacred mother becomes an antidote to a shy, tired man who is refused and not able to bed who he wants. Shifts in self-concept, anatomy, and worth continue. The character wears tight pants that allows her to "watch my cock rise and fall it looks like a small animal only I know it's me" (35). Still later she is "in a French boarding school ... growing up too quickly to have a childhood" (38).

At other times her quest to find out what it is to be real and to live in a reality outside the meaningless, drab, mainstream existence has her become an animal or "take sex with animals" (26). She is at once "a black dog" and "the black leather Virgin Mary," elucidating the dramatic dichotomies of a subversive switch identity. Acker's characters are crafted to be able to switch gender as if it were a costume. She provides us with playful characters who switch identity quickly and effortlessly: "[A]t this point I change my costume; for the rest of my life I wear only men's clothes" (28). Acker has her characters *choose* their switching to suit their needs and wants, establishing the switch as an empowering action *and* identity.

The rest of her life passes in a glimpse, of course, as time in all of Acker's narratives is as utterly unreliable as a gendered identity or fake promise. Later she will write that, at the same time, she "became a man and a woman" (49). She doesn't have to choose, and if she does, she can switch in her gender and sexual choices and variancies, as it may serve her in the moment. This is the work of an author who has distaste for static, unchangeable consistency and insists on her freedom to switch at will: she writes, "I don't want to hide. I want to hide" (39).

Her experiences illustrate an honest and clear discomfort with the growth and change process:

> [T]he ground pulls out from under my body I feel the anxieties I felt as a kid ... I stay with the anxiety to find out what's happening I forget who I am I don't know who I am I see a huge soft black widow no identity a large tarantula I have no feelings I begin to float.
>
> (50)

As with Eileen Myles and Jeanette Winterson, sexual deviancy and the body can move into existence and identification with sister and mythic animals *as well as* through an ethereal space and time.

Acker then switches to wonder if her "work means less to me than my sexuality" and, if so, does the compromise into the perverse depths of her desires constitute her life as "a failure" (50). In this moment, and other such slippages that show in the rest of the work, Acker is writing on writing, bridging her character's sex work, sex addiction, and sexual desires with writing. To fail is not to be able to bridge her work (which is writing) with sex. To fail is to let sex become personal and thus grab a foothold on her identity and the safely constructed world of self. If "the complete sexuality occurs within" she writes, and is "not expressed by, the writing" she has somehow failed her identity (50). To live a fully expressed life, without constraints, one that encompasses all the variant switching of who and what she is, is her sanity, her aliveness. Without her writing of her external and internal sex worlds she is in a perpetual state of anxiousness (50).

Floating becomes a common theme for Acker's characters, who are either swimming in an ocean of heady reflection and experience or attempting to feel alive and exist in a sea of pornographic sex that is extremely perverse, subversive, and situated in BDSM. Throughout Acker's texts, primarily two spaces exist: spaces of "complete disorder" (60) *and* spaces of sexual switching—both reveal just how urgent her "explaining everything about my sexual life as fully as possible" is when considering that what is on the other side for her characters is death (and their fear of it). At the same time, Acker uses her writing to "get rid of all feelings of identity that aren't my sexuality" (50), which complicates any theory that her writing is all sexual practice.

Acker has her character's identity inextricably joined with a dysfunctional, unsatisfied sex life while simultaneously questioning if the character can have a sex life that is somehow functional: connecting, personal, complete, and satisfying. A typical trope in the switch narrative occurs with the constant back and forth switching between ambivalence and hope, resignation and responsibility, past and present. Acker's character repeatedly chooses to swim in the fluidity of losing of her identity (and the dysfunction) of her life. She then laments it, repeating the conflict that sometimes occurs as insanity, dwelling in it until she is spent with pain or hollowness.

Having sex and orgasm, masturbating herself and others, pleasure itself becomes a vicious cycle for all of Acker's characters. She is desperate for it, and yet it makes her sick, diseased, and causes her extreme pain. Sex becomes both a tool to cope and a chosen weapon; one that also hurts her, the one inflicting the violence, in deeply affecting ways. Having sex outside with a female lover, she writes, "I have to orgasm to blank everyone out" (55).

A characteristic of the switch is dwelling in difficult, conflicting terrains: the characters are in a constant state of accepting versus questioning their worth, ability, and identity: "I don't know what would help me and I'm too far gone to do more than act through my delirium." She writes, "I'm completely involved in my delirium" (59). Moving from fluid to solid, the switch navigates choice every step. She repeatedly clings to outworn patterns and then surrenders into the desire for a new life through metaphors of animal strength and power. Seeing to know another way to live by shedding a dysfunctional, delirious identity that does not serve the character:

> As the man's cock enters me, every muscle of me begins to shake, every nerve begins to burn and quiver. I'm both liquid and solid. I'm completely pleasure. At this moment. (1) I'm opening enough to contain all identities, things, change everything to energy, a volcano. (2) I'm constant energy and I can never be anything else. (3) I have no emotions; I sense textures of everything against textures; I'm completely part of and aware of the object world. I don't exist. My nerves quiver, quiver burning, up and down the secret inflamed passages of my skin, the nerves tensing my muscles so that my blood zooms to the edge of my body, swells and inflames me, and unable to burst, I begin to come. These sensations—I don't know how to describe them—last for hours. I come again and again and again I am now equal to everything and nothing am completely dependent on the pleasure this stranger is giving me.
>
> (60)

There exists a temporary salvation in moving out of the drama of the delirium, yet it is an evasive and penetrating action that the character seems constantly thwarted by and at war with. The "I" of her ego and past is familiar and at constant war with the "I" of higher self and future. Acker's characters are "completely dependent" on sex, touch, physicality, and being wanted in order to survive in a nightmare of core needs not being met (55). A continual and persistent needing, being left, seeking, running after, listlessness and control of the love, lust, and sex addiction runs throughout each narrative.

For Acker's characters, the quest for what is reality and what is rebellion coexist in the tenuous spaces of sexual fluidity and identity switching. S/he engages in orgasm "until there's no difference between coming and reality" (49). Her escape into fantasy is in constant proximity and battle with the harshness of reality as she forages for an identity that would work for all her sides. She writes,

> I'm still me, still scared by my passion and sex. Reporting involves memories involved identity: I have my identity and I have my sex: I'm not new yet. I have to be careful for I may be visited at any moment.
>
> (49)

Constructing and reconstructing the self and identity in the present, but trapped in working from the past and memory, creating a future not based in fear seems impossible—and it is.

Acker's characters know no boundaries and, as a result, a hyper-mania and instability lurk. The Black Tarantula writes she "would have slept with my brother, after my mother died, but he chases me away" (61). There is a repetitious rejection throughout all of Acker's work. This is not a powerless victim character, however, even as she may totter and fall more often than she stays in the saddle; she straddles both empowering and disempowering locations, often falling into her familiar victim-self, yet also firmly articulating that she mostly feels "the pleasure of the masochism which occurs *only* when I give my consent. If I consent, now, I can do anything" (61). Off-putting for some? Maybe. Courageous and confronting? Yes.

Acker's texts, while pornographic and perverse, are locations of possibility: feminist *and* switch manifestas, cries and speeches, shouts and sobs, as to what it means to walk the world as a switch woman and sexual being, as related to and with. "I'm scared to always follow my desires in this sick society" (90), she writes, as she fuses her writing and character with Marquis de Sade-like notions of pleasure, offense, and society's prudery. She writes,

> I love only what occurs in my mind. I've remade the outside prison inside me because there's no difference between outside and inside my mind: they release me from prison and I am still in prison.
>
> (83)

Acker's characters are people who "fear everyone," while also seeking and asking "is it possible to come to the end of my fear?" (82). Through each of her narratives, Acker steps closer to answering her evasive question on fear. What remains is a body of work that screamed liberation through language and the exposure of a raw self for the purposes of discovery *while at the same time* remaining muddied and mired in self-imposed constraints and fears. Acker's characters are hated, told they are disgusting, unwanted, stupid, and ugly, while also being wanted and desired and possessing surreal intelligence and abilities. In the darkness, and also in the light, of Acker's fiction dwells a deep fear of moving forward into an unknown freedom with identity. Acker creates and feeds her characters' needs in a survival-based, escapist, addictive, dark chaos; they are offered the choice to explore themselves and triumph, knowing a freedom wherein the character's sexual perversity and switchiness can thrive, or not. Acker's characters attempt, but are unsuccessful in, living and creating a loving world of balance and trust; rather, they are kept at arm's length and left unknown.

Notes

1 Public celebrations of variancy and freedom of gender and sexual identity occur at the individual, family, group, community, organizational, governmental, and global levels. In this chapter, I will be concerned with individual and language-based celebrations.
2 Gender-neutral pronouns are not new. From the fourteenth to the seventeenth century, when the gender was not known or in question, "they," "their," and "themselves," were actually quite common pronouns, with "they" standing in for "he" "she" or "you." Midway through the seventeenth century, the masculine pronoun "he" began to be espoused by some as the preferred and proper pronoun to describe all things. Almost every book of Jane Austen's used "their," "them," and "themselves," and many of the canonical authors throughout the centuries—such as Shakespeare, Thackeray, Fielding, and Byron—liberally used gender-neutral pronouns. Using gender-neutral pronouns challenges the either/or gender binary of male and female, which is simplistic and singular and thus doesn't work for some folks who locate their gender identity on a much larger spectrum. While many LGBTQ and gender variants use and embrace gender-specific pronouns, it is very important to recognize and welcome the diversity of gender identities: respecting people's choices with regard to pronoun and language use is one way to do that.
3 Connecting with the gendered aspects of one's heritage and ancestors can be a complex and difficult navigation in and with LGBTQ identities. The intersections of the body, representation, gender, and sexuality with the traditional, ancestral, spiritual, and/or ethnic and cultural aspects of identity are interesting, ripe topics for scholarly discourse and my theory of switching. I have further writing forthcoming on this and hope that others consider this as a site of research, scholarship, and activism.

4 Memoir, girl and teen-hood
The body and deviancy in Kathy Acker, Anne Carson, and Sappho

This chapter dwells in and reveals how Kathy Acker, Anne Carson, and Sappho, as translated by Carson, traverse the ever-changing landscape of youth/teen affection, desire, love, identity, self, gender and sexual deviancy. Angles and perspectives, proximity and location, boundaries and autonomy become blurred and then recrystallized as subversive, intersecting worlds of investigation and self-growth when seen and then written from a child's or teen's perspective. I address how the teen narratives of Kathy Acker and Anne Carson play with conventional and accepted behaviours and established practices of sexuality and desire, recreating them in fluid and exploratory ways.

Kathy Acker's *Blood and Guts in High School*, Anne Carson's *Autobiography of Red*, and Anne Carson's translation of the entire collection of Sappho's poems, all of which exist in fragments, in *IF NOT WINTER, Fragments of Sappho*, create narrative occasions that carve out spaces for the reader to inquire into how youth are written to traffic in queerness, perversity, identity, and sexual practices; further, readers are privy to witness the raw experiences and sensations of the youth of these texts wherein a youthful curiosity carries excitement, shame, possibility, and confusion.

This chapter sheds light on how characters' explorations into variant identifications and consensual roles—as a girl, boy, or non-binary other, as a daughter, son, daddy, or brother, as a top or a submissive—get played out. These identifications can move through moments of switching within and from each young person's identity and perspective, creating compelling turns in mapping out new gendered and sexualized locations, identities, and boundaries. The readings in this chapter deconstruct and demonstrate how undoing "the latches of being" (4) both complicates and informs notions of sexuality, identity, and roles.

With switching there is an emphasis on the uncertainty and discomfort *while at the same time* there is often is a joy and liberatory freedom that emerges out of the playful and exploratory nature that can accompany gender or sexual switching and variancy. In addition, there exists an elusive future. The youthful character experiences of Acker, Carson, and Sappho shine star-bright and surreal in these uncertain locations. Their characters create space for identity-play, construction, and reconstruction.

As children and teens exhibit beginners' minds by default, their narratives are excellent examples of trafficking in the unsettling and destabilizing territory of the switch. In these narratives there are moments when the child/teen character engages in switching effortlessly, without adding any meaning or significance to the switch moment or switching action, and there are moments when an inner storm is brewing, a character feeling/experiencing being blinded, out of control, and at the affect (mercy) of others and an external world of circumstances. In the struggle of these tumultuous switch moments, meaning is often added, and switching clearly signifies an identity (re)formation and a changed and altered relationality (with the self, others, and the external world). In uncollapsing these switch moments, we witness the calm, ease, peacefulness, and internal knowing that can occur for these characters.

In Chapter 2 I referred to part of Valerie Traub's creative list of deviant topics. The overlap and remainder of them serve as connecting points for the reader as s/he/they grapples with the societal definitions and challenges, social significances and explorations of this chapter. The more perverse of her crafted list of deviant topics and tropes of homoerotic writing, which Traub asserts have "more consequence to female bodies," and which also have relevance to the child/teen body regardless of gender, are listed below as they are threads that are pulled through both Acker's *Blood and Guts in High School* and Carson's *Autobiography of Red*. As the female body is particularly at the effect of the below relationships and axis so, too, is the teen/youth/underage body affected. Traub makes connections and means of relationally range from

> the relationship between erotic acts and erotic identities ... the status accorded to the genitals in defining sexual acts ... the fine line between virtue and transgression, orderly and disorderly homoeroticism ... the relationship of eroticism to gender deviance and conformity ... the symbolic and social functions of gendered clothing ... the relevance of age, class/status, and ethnic/racial hierarchies to erotic relations ... the role of voluntary kinship and familial nomenclatures in mediating and expressing erotic bonds; the relationship of homoeroticism to homosociality ... the role of gender-segregated spaces, including religious, educational, criminal, and medical institutions ... the existence of communities and subcultures, including public sexual cultures and spaces ... the division between public and private sexualities ... the effects of racial, geographical, religious, and national othering ... the effects of social and geographical mobility and "traveling" sexualities ... assessments of appropriate erotic knowledge, including the ambiguous line separating medicine from obscenity ... the credibility of religious, medical, scientific and legal discourse in the production

of sexual categories, including definitions of nature, the unnatural, normality and the abnormal ... the differences between concepts of erotic identity, predisposition, and habitual behaviors ... the dynamic of secrecy and disclosure, including covert signs, coding, and open secrets.

("The Present Future of Lesbian Historiography," 133–134)

In addition to the axis above, which I will pull through this chapter, switch moments are elucidated by looking at, and including, *"the relationship between erotic subject and erotic identity."* Both Acker and Carson explore this relationship via the fine lines between addiction, pleasure, pain, and identity and the even-finer lines of escapism, avoidance, and fantasy with both reality and the undesired. These three writers address the impact of these choices and locations on a life, both internally/personally and externally/within community, and how they influence and alter integrity, responsibility and connection—the blurred or strict relationship between consensual acts and non-consensual acts, between victim and perpetrator, subject and object, what is inappropriate, taboo, forbidden and/or unspeakable and what is appropriate—the relationship between the variant and the sometimes disconcerting and/or uncomfortable.

In looking at the historiography of LGBTQ writing, Traub astutely observes that many deconstructionist readings "yield ample evidence of queerness located within ostensibly heterosexual literary texts" (137). This definitely applies to Acker, Carson, and Sappho's work: their writing concerns a *variant* loci, can be read both outside of a sexual identity while within a queer loci and also with a "ostensibly heterosexual" lens.[1] These types of texts, according to Laura Doan, "enable us to ascertain the 'imbrication of alternative possibilities within normative sexualities'" (*Fashioning Sapphism: The Origins of a Modern English Lesbian Culture*, 137).

It is precisely *the overlap* of "alternative possibilities within normative sexualities" that interests me with these gender-bending, youth-driven narratives, while also, and perhaps even more intriguing is the *overlap* of alternative possibilities with non-normative sexualities, which can be either masked or presented as normative. This chapter will reveal the exuberant and lush perversities, both sexy and sexualized, that gestate here.

Aberrations a go-go: switching our way out of expectations

The accessing of taboo subjects and language that many feminists might experience as violation—even when experienced consensually—are, in Acker's writings, presented as ripe, switch-like sites of confusing topics one wants to linger over and digest. Her writing can be unnerving and raw, disconcerting and repetitive, to the point that a reader can tire of the addictive nature of the sex and drama, as well as the seemingly endless circularity of victimization and perpetration. Acker's repetition is no accident however, and, in fact, is key to the innovative grappling of her switching characters and narratives.

Another way in which Acker uses repetition is in the writing of others. Acker would drop published writing into her narrative, thus changing and recontextualizing the original to accompany hers, as if in a dance. Another repetition, which I share at the risk of conflating the author and her work, is that Acker herself periodically appears to get looped into a drama of survival, victim, and "story"[2] that is the mirrored world of her characters. Winterson, who wrote the introduction to the 2002 Grove Press selected writing compilation, *Essential Acker*, writes that "Acker saw herself as dispossessed," and that Acker, along with her female characters, react to life with acts of "revenge" ("Introduction," ix).

Acker's provocative writing is regarded so highly and with such reverence in part because it pre-empted second- and third-wave feminist, LGBTQ, pro sex activism and analysis while she was writing an entire oeuvre that tackles these exact subjects. In her writings, she was much more gritty, direct, intense, and uncompromising, often harshly so, than any other woman writing during her time; one could argue subsequently as well, accessing a very personal attraction to and survival in the perverse. Acker was, unquestionably, at the forefront of dangerous, frontier-like fictional writing.

Of course, Acker was in a large sea of daring, with other women, feminist change makers who were addressing intense subjects and subjectivity, most often in non-fiction, shorter work, music, art, performance, and activism. Individually, and also collectively, they recreated women's roles, perspectives, and as-lived experiences as each woman's own to tell while also creating the space for both old and new stories to be told. Feminist storytellers were (and still are) part of a large ocean of creators and wave makers:

> ...But you who dream of liberty
> Must not yourselves be fooled
> Before you get to plea for freedom
> You have agreed to be ruled
> If the body stays a shackle
> Then the mind remains a chain
> That'll link you to a destiny
> Whereby all good souls are slain
> You know love has finally called for me
> I will not wilt upon its stage
> ...Do we have to live inside its walls to identify the cage?
> I am my mother's daughter
> And I've seen myself in you
> It's this blessing that I follow now
> And so I must speak true

I dreamed of thousands dying
It was you and you and you
And while the city sleeps so quietly
There is something we must do and it won't take long
… And you may say "I don't think this has anything to do with me,"
But did you ever think you could be wrong?
Human strength will fill the streets
Hear the sound of angry feet…
and you may say "I don't know how to be a part of that"
and it makes me want to say, "don't you want to see yourself that
     strong?"
And though our homes be torn and ransacked
We will not be undone, for as we let ourselves be bought
We're gonna let ourselves be free
And if you think we stand alone
Look again and you see
We are children in the rafters
We are babies in the park
We are lovers at the movies
We are candles in the dark
We are changes in the weather
We are women grown together
We are men who easily cry
We are words not quickly spoken
With a deeper side of try
We are dreamers in the making
We are not afraid of "why?"
I will not be complacent
          (Ferron Foisy, "It Won't Take Long," *Boulder*)

Feminists writers, artists, and activists know we have a rich herstory and
that our movements today stand on the shoulders of our foremothers; sadly,
our foremothers names and work are not remembered and valued in mainstream contemporary culture as they could be. A very short, and incomplete, interdisciplinary list of feminist women writers and cultural producers
who paved the way for experimental women writers like Acker might
include Cindy Sherman, Patti Smith, Adrienne Rich, Audre Lorde, Barbara
Kruger, Lorna Simpson, Gloria Steinem, Valie Export, Germaine Greer, Judy
Chicago, Annie Sprinkle, Hannah Wilke, The Guerrilla Girls, Carie Mae
Weems, and Adrian Piper: all were direct, unapologizing women who were
courageously producing and releasing experimental feminist work that dealt
with gender and female sexuality in the face of rejection and ridicule. Their
work bridged daring feminism, social commentary, personal experience,
and point of view in response and/or reaction to the conditions of sexism,

racism, heterosexism, homophobia, capitalism, classism, and/or elitism they witnessed and/or experienced.

To release and publish their work, women helped to create a demand for experimental, feminist, LGBTQ and/or alternative publishing houses, record labels, art and theatre spaces, and/or formed their own. Acker's writing was published in the United States by Barney Rosset, who, from 1951 to 1985 established and ran Grove Press, an avant-garde, independent publishing house that also published *The Evergreen Review* and distributed films by brilliant film-makers such as Jean-Luc Godard. Grove Press brought independent, political, cutting edge, erotic, pornographic novels, literature, and counterculture to North America. Grove took many a risk on writers whom no one else would publish, as well as many works that would be banned in various states and countries. Despite the subcultural demand, publishing some of the most daring and controversial of writers at the time: Malcom X, Amiri Baraka (LeRoy Jones) Samuel Beckett, Jean Genet, Henry Miller, D. H. Lawrence, Franz Fanon, Jorges Louis Borges, Che Guevara, and the Marquis de Sade to name a few, and being lauded as a cultural contributor and facilitator of the arts, Rosset would sell Grove in 1985 to the Getty family due to many years of court battles fighting obscenity laws, government investigations, death threats, and break-ins as well as union and feminist conflicts and protests (See Rosset's *Rosset : My Life in Publishing and How I Fought Censorship,* his autobiography *The Subject was Left Handed:* a phrase taken from his FBI file) or the 2007 film *Obscene: A Portrait of Barney Rosset.*

Poetry, performance, and non-fiction were the mediums Acker's contemporaries used, whereas Acker wrote fiction, primarily novels. Winterson wrote,

> her vulnerability as a woman in a man's world set her to use her body as text. She would be a writer—fuck 'em—but she would write from the place of denied, despised, and desired by men. She would not deny her own body, indeed she treated it like a fetish item, adoring, tattooing, and piercing it.
>
> ("Introduction," *Essential Acker: The Selected Writings of Kathy Acker,* ix–x)

What has Acker stand alone, maverick-like, is her fetishization: not only did she write on sexual behaviours that are generally regarded as obscene, abnormal, or unacceptable, she also crafted *a style* of writing, like Stein, that was non-normative. Acker's writing (and living) was consistent in being utterly unreasonable.

Some readers have confused her grit, street savviness, and perversity—her "fuck youness"—with the uneducated and/or unrefined; however, Acker was raised upper-class and was very well schooled. She always kept her upper-class appreciation for fashion and turned to buy her haute couture clothes second hand when finances permitted. Acker chose her writing style with intention: as a personal and a political act of protest. Certainly, part of that protest existed in her taking reversed refuge in choosing to live a life outside the circles of her upbringing. In her 1988 interview with William Burroughs,[3] Acker can appear to mimic the "starving artist" stereotype rather than the painter of her own canvas and creator of her life choices, yet any of us looking at her impressive lifework would never deem her a victim of circumstance. Notably, her loss of social status and monetary prowess in the conventional, mainstream world of literature gave way to an iconic status within *many* avant-garde subcultures and genres.

Blood and Guts in High School holds a large mirror up to teen perversity, confusion, the body, incest, fantasy, and desire, and it is this I want to delve into by offering some new switch readings of Acker's teen girl, Janey.[4] Acker's post-porn-punk-feminist novel of psychology and perversity is layered with the personal and political, yet it is the young Janey who is most compelling in her navigations. Janey is the keeper of a perverse identity and perverse experiences; a switch nature speeds through her narrative as she lives in the complexity of that identity and experience.

Looking at Janey's walk with heterosexual sex, incest, rape, exhibitionism and voyeurism, and BDSM—not simply with likely physically, gendered, identified, or politically similar partners/viewers, but with those dramatically opposite, taboo, undesired, and/or usually negated (as well as other sexually taboo fantasies)—Acker engages in a revolutionary and courageous act by presenting alternative sexualities, identities, and lifestyles. What is groundbreaking is that Acker writes and reveals these paths of Janey's as confusing *and* troubling *while also being* life-sustaining, alluring, and stimulating. Acker asks her readers to loosen into trust with her as we read the act of surrender and trust into the narrative, into Acker's weaving of mindsets, points of view, and narrative turns—essential if we, as readers, are to allow the narrative to unfold.

Acker's experimental, shape-shifting narrative is divided into three parts: "Inside High School," "Outside High School," and "A Journey to the end of the Night." The first section of the novel begins with the subtitle "Parents stink" and lays out the incestuous and tormenting relationship between Janey and her father, Johnny. It is this complicated and dysfunctional relationship that opens the novel: "Janey depended on her father for everything and regarded her father as boyfriend, brother, sister, money, amusement, and father" (*Blood and Guts in High School*, 7). And, thus begins a narrative that sails over waves of insanity, jealousy, and codependence, using sex as a seeming anchor to feel and know the self through the body, being wanted and wanting. Sex as an anchor for being and experience is not only Janey's but also her father's, her abductors', and the other characters of the novel; Acker uses the writing of sex and sex obsession to traffic in the stormy seas of identity-construction, knowing, control, relationality, power, intimacy, relationship, love, and—sex.

Returning to Valerie Traub's list above, what I like about her gendered, sexual, body, identity, and action-based specifics is that we can map them onto Janey's deviant narrative in *Blood and Guts in High School*: Where and in what forms do these turns of relationality show up in Acker's adolescents? What does switching between these acts and identities look like for an adolescent character or narrative?

For Janey, this occurs in locations of switching. Acker creates Janey's switching in the first part of *Blood and Guts in High School* as especially jarring and disturbing; the exterior worlds of discomfort mirror Janey's inner turmoil. The switching occurs as fast and furious, challenging, and complex. With her father, Janey is constantly switching between her need for her father's attention and the need for her father-as-her-lover's attention. Janey vacillates and switches between a jealous and needy desperation and a passive-aggressive pushing away; there is also a fast-paced switching between a narrative of introspection and awareness to a narrative of utter abandon and swallowing of addictive patterns.

Janey's incest with her father and the language she uses is anamorphic—with a lusting after the subject. Janey's high school daze follows with long graphic scenes of abortions following her rejection from her father. Alongside Janey, we are abandoned into a world of procedures and being done to. The narrative then moves to a more disjointed switching when Janey is seen to go into Bloomingdales to steal. Here the scene will have a switch every paragraph between Janey planning her theft in Bloomingdales to her being with her daddy in a hotel in Laguna Beach, yet her father is absent, in another room with his lover. Janey's room is the room "no one else in the world wants" (36) and this really is the drive of the narrative: Janey exists to be wanted. Through coarse, dramatic sex, often via rape, abduction, and slavery, Janey questions her sense of value and experiences these circumstances as a reliving of her past, where she sought the approval and love of her father, and also, herself.

Janey's identity is constructed by others and her experiences with the characters in her life rather than created or generated by herself: their influence and control, and Janey's being so influenced by them, determines who Janey is and chooses to be. Self-construction seems absent even as there is a pervasive self-referentiality; Janey is a character who stands in contrast to others wanting her. There is no self-love or worth, she must receive it from external sources, and in most cases not receive it, and/or give it away, through violence and sex. Amy Scholder writes that Acker brought to her work a "visceral understanding ... a totally unromantic perspective on relations between men and women" ("Introduction," *Essential Acker: The Selected Writings of Kathy Acker*, xiii), and while this is very accurate, and gives a very solid grounding for reading Acker, Acker will construct Janey to sometimes frantically cling to cultural norms of romance, attempting to place them on top of a perverse situation, such as being in love with her father. These oscillations and moments of switching provide ripe places for the examination and deconstruction of the topics of love, sex, and power as they relate to gender and identity.

While all of Acker's narratives consist of an experimental writing style, *Blood and Guts in High School* has many additions to the pornographic, troubled narrative as well as many more switching moments: drawings of female and male genitalia and naked bodies move from being object to subject; maps and diagrams depicting dreams move to visions with both hyper-descriptive words in tiny print and drawings to accompany the storytelling; a hyper-large, hand-printed poem consists of Persian and then English translations, the language switching every line, with Janey attempting to teach herself Persian; and a multitude of different typesets and narrative formula such as repeating the same paragraphs and words, "no," for example, which communicates both an adamant refusal and openness.

For example, Acker switches from narrative story to the hyper-sexed "SUCK ME" for paragraphs or sections of text in bold type (*Blood and Guts in High School*, 109–110). The "no" seems directed to "all you creeps in the streets," yet switches to a familiar knowing with "oh suck my cock honey suck my cock / that's what it's all about / I love how you turn yourself / around and upside-down inside-out / for me / just for me / oh I know / I must taste sweet" (109–110). There is an intimate instruction to please and do, which speaks to an aspect of desire that is often not theorized. Acker creates a scene of action, verbal sex play that includes word cues, possessiveness, connection, and role-play. Is he really a stranger on the street, a creep? The use of "honey" and the familiarity of the scene with "I love" could imply a past encounter and/or the language is used to bring familiarity and intimacy forth. Acker adding, "how you turn yourself around and upside-down inside-out *for me just for me*" also implies a familiarity of service and/or possessive desire and role-playing that is already in existence (109–110).

Acker is in the company of many erotic literary writers whose work was banned in some countries for exploring of the taboo desires and turn-ons that can be located with the language of verbal play. The raw sexedness and pornographic/erotic charge of her writing has meant that there is not a lot of academic discussion on the rich sexual identities in such narratives. A quiet shyness hovers over these muted conversations. Avoidance and shame can fill the space, theorists will talk *around* pornographic desires, sometimes (if we are lucky) addressing the erotic and sexy, yet not the titillating or vulgar, and so the dynamics of sexed word play and language are missed. Discussing the subversive and perverse desires—and verbal, raw, sex language and play is one such aspect of desire—even as it may not be comfortable or canonically based in academia, is a language and writing to explore for those exploring sexuality, gender, and identity.

Why? Simply put, not speaking about transgressive desire in literature and writing works to keep variant desires and identities hidden and silent. This is apparent even with those texts in which the subject is dominant: a quiet, demur-turn ensues, as if to cast a quaintness to the sexual act, saving "good, high literature" and "good women" from being perceived as "low literature" and "sluts" and "gentlemen" from being perceived as "predators." While Acker's male characters are far from a trusting or loving male archetype, and the language Acker uses is hard rather than romantic; reading and deconstructing her challenging approaches to the variant ways her characters clock desires opens an important door in understanding switching in identity and desire.

Verbal sexing is a language and bespeaks desire that, even when in literary work, is left to the nether realms: usually of written pornography proper. We circumnavigate the pornographic, most often privately, perhaps a little scared of what we will see or feel in between the lines and as we turn the pages. In the above scene of Acker's we witness the repeated pornographic words, which are trigger/cue words of desire and switching: the giving of instruction, and the act of talking about the giving and receiving of instruction, is part of language of desire and playfulness: the man sharing how he loves to have her give herself to him: "turning yourself around and upside-down inside-out for me" opens up her hunger and willingness, the possessive turn on of "just for me," offers the context of play with possession and giving, which is a BDSM location (109–110). The turning inside out "for me / just for me" communicates an intimacy that, when adjacent to the repeating verbal play of "SUCK ME" holds a space for a comfortable, confident lover to ask for and speak what is wanted in the sexual intimacy and, no doubt, it is Janey that seeks this and pulls it out. Janey is the space or clearing for the verbal play to show up, the space for needs to be expressed safely, given and received no matter what they look like.

There exists a lot of switch-hitting in this one scene: he is telling her to suck him yet also creating the wondering/almost question-like of how sweet he will taste; he is instructing but it is potentially she that is driving the scene. It's a topping from the bottom that might exist for both characters: him in instructing, her in being the one controlling the scene via the action, he in speaking, her in doing, he in encouraging her to do what is needed so that she can then get what she wants, he getting what he wants all the while. The language of the scene is so simple, yet the dance rich. This scene is followed by a full paragraph of "SUCK ME SUCK ME SUCK ME" pornographic, turn on, trigger language full out, which is then followed by the delightful last line of "sex is sweet" (109–110), which utterly destabilizes the pornographic, D/S edge of the instructive language.

These spaces side by side are what Acker excels at brilliantly, yet how easy it would be to miss the intimacy and, for some, the raw sexiness of these scenes by focusing on the abruptness or unlyrical, untempered aspects of her writing. Scholder adds that Acker "discovered a political use for pornography, a way of disrupting polite society;" further she is "always oscillating between worlds—bourgeois and bohemian, narrative and avant-garde, couture and biker. Inserting porn into the literary, she refused to choose sides. What cannot be overestimated is the pleasure Acker took in writing porn, finding the exactly right cadence and rhythm: using language, pushing limits, turning on" ("Introduction," *Essential Acker: The Selected Writings of Kathy Acker*, xiii).

It is precisely in this tradition of "turning on" that Grove Press published and Kathy Acker wrote: to sidestep the pleasure of the text, the joy and turned-on factor of the text, is worthy of our scholarly rigor of upturning and delving into. As Barney Rossett would reveal in his 2008 interview with *Newsweek*, he printed erotica because it "excited me" (quoted in *The New York Times*, February 22, 2012). Why do we write or teach literature and writing? In *some* manner, we find the writing process, and the voyeuristic activity of reading, pleasurable and exciting, life giving and affirming. If we read Acker in the tradition of other erotic and/or pornographic, taboo, and/or BDSM writing, like the Marquis de Sade, Georges Bataille, Pauline Réage, and Anais Nin we find a similar literary sexed language beneath what could be missed, hidden, and/or interpreted as crass, undisciplined, or unliterary.

The writing of Georges Bataille and Pauline Réage no doubt heavily influenced Acker's writing style and subversive pornographic content in *Blood and Guts in High School*, as well as the psychology and perverse boldness of her characters. Bataille's first-person male narrator as well as the character of Simone, both perverse, sex-driven youth, in *Story of the Eye*, and Réage's submissive slave character of O most particularly, and also the young Natalie who seeks to be a slave, and the masters Rene and Sir Stephen, in *Story of O* are sources for Acker's Janey. Bataille's novel, like Acker's, engages in extreme boundary pushing and is a graphic, perverse, and pornographically written narrative, while Réage moves deeply into the layerings of identity (re)formation(s) and notions/explorations of love and BDSM, as does Acker, but in a writing style that is not graphic, but rather, much more erotic.

When Réage has O turned over, face down, over an ottoman, to be examined by a mistress who is considering borrowing her for a week, the woman orders O not to move and seizes her lips. *The Story of O* follows O's thoughts:

> After all, she was no longer mistress of her own fate, and that part of her of which she was no longer mistress of her own fate, and that part of her of which she was least in control was most assuredly that half of her body which could, so to speak, be put to use independently of the rest. Why, each time that she realized this, was she—surprised was not really the right word—once again persuaded, why was she paralyzed each time by the same feeling of profound distress, a sentiment which tended to deliver her not so much into the hands of the person she was with as into the hands of him who had turned her over to alien hands, a sentiment which drew her closer to Rene when others were possessing

her and which, here, was tending to draw her closer to whom? To Rene
or Sir Stephen? She no longer knew ... but that was because she did not
want to know, for it was clear that she had belonged to Sir Stephen now
for ... how long had it been?

(145)

We witness a similar giving over of the self: both Janey and O give up being
responsible for their life, preferring to give themselves over to fate. Both O
and Janey also switch between being curious about their submission: both
surrender into it while also, at times, questioning it. However, what coincides
(and trumps) the questioning is the deep pleasure and satisfaction that both
women derive from relinquishing control. Janey and O have a submissive
love, attachment, and inclination toward fully surrendering themselves over
to the men who possess them, want them, and vie for them. This attachment
(and often jealousy) extends to the lovers of the men who love them as well.

The exhibitionism/voyeurism as well as ownership/possession aspects in
both characters and narratives are delicious and ripe: Réage would write O
as being taken by her love, lover, and master Rene in front of Sir Stephen, hair
pulled, hand around her throat, after which she would open her eyes to be

completely stunned and bewildered ... gasping with joy ... able to see
that he [Sir Stephen, who she has just met] was admiring her, and that
he desired her. Who could have resisted her moist, half-open mouth,
with its full lips, the white stalk of her arching neck against the black
collar of her page-boy jacket, her eyes large and clear, which refused to
be evasive? But the only gesture Sir Stephen allowed himself was to run
his finger softly over her eyebrows, then over her lips. Then he sat down
facing her on the opposite side of the fireplace.

(72)

The male characters of both novels—Bataille's first-person narrator to some
degree and Réage's characters of Rene and Sir Stephen even more—find
themselves in Acker's male protagonists. The former novel was first published
in 1928, the later published in 1954. Jean-Jacques Pauvert published both
novels in Paris. In addition, both novels were published under pseudonyms,
most probably due to the pornographic language and the sexually subversive, boundary-pushing BDSM content and context of both works.

While taking on similar subject matters as Bataille and Réage, Acker
chose to publish under her own name, to be an "out" writer of avant-garde,
literary pornography, BDSM, and the eroticism and complicated nature of
sexed, perverse identities. The scenes of Acker's novel are revisions of similarly evocative scenes in both writer's work: scenes of urination, the language
of pornographic, and at times exploitative, sex is common, yet Bataille and
Réage wrote with an ease and grace that Acker never possessed or chose to
engage with. Acker is disjointed, truncated, and, at times, wearing, whereas

the writers she would copy directly from, admired, and was influenced by—writers such as Bataille and Réage, Artaud and Verlaine, Rimbaud and Genet, Sade and Burroughs—had a grace Acker refused. While she would "borrow" their writing, revising it to suit her narrative and vision, her use of the word "cunt" is hard and affecting, their use much softer; this speaks to her challenging and confronting mainstream notions of what women writers could write, male writer's privilege, and the structures and boxes of "literary" tradition. Acker looked to these male writers with a longing, even if her lifework was consumed with challenging the paradigms of patriarchy and the literary world, because, like her, they challenged normative thinking and writing.

Acker would say in an interview with Larry McCaffery that she "definitely" placed herself "in that lineage … and I very much hope I do enough significant work that I can someday be seen as belonging to that lineage. If someone tries to place me in another lineage, they're mistaken" (*Some Other Frequency : Interviews with Innovative American Authors*, 19). She would also state that she and these writers share an intense,

> deeply sexual perspective, which insists upon the connections between power and sexuality. It's basically a world-view. There's also the use of non-social realist language and imagery that is very involved with areas of the mind which are not rational.
>
> (20)

Acker's Janey also specifically evokes Jean Genet. She writes directly to him, ushering the perversity of Genet into her own text by naming a character Genet. Acker also brings forth such authors by directly inserting their writings into her plagiarizing as a way of homage.

Part of the end of the novel takes place in Egypt, and Acker writes the narrative out in scenes as if to be acted on a stage. The scenes move from reflection and social commentary to perverse speaking and desire. As with *Story of O*, one scene begins in a brothel where "it is clear that the whores regard what most people regard as (them)selves as images. Sex, that unblocked meeting of the selves, is the most fake thing there is" (*Blood and Guts in High School*, 129). Scene one is compelling because Acker's voice of Janey as social and gender commentator, as well as switches in gendered bodies, begins:

> Janey to herself: Genet doesn't know how to be a woman. He thinks all he has to do to be a woman is slobber. He has to do more. He has to get down on his knees and crawl mentally every minute of the day. If he wants a lover, if he doesn't want to be alone very single goddamn minute of the day and horny so bad he feels the tip of his clit stuck in a porcupine's quill, he has to perfectly read his lover's mind, silently, unobtrusively, like a corpse, and figure out at every changing second

what his lover wants. He can't be a slave. Women aren't just slaves. They are whatever their men want them to be. They are made, created by men. They are nothing without men. I have to decide what the world is from my own loneliness.

(130)

In scene 8 the Genet of *Blood and Guts in High School* and Janey are locked in adjacent cages. Acker's Genet calls Janey a "lousy stinking pervert" (136) to which Janey replies in a whisper "the night is opening up, to our thighs, like this cunt which I'm holding in my hand cuntcuntcuntcunt. And we descend, / like we're in a tunnel or a / cave inside the mind, / night is opening all (136). It's a turn, a switch, of absolute freedom and possibility when Janey powerfully responds to Genet: she grants them both an adventure rather than finality. She maps confinement onto her body and imagination. She transcends insult into her own power, pleasure, and agency.

Scene 10 is also opening, as it is here, that Janey moves into an even more independent state of mind, wherein she takes some control and ownership over her body and experience holding herself in her hands, and asks for what she wants. The italics in parentheses show an internal dialogue that illustrates that Janey is still run by some self-doubt—one does need to gain courage when one is filled with courage, it's simply present or not and when not, either absent altogether or in need of summoning—at the same time she has a directive quality in her dialogue with Genet that evokes a deep, solid control over her choice of submission:

JANEY: I'll obey you. But I want, (*gains courage and firmness, decision*) I want you to forget who you are. (*Corrects she.*) Been. I want you to lead me without hesitation into the land of the shadow and the monster. I want you to plunge into endless misery and hardship. I want—because it's my ugliness, my lack of femininity my wounded body, earned minute by minute that is all that is left to speak—I want you to be without hope. I want you to choose evil. I want you to feel hatred and violence. I want you to refuse the delicacy of thistles, the softness of rocks, the beauty of the darkness, the emptiness. I know where we're traveling, Genet, and I know why we're traveling there. It's not just to travel, but it's so those others who kicked me out have a chance of being at peace, have a chance of knowing the land of the monster without going there.
GENET: Do you think that's possible?

(139)

The passage above echoes the *The Story of O*: like O, Janey takes ownership over her consensual submission and creates the space to ask for the dominance and healing she seeks. She takes control and responsibility of the giving over of herself, the play and dwelling in roles, the directive and accepting nature of BDSM relations, and the pleasure that comes from exploring sexuality within a dominant/submissive relationship where one is free to speak one's needs and read another's in the dance of pleasure-seeking, giving and receiving. Réage's groundbreaking narrative and main character O no doubt influenced Acker's character's constructions, for not only do we see O in Janey (among other Acker characters), Acker names the main character of *Pussy, King of the Pirates* O.

The youth of George Bataille's 1928 *Story of the Eye* (republished by the progressive San Franciscan publisher and bookstore City Lights) can also be noted as influential: they are equally as perverse as Acker's characters. Bataille's young women and men quested and sought out how they could push every sexual drive and experience into that which would turn over another layer of the self. Like Janey, X and Z were boundary pushers.

Other experimental—and repetitive—boundary-pushing pornographies in the novel traffic in child-like and juvenile word choices, as in "**I CAN SCRAWL AND I CAN CRAWL** ~~ONLY MY PEN~~ **I I I I I I I I I I** (~~I W~~ ... **GLOOGLOOGLOO FUCK YOU SHIT PISS** (*Blood and Guts in High School*, 108). And, yet, what more is Acker attempting to deliver and/or uncover in these lines? Winterson insightfully wrote that Acker's

> female characters are both dispossessed and abused, but they are strong too, and full of hope that is not disgust ... there is no disgust in her work. Vomit, shit, urine, cocks, cunts, assholes, blood, and the body are intimately described, and not in the language of cloudy romance. Yet there is no disgust. Disgust is reserved for the hypocrites, the morons, the authority figures, the moneymen, the politicians. Transgression is never disgust—it is a way of surviving ... she was a moral writer—she had high ideals and a cause ... she was edging fiction forward, just as she was trying to jab humanity into a little bit of consciousness.
>
> ("Introduction," *Essential Acker: The Selected Writings of Kathy Acker*, ix–x)

This jabbing into consciousness is exactly what the switch moments are making room for as well as locating; switching occurs throughout the text in clearly visible depictions such as Acker adding the self-referential, identity-questing statement with an arrow pointing to an in-between the third and fourth "I" in the quote of "**I I I I I I I I I I**" above: "I wish that there was a reason to be-lieve this letter" (*Blood and Guts in High School*, 108). To question the "I," in a hopeful yet doubtful way, at the third "I" or "eye" location of the text is telling: Acker could also be referencing the Hindu concept of the third eye being the centre point of wisdom and power located in the forehead, the location of insight that is activated through medita-tion and yoga, as she questions her own existence. To skew the I of the sacred Hindu teachings and texts speaks to the depths of listlessness Janey experiences: a hardness *and* a compassion that Acker navigates; it speaks to the many who, no matter how honouring of their transgressive, variant, or switchy selves, can, at certain times, be pulled into a quicksand that reeks of a disempowering, helpless havoc.

The novel ends with a chapter entitled "A second of time," which does not occur as a normal chapter heading would, but rather at the end of the last chapter. We only know it's a chapter title by following the table of contents. Then, on the following page occurs a section entitled "The World," which is the only section in the novel without page numbers and contains a mystical, hieroglyphic depiction of images and words, none of which are troubling, but rather liberating. Again, fonts and typesetting are played with, and there is an innocent, beginner's mind to the section. Acker asks,

> [S]hall we look for this wonderful book [an ancient, most important book on human transformation wherein the ways humans can become something else is explicated]? Shall we stop being dead people? Shall we find our way out of all expectations?
>
> (147)

"The World" of Acker then moves into "The Journey," which loses the innocence of "The World," and pulls for humanity to win. One page has the words, "the Devil uses every trick in the book to win." There are pictures of birds in flight holding onto elephants by talons, Kali (Goddess of destruction, and correspondingly rebirth), dismembered bodies, and people having sex. The caption "The Devil is an image. Imagine Hell. We grab the book, and run" implies a deep belief and hope in humanity as well as playfulness in not only imagination but in testing, thwarting, and challenging the fates.

The following page presents yet another switch, bringing the reader from ancient Egypt and India to New York City, the East River, a black and white division, birds flying up and down to the words "light is before us / darkness closes behind us / and we fly." The section ends with the words "so we create this world in our own image" is profound because it speaks to the notion that her characters (and we as readers) have the power to create their world: How we see and experience "this world" is based on our imaginings/ points of view, which may be determined by a "that world" context, mostly based on circumstances, past experiences, and which we have agency to consciously create/choose.

Following is the last chapter, entitled "So the doves …" which is Acker's one-page finale of the novel. Janey has passed and is in a grave in Luxor. Doves coo, "whispering of their own events" over Janey's grave. We read that "soon many other Janey's were born and these Janey's covered the earth" (165). And, here, Acker concludes with a healthy Janey, a world of healthy Janeys, who know what it may be to love outside the world of high school, parents, boyfriends, teachers, who are in control of their life, their sexuality, their wants and desires in a way that resonates the freedom of travel by train or ship, the freedom of open roads and ocean, a life of choice.

At the same time there is also the world and identity of Janey as sexed, the world of her life revolving around sex, being wanted, and wanting. This last passage has a grown-up Janey appear and be present to a push and pull desire that is a recurring theme:

> Blood and guts in high school
> This is all I know
> Parents teachers boyfriends
> All have got to go.
> Some folks like trains,
>   Some folks like ships,
> I like the way you move your hips
> All I want is a taste of your lips,
>   boy,
> All I want is a taste of your lips.
>   (165)

In the process of this desire, Acker gives us the sexiness and resonance of the word "boy." We are pulled into the world of very alive women in Acker's work: alive in desire, in the wanting, the longing, the craving, and the imagining the be-ing and becoming. Acker's women are "sexually voracious, they have exploits which leave them ravenous, humiliated, and victorious all at once" ("Introduction," *Essential Acker: The Selected Writings of Kathy Acker*, xiii). Scholder would write that for Acker her women exist in the space of desire as "a place of not yet having" (xiii). And it truly is this "not having" that pushes the narrative with relentless fearlessness.

Autobiographies coloured red; fragments coloured ripe

Anne Carson was born in Toronto on June 21, 1950 and raised in small towns in Ontario, Canada. She is an incredibly prolific poet and essayist, who also works in the classics and comparative literature, and as an artistic collaboration professor and translator who specializes in Greek translations—Sappho, Euripides, and Sophocles being among the most notable. She also collaborates regularly with her husband, Robert Currie and a wide variety of other artists in moving her texts into performance/art pieces. Carson has been the recipient of (as well as short and long-listed for) many prestigious awards, fellowships, and prizes, including the Griffin Prize for Poetry, the Lannan Literary Award, the Pushcart Prize, a Guggenheim Fellowship, a MacArthur Fellowship (known as the "genius grant"), and she has the honour of being the first woman to win the T. S. Eliot Prize for Poetry for *The Beauty of the Husband* in 2002 (for which she was lambasted and criticized by a few male writers). She has published twenty books to date, and her first book, *Eros of the Bittersweet*, published by Princeton University Press in 1986, was named one of the 100 best non-fiction books of all time by the Modern Library.

Carson's dense, lyrical, and brilliant word-smithing has garnered her high esteem and acclaim with many modern, post-modern, experimental, avant-garde loving readers and scholars; like Acker, Carson is considered a trailblazer in the world of exciting verse. She brings a wonderfully articulate and smart, deep and measured approach to words and language that move and navigate between the contemporary and historical. There is also a very strong womanly elegance *and* feminist presence to her work, which a few may not perceive, but which is present to this reader all the same.

In a 2006 interview by Emma Brockes, published in *The Guardian*, Carson shares on the thought and writing process that some of us writers intuitively experience and know, and indeed, respect:

> I don't know that we really think any thoughts; we think connections between thoughts. That's where the mind moves, that's what's new, and the thoughts themselves have probably been there in my head or lots of other people's heads for a long time. But the jumps between them are entirely at that moment … it's magical … You write what you want to write in the way that it has to be.
>
> (Brockes, *Guardian* Book Section, December 30, 2006)

Anne Carson's *Autobiography of Red: A Novel in Verse* offers readers a beautiful, lyrical journey through adolescent inquiry, perversity, and the cloaked sexual and gender identities of a modern teenager turned winged, red creature. *Autobiography of Red* is profound in both composition and scope and could be considered one of the greatest contemporary lyrical compositions. Carson blends the coming-of-age story with Greek myth to allow for the erotic and desire, the body and identity, fantasy and BDSM to be explored; sex and intimacy with the self and in relation with others, brother/brother incest, mother/son relations, other-worldly, animalia anamorphousness, and the spaces of lostlessness and seeking that these locations elicit.

Many years ago, I coined the term *lostlessness*, which speaks to a location that can present itself, usually early on, in a narrative of switching. *Autobiography of Red* is ripe with it. Lostlessness is a space of uncertainty and unsettled unknowingness, where, in occupying the space between and betwixt, something unknown has the potential to be birthed, occur, exist, and/or hover. In being a between and betwixt location, lostlessness evokes movement and fluidity. It is not a static, stationary, or settled place or way of being. This in-between space of knowing and unknowing can be one of vacillation or pause. It is a solitary experience that is marked by a quiet and self-reflective internal dialogue and dwelling; one must go through the eye of the needle alone. The energy around a narrative trafficking in lostlessness can occur as sombre, yet it is not necessarily sad; when switch moments happen, the energy can turn toward being curious, seeking, and discovery-oriented beginner or child mind.

A key signifier is that switch moments are often bookmarked. Examples would be curiosity and confusion, freedom and loss, peace of mind and loneliness; a wide range of emotions (such as anger, sadness, and shame; surprise, joy, agency, and pride) and beliefs (self-worth, notions of deserving and being worthy or loveable, sense of self and place), and habits (actions and choices that are either supportive or destructive) can all occur and accompany the switch travelling through unknown spaces of discovery. *Lostlessness* disappears identity as it creates it; who one thinks one is is set aside to create a space where identity is allowed a reinvention, a trans-formation. While *lostlessness* may initially be read or experienced as deeply uncomfortable and unwanted, and often resisted, the switching that arises can become locations of excitement and celebration, where newness, playful-ness, and adventure arise. I seek to introduce the term to imply the uncertain and unsettled, vast and expansive, changing spaces that can swirl around a character and their narrative experiences, *especially in the context of iden-tity and switching*.

Carson invites us in to play and switch. Right from the beginning of the novel, switchness exists in Carson's characters. Like Stein's, Carson's per-versity has been downplayed and ignored, with more sedate readings offered. And, like Acker's work, *Autobiography of Red* is a labyrinth of poetic per-versity and adolescent seeking where the main character, Geryon, dwells on interiority and "the difference between outside and inside" (*Autobiography of Red*, 29). Carson's character reconciles that while his brother may nego-tiate to own his exterior body the "inside is mine" (29). He then begins to write his autobiography, in which he will "set down all inside things / par-ticularly his own heroism" (29).

Geryon, like Janey, is self-referential. However, Carson creates Geryon to coolly omit "all outside things" in the exploration and telling of the self. This deliberate act of looking inward for the answers illustrates a character willing to take responsibility for his own world and experiences. His world intersects with others, but he alone is responsible for how the world occurs to him, and it is this narrative he will tell.

Carson invites the reader to look at what happens—at the level of lan-guage and identity—when her small town Ontario boy child switches to and from a genderless child, a (homo) sexed child and teen, an animal, and the Greek mythic hero Herakles. Changes of subversive agency, subject, and object are presented as Carson's main character writes his autobiography far outside the charmed circle of "normal" adolescence. For Geryon, "andro-gyny seeks to liberate the individual from the confines of the appropriate" (Heilbrun, x).

I will now map out Carson's main character's desires and subversive switch sensibilities, chart how "the fantastic fingerwork of his wings is outspread on the bed like a black lace map of South America" (97), and how "a romance" (21) with his brother and others play out sadistic and masochistic fantasies, desires, and roles. If we readers are willing, we are allowed to get in bed with a gay genderqueer and know his gender-variant body and sexually variant thinking intimately. The gender switching and performances of Carson's characters, the queerness, the incest, and other fantasies that she explores, directly challenge what it is to hold an epic court.

The intimacy between Geryon and his mother is layered, beautiful, and rare. She is described as being the "engineer of his softness" (10), which is a generous and tender way to describe a mother's gift to a son. It speaks to the boy and young man's openness to the love of his mother, the mother as embracing her own archetypal feminine and her willingness to share it with her son and nurture him into what he needs. It also speaks, of course, to who Carson is: a scholar of ancient Greek writing and culture who has fully taken on some of the most profound teachings of that time. She not only reflects on the oracles of Delphi, the goddess-worshipping, the honouring of the feminine and the feminine archetype in all her manifestations, but brings the sacred herstories, mythologies, and qualities of the feminine forth into our own time as a way to honour and presence the divine feminine now.

And so Geryon's relationship with his mother is one that is incredibly tender and profound. Even the title of the poem, entitled "Geryon's Reversible Destiny" contains a switch: the notion that destiny—fate predetermined—could be reversible. In this poem it is written: "His mother saw it mothers are like that / Trust me she said Engineer of his softness" (10) to which she tells him that he has time, he can take time, to make up his mind, to choose, meanwhile she is fiery, even as she is the Engineer of his softness: "behind her red right cheek Geryon could see / Coil of the hot plate starting to glow" (10). Geryon acknowledges the wisdom and knowing of his mother as he is faced with making choices. She is softness, yet she is switchable: she is fiery and red, hot and glowing, while she is also soft and trusting. She is "a Nymph of a river that ran to the sea" while his father "was a gold / cutting tool" (14).

Geryon's relationship with his mother, which is one of hand-holding on the first day of school, one of safety and nurturing, sits in juxtaposition with his relationship with his brother and father: tools that cut are switched in and out for the naturalistic spirits of nature and water. Switching is ever-present in this narrative: Geryon's hand moves from the safety of his mother's as she walks him to school on his first day to his brother teaching him hard "justice" through layers of toughness and verbal put-downs of "stupid" in telling him to go into school alone (23–24). The sensitive Geryon does not, cannot, rather he waits in the bushes until he is noticed and brought in: standing motionless, gripping his book bag with one hand, stroking a lucky penny in his pocket with the other, he stands so still that the first snow of winter lands on his eyelashes to match the snow-covered branches that surround him in silence (25).

Geryon's world switches often from the loving experiences he has with his mother to the tenuous ones he has with his brother: juxtaposing and switching spaces, ways of being, and navigating these switch moments occupy a lot of space in the narrative. And it is these spaces, these navigating spaces between outside and inside, tender and hard, mother and brother that occupy the switch narratives. The incestuous relationship exists under ominous threats to Geryon's sense of self as well as his relationship with his mother. For example, Geryon's brother states that he will tell their mother that no one at school likes Geryon, which the older brother knows will embarrass and shame the younger boy.

An "economy of sex" is established as the older brother promises Geryon a prized cat's eye marble in exchange for masturbating his brother and then, later, letting the brother play with Geryon's penis in some way (masturbation and/or oral sex is implied). The brother becomes kinder in speech and action after sex is established; yet the younger brother Geryon moves more and more inward. The older brother witnesses this process, as does Geryon himself, yet no action is taken by either to confront this slippage.

The mother then takes on a heroic, shiny, rhinestoned bravery. Geryon stares at his mother in "amazement ... she looked so brave. He could look at her forever" (30). There is then a moment which eludes him, and the brother switches into the scene: the mother nears the door and then is gone, the room circles in for the young boy, breath becomes harder, he wants to cry but instead turns inward. It's an agony to watch him be silent with the wanting to be near his mother when she is unavailable. The brother and a babysitter take her place, switching the scene from one of love, longing, and missing, to that of the playfulness and mockery of his older brother and the "wrong voiced" (31) stand-in for his mother, a babysitter whom Geryon tolerates with a politeness rather than a connection that enlivens.

The switch between the brother snapping elastics against Geryon's legs bleeds into the day of Tuesday. Every second Tuesday of the winter season exists as, simply, the "best," for that is the day Geryon's brother plays hockey, which allows Geryon and his mother to have supper and evening alone. Geryon's mother describes Geryon to her friend on the phone: "[h]e's right here working on his autobiography ... a sculpture [as] he doesn't know how to write yet" (35). The mother *seeing* Geryon's creation *as autobiography* and adding the descriptor of sculpture speaks to her creating him as powerful, intelligent, artistic: all the things he does not experience elsewhere. This particular Tuesday evening ends with the mother lightly suggesting, "maybe next time you could use a one-dollar bill instead of a ten for the hair," and one is left to wonder: What is not to love in this mother: she is all compassion, all loving, and the archetype of the mother figure (35).

I want to pause and convey how revolutionary this relationship is, how remarkable this mother is, how rare it is to have a mother show up as *all* loving and compassionate, as utterly worthy of worship and honour: as bravery itself. This is not standard teen narrative perspective nor is the listening they provide for each other typical or normal. An elevated way of relating exists here. This is not how mothers or mother/son relationships are written or depicted in North American writing, media, and culture. Mother/son relationships are often depicted as fraught with some percentage of blame/guilt, dependence/independence, separation/(s)mothering. Carson's mother, with her simple, humorous request, allows her son the freedom to make mistakes without fear or anger. Carson gives us a mother who encouragingly says to her resisting to-going-to-school son, "[T]his would be hard for you if you were weak but you're not weak," as she neatens "his little red wings" and encourages him out the door (36).

The mother helps to build Geryon's foundation for his healthy evolution and development, a rare depiction of love and parenting, especially for the mother figure and role. The freedom of flying is so present for Geryon, his big wings seen only by his mother at this point in the narrative, so that when Geryon learns to write, he begins to write his autobiography. He writes his mother as "a river that runs to the sea the Red Joy River" and his father as "gold." Here, Carson is evoking the most evocative of Stein's poems, which I referred to in Chapter 1, *Pink Melon Joy* as she creates the mother as "Red Joy River." Geryon himself is the red-winged creature, his mother the red joy river.

The narrative moves on to Geryon falling in love, at the age of fourteen, with a teen boy of sixteen named Herakles. They spend time together at night, and Geryon spends less and less time with his mother. As the relationship dissolves, without any real mechanisms that would indicate a dissolving or ending, yet seemingly the ending coming from Herakles, who says they will "always be friends," which turns Geryon's heart and lungs to a "black crust," Geryon moves more and more into the interior realm of his mind and safe space, as he did as a youth, hiding, telling himself to listen to what the outside world is saying while retreating, unable to find his breath, red walls come down all around him slicing "the air in half" (62). Red is the colour all around Geryon, flames all "along the floorboards inside" of him (63). Lava, that deep red molten substance that has no end and no method of rivering, becomes their destination: visiting volcanoes and "bouncing from rock to rock / as if looking for lost kin," Geryon and Herakles traverse the lava of memories, belief and fact, dancing in a "memory burn" (65).

The narrative then switches back to the home and Geryon's mother, who is there, "sitting at the kitchen table" (68) as he comes home after a seven-hour car ride of tears and weeping. Geryon wants to retreat to his room, yet when he sees his mother, he sits down. His mother reads, in appreciation, what is written in "red singlet with white letters" across the t-shirt Herakles gave to Geryon: "Tender / Loin" (68). The loin, the sexual centre, tender, hurt, wounded for Geryon.

Fragments of identity, tender, follow. The reader has watched the youth move through a child and teen-hood of innocence, identity building, love, and shame. Volcanoes, lava, the colour and evoking of red, wings, mythic names and creatures, silence and hiding, risk and pleasure have moved back and forth, switching between safe and dangerous spaces as this young man ponders "the cracks and fissures / of his inner life" with a "kiss":

> A healthy volcano is an exercise in the uses of pressure.
> Geryon sat on his bed in the hotel room pondering the cracks and
>   fissures
> of his inner life. It may happen
> that the exit of the volcanic vent is blocked by a plug of rock, forcing
> molten matter sideways along
> lateral fissures called fire lips by volcanologists. Yet Geryon did
>   not want
> to become one of those people
> who think of nothing but their stores of pain ...
> "... I will never know how you see red and you will never know how
>   I see it.
> But the separation of consciousness
> Is recognized only after a failure of communication, and our first
>   movement is
> To believe in an undivided being between us ..."
> As he read Geryon could feel something like tons of black magma
>   boiling up
> From the deeper regions of him.
> He moved his eyes back to the beginning of the page and started again.
> "To deny the existence of red
> is to deny the existence of mystery. The soul which does so will one
>   day go mad."
> A church bell rang across the page ...
> *I am not the one who is crazy here,*
> Said Geryon closing the book.
>
> (105)

It may happen, Carson writes, that "the exit of the volcanic vent is blocked by a plug of rock, forcing molten matter sideways along / lateral fissures called fire lips ... yet Geryon did not want to become one of those people" and he does not. *Autobiography of Red* reveals the boiling points of a youth, gay or not, and the volcanic interiority of what it means to be an adolescent. The switch nature of every unpredictable moment, and a life of red-winged flight, Geryon is painted to be the son of a red river flowing towards a miraculous love and acceptance.

Geryon, ever the switch, has a hopeful heart even as he runs from his feelings.

> There are no words for a world without a self, seen with impersonal clarity. / All language can register is the slow return / to the oblivion we call health when imagination automatically recolor the landscape and habit blurs perception and language / takes up its routine flourishes.
>
> (107)

Carson's Sappho: sites of crossing and dissent

IF NOT, WINTER: Fragments of Sappho is Anne Carson's recreation and translation, from Greek to English, of the entire collection of the fragments that exist from Sappho's nine books. I have chosen to discuss the ground-breaking and gorgeously lyrical *IF NOT, WINTER: Fragments of Sappho* in conjunction with Carson's *Autobiography of Red* as they are in direct alignment. Both Carson's revision/recreation of the fragments and the fragments themselves speak directly to the gender and sexual ambiguity and switch locations.

Sappho was a Greek poet who was born to an aristocratic family around 617 BC on the Greek island of Lesbos and died around 570 BC. Sappho has had a profound and lasting impact on our world, one being her enormous influence on fellow poets and writers during her time and since, another her contribution to women's sexual rights and linguistic/social history: the word "lesbian" originally comes from the Isle of Lesbos, where Sappho was born, and has morphed from referring to a type of bendable, flexible lead mostly used to make the curves of moulding (how feminine), to "pertaining to the Isle of Lesbos" in the sixteenth century (referencing wine amongst other things) and then later, around 1870, to refer to "homosexual relations between women, characterized by erotic interest in other women," which was directly attributed to Sappho's poems celebrating her love of women and women's sexually.

Much myth—and controversy—has long existed around Sappho's life and work, especially on the topics of desire, love (thwarted and experienced), passion, romance, and sex, for which she and her writing are best known (even as she wrote prolifically on many other topics). Did she throw herself off a cliff and into the sea due to the unreciprocated love for a ferryman named Phaon, or did she die of old age in her sleep? Was she a mother? A wife? Was Sappho's work ordered to be burned by the Pope in 1073, or was the papyrus left to decay due to the inaccessibility of the dialect in which she wrote. In part, the mythmaking is due to her songs and poems surviving in papyrus fragments. There have been many varied interpretations of her work and life, and the truth is that much historical interpretation is speculative: the constructions of a fragmented past are all tentatively reliable, at best: interpreting biography into her poetry as well as taking historical informers interpretations, which are always coloured by one's own individual values and temporal societal norms, have been both incredibly thorny and unreliable. Two other important factors lead to her mythologization: one is that Sappho may have married a man, and she also had relationships with women: love-ships with both men and women were the subject of some of her lyrics; and, two, the problematic views—and silencing actions—that humanity has long held of vocal women creatives who harrowingly traffic the various ranges of emotion, desire, intimacy, and love, especially same-sex.

Unarguably, Sappho was *the* female poet of her time. Homer was regarded as her male equivalent. Sappho composed her writing in the Aeolian dialect, and many of her poems were sung to the accompaniment of a lyre (hence, the name lyric poetry). It was a time when writing was passed down orally at collective informal and formal gatherings, and a time when the Goddesses were regarded as equally holy as the Gods: in this climate Sappho was able to shine in her life and contributions. She was regarded as a muse: a "minor" Goddess of inspiration in the fields of literature, music, and arts, especially, and also, history and science, in ancient Greek: the tenth muse in an honoured system of the nine muses, all children of Zeus, to be exact. Pottery of the time, depicting her holding a lyre, illustrates Sappho as an incredibly beautiful woman; coins and status were both awarded her, scholars laboriously catalogued her scrolls in the Library of Alexandria, and her work was read and celebrated as the epitome of lyrical beauty for centuries until the Middle Ages. In the last twentieth century she regained popularity as her "Hymn to Aphrodite," also known as Fragment 1, survived time due to Dionysus, the Roman orator of 30 BC, quoted it in full in one of his works.

Like my other writers, Sappho is held in the highest esteem as a creative and courageous genius. Also similar is how Sappho's poetry transcends location, circumstances, and time: she creates and displays a raw desire, shifts and switches in roles, and births not only a reinvented language, but also identities, and with acutely subversive meanings. Anne Carson's *Autobiography of Red*, when read along with her reading of Sappho in *IF NOT, WINTER: Fragments of Sappho*, creates revolutionary displays of desire: the characters shift in roles and identities, and thereby they birth a reinvented language and alternative, subversive meanings.

Carson's translation of Sappho's lyrics provides a long-needed, accurate, and true translation of this epic lesbian poet and lyricist. Elliptical brackets that look like [and/or] throughout the text where destroyed papyrus or illegibility omissions occur (and is the first of any of Sappho translations to do so); this addition, combined with Carson's eloquent translation itself, allow readers to have a closer relationship to the subversive desires Sappho was exploring and ushering into existence. Carson writes,

even though you are approaching Sappho in translation, that is no
reason you should miss the drama of trying to read a papyrus torn in
half or riffled with holes or smaller than a postage stamp—brackets
imply a free space of imaginable adventure ... at the inside edge where
her words go missing, a sort of antipoem that condenses everything you
ever wanted her to write.

("Introduction," *IF NOT WINTER, Fragments of Sappho*, xi, xiii)

I love what Carson is alluding to here with "everything you ever wanted
her to write"—What is this for you? What might this be for Carson? What
might have been in the missing, which, if present, would have made a difference: such an interesting concept, to look at what is missing, the presence
of which would make a difference and lead to a new adventure.

In a very similar fashion to Stein, Sappho's poems and songs are laden with
desire, sex, and instruction. Both women poets were consumed with *being* in
action around their desires: Stein and Sappho offered up prayers of desires
that sought a craving. The body's need for intimacy, touch, and connection is
the silk that holds each woven lyric together. Carson translates a Sappho who

> prayed
> this word:
> I want
>
> (*IF NOT, WINTER: Fragments of Sappho* #22, 41)

>]of desire
> ...
>]from every care
>]you could release me
>]dewy riverbanks
>]to last all night long
>
> (#23, 43)

Sappho creates a language of choice. Burning, longing, dripping, loosening,
opening, and the gaps provide much more. Sappho explores what it is to have

> two states of mind in me
> (#51, 107)

exploring, as my other authors do, what it is to wrestle with complexities of
desire, roles, gender, and sexuality as Eros shakes her

> Eros shook my
> mind like a mountain wind falling on oak trees
> (#47, 99)

It's *that kind* of thundering that Sappho dwells in: fragments of masterful seeking

> I long and seek after
>
> (#36, 73)

submissive invitations like

> as long as you want
>
> (#45, 95)

The love affair, the hunger, the desire of Sappho's writing, when read like this, as well as the switching and "two states of mind," are utterly rare and a gift only a "minor" Goddess could bestow all these centuries later. Carson's translation is, without doubt, the fairest and most historically accurate that a scholar or historian has been to Sappho: it is alive with lust and want, her lyrics drip sexiness. There is at once a powerful agent of her own desires being met and a level of submission. Sappho's switching is clear, her two states of mind seductive even as they provide a space of confusion for her. A poem without gaps reads:

> I want to say something but shame
> prevents me
>
> yet if you had a desire for good or beautiful things
> and your tongue were not concocting some evil to say,
> shame would not hold down your eyes
> but rather you would speak about what is just
>
> (#137, 279)

Sappho has another moment of quizzical wonderment when she writes:

> what country girl seduces your wits
> wearing a country   dress
> not knowing how to pull the cloth to her ankles?
>
> (#57, 119)

Thinking back to earlier narratives deconstructed in this chapter, we are presented with links that represent the child/teen world as playful, confusing, and osculating. These songs, spanning thousands of years, speak of a child/teen-hood darkness and the light that will come ... even if it is in noticing the prudery all around the writer.

This conclusion is sinful

In this chapter, I have addressed how, through verse and deviant teen-hood, my chosen authors dwell in, complicate, and reject conformist gender and sexual binaries and carve out room to play with their gender and sexual variancy. Kathy Acker, Anne Carson, and Carson's rendition of Sappho disclose a perversity that can be both unchecked and free while also hesitant and restrained. Both the sexy and sexualized exists as these girl, boy, and gender-neutral characters switch. These writers invite an authentic conversation about teen sexuality and variance where something new can be created. The spaces of possibility are located in conversations around torn fragments, with room for new interpretations:

>]
>] nor
>] desire
>] but all at once
>] blossom
>] desire
>] took delight

(#78, 153)

Further, the perspectives, locations, boundaries, autonomy-seeking, and creation-based living as seen from a young person's point of view provide the reader with the invitation to look boldly at the variancies, layers, and unknown/unforeseen possibilities of gender and sexual switching in youth. I hope that this chapter might inspire readers to consider how the desires, roles, and identities of a young person get negotiated, traversed, and birthed—and how do we support or shut down the process of discovery? How might we as adults expand and nurture our conversations with teens and youth and also amongst ourselves, to incorporate switch identities?

After writing on the longing and seeking-after, the dripping and longing, the holy and the beautiful, Sappho beautifully writes on identity and desire being created, gifted, and born, thusly:

> you will go your way among dim shapes. Having been breathed out.
> (#55, 115)

A surrender is needed to follow the switchback journey these writers so skilfully navigate and write for us: their characters often do wander in a world of dim shapes, as Janey does, never really shining a light on the cobwebs of her mind and world, while others experience a sweetness in releasing their attachment to a solid and singular identity as they discover a destabilized, switch identity. What is true is that gender and sexual switching in its uncertainty and changeability shows up as colour-filled and alive next to the dimness of a predictable shape.

To dwell in the space of being breathed out, the space of switching, in *that between and betwixt place of variance,* is to know the self as free beyond any difference; the freedom to breathe, outside of the body rather than what is held within, contained, and shrouded. Sappho writes that this state is both a wisdom and a rarity:

> not one girl I think
> > who looks on the light of the sun
> > > will ever
> > > have wisdom
> > > like this

(#56, 117)

She tells us when, too:

>]
>]right here
>]
>] (now again)
>]

(#83, 161).

Notes

1 Acker's movements are all within a sexual and identity-variant milieu, whereas Carson's subjects and thematics span much broader.

2 I refer to "story" here as fictional *and* inaccurate: that which is conceived/ perceived as real when in fact the narrative is a distortion; a story is "used to lament the fact that a particular misfortune has happened too often in one's experience," and, often to the listener as well as the storyteller, the story "indicates that a particular bad situation is tediously familiar" (*New Oxford American Dictionary*). The "tediously familiar" occurs out of the story being past-based, individualistic, self-centred, and inaccurate: often blame, complaint, upset or judgement accompanies a story. What is thought has nothing to do with what actually happened or is happening in the present reality *even as it may seem* to be real or "factual." Stories are likened to dreams in Buddhism, and most of life considered a dream/story. For Carl Jung, derangement also accompanies story.

3 The thirty-five minute interview is directed by Fennella Greenfield and took place at The October Gallery in London on the occasion of William Burroughs's first exhibition of paintings in the United Kingdom. It was part of the "ICA Guardian Conversations," via The Institute of Contemporary Arts (ICA) in London.

4 I want to be clear that while this chapter will address fiction that concerns incest and the pornography and eroticism of youth, in no way does this mean that I condone or support, in any way, the sexualization of children, youth, or adolescents, especially incest or pornography, in any form or in any real-life. The texts I am engaging with are *fictional narratives written by adults for adults*; the author's work, and mine, imply an adult readership that is consensually choosing to engage with transgressive subject matter. Within a deconstructionist, feminist context, readings of such difficult, challenging, and subversive material can be done within an empowering and liberating context, rather than a silencing or sex-panic lens (as discussed in my first chapter).

5 Concluding possibilities for switching
Gender, sexuality, and identity freedom

Gender and Sexual Fluidity in 20th Century Women Writers: Switching Desire and Identity has brought together five evocative, powerful, experimental women/LGBTQ writers and introduced the notion and theory of switching by which to deconstruct, understand, and celebrate the non-normative, variant genders, sexualities, identities, and desires they navigate and write about. My specific aim with this book is that the typology of the switch—and the new and expansive realms of gender and sexual identity that switching illuminates—be seen, understood, and utilized as an access and pathway to freedom.

To elucidate this I have shone a light on the subversive and perverse desires and identities located in selected, avant-garde writing of Gertrude Stein, Jeanette Winterson, Kathy Acker, Eileen Myles, Anne Carson, and Sappho. Through various forms of switching, the writers and narrators de-centre the discursive cultural norms of sex and sexuality, desire and identity.

Notions of identity are destabilized through deconstructing the language and pattern of switching gendered bodies, sexualities, desires, roles, and identities. The action of switching serves to allow the characters, texts, and us as readers the experience of being free from the constraints of familial, societal and cultural norms and notions that normally confine the gendered identity and/or sexual self. Read together, these five authors and their texts are connected by a similarly felt thread: the fabric and structure of these works, and of this book, weave variancies of desire, role, sex, gender, and identity through a new lens: the lens of the switch. In the vibrant, multi-coloured pattern of switching, liberating and freeing actions are revealed and taken.

This book gives the switch some room to play by illustrating sites of switching that are excitingly prevalent in literature; it also demonstrates that the concept and theory of switching are important additions to our current theoretical models. It is my hope that the disciplines of literature and writing, literary and feminist theory, queer theory, women's and gender studies, identity studies, sexuality studies, and LGBTQ studies (as well as others) will benefit enormously from introducing the terminology and ideas associated with the switch: as a noun, verb, adjective, descriptor, and multifaceted practice, the switch and switching elicit numerous and infinite possibilities.

The option to deconstruct identity

The scholarship and conversations around variant gender and sexual identities, especially trans ones, has never been more alive; yet we also still live and breathe in a society that leans into having gender and sexual identities known, stable, and certain. Fixed identities have a seductiveness. In the tumultuous sea of sexism, normativity, and semi-compulsory heterosexuality, familiar and known gender and sex identities support the illusion of identity being calm, consistent, and reliable.

The process of gender and sexual identity construction and socialization, begun in early childhood and more fully formed in teen-hood, reveals a gradual adaptation of ways of being and acting in order to be accepted and successful. By the time later teen-hood and adulthood are reached, a set of beliefs and truths, practices and approaches, attributes and characteristics, *which mean both our survival and success*, make up our identity. Being wedded to an identity—*who we consider ourselves to be, the meaning of that identity, and what we attach to it*—is thus understandable. Considering these social norms and cultural conditions, an authentic, self-generated identity might seem daunting. Even more, it might occur as improbable or impossible.

Considering the potentially of identity arising and being constructed inauthentically might identity be a location that is ripe *to be deconstructed*. Could the deconstruction of variant gender and sexual identities (along with other forms of identity) be a key and necessary step in allowing new, authentic, self-created narratives to be constructed, written, and *experienced?* A much larger space to play is made visible when the freedom to deconstruct—and create or (re)construct—gender and sexuality identities is made available. When switching along these new continuums of identities is chosen, the playground gets even bigger.

Judith Butler drew attention to the paradox of identity frameworks that could fix or constrain "the very 'subjects' that it hopes to represent and liberate" in her groundbreaking book *Gender Trouble*. She asked us to consider that

> if identities were no longer fixed ... cultural configurations of sex and gender might then proliferate or, rather, their present proliferation might then become articulable within the discourses that establish intelligible cultural life, confounding the very binaries of sex, and exposing its fundamental unnaturalness.

(189–190)

While the mainstream tendency is to grant a vast amount of importance to gender and sexual consistency and the familiarity that it brings, others embrace and advocate for a gender and sexual politics that call out for "confounding" binary disruptions.

The notion of unlatching and deconstructing fundamentally unnatural, fixed identities, and embracing the concept of the switch and switching, allows for great freedom of choice. Yet we can also ask: What actually occurs when binaries are disrupted? What affect does it have? If Stein were alive today, with all her butchy and stoic mannerisms, yet wearing a skirt, how, where, and by whom might her variant, switchy writing and narratives be regarded and read?

For some feminists and queer theorists, scholars, students, writers, intellectuals, professionals, and/or activists, especially those who locate themselves along axis of interconnected social justice, gender and sex advocacy work, the expansion and visibility of switching in desires, roles, sexuality, and gender might be both welcome *and* uncomfortable. If we value (and are committed to) the long-term goal of *all people* living with more freedom in their identity, is it not incumbent upon us to notice, and challenge where subtle and nuanced fixed and restrictive ways of being and thinking exist? What new strategies and theories might we develop *and use* to challenge the static gender and sex binaries and the confines that continue to limit and restrict our reading, teaching, and understanding of sexuality and gender? At the individual, group, organizational, and societal level, where and how can we continue to foster and create visibility and space to serve and support complex sexual and gender identities such as switching?

All of my writers—Stein, Winterson, Acker, Myles, Sappho, and Carson—broach these questions in various ways through the language, locations, and actions of switching, and we can, too. The action of gender and sexual switching—the switching on and off, betwixt and between, moments that exist through choices in language, roles, and desires—allow for something new and unhinged to be expressed and freed. I want to urge us all to use these and other authors who work with complex and difficult switch narratives to further a more *dynamic and accessible* literary, feminist, and queer theory and activism. I want us all to continue to mine the depths of our reserves and ask: Where might we as educators, students, and activists work to remove the blind spots, which our theories, pedagogy, and classrooms have, to being more inclusive of variant gender identities and sexual practices? Contrasting questions may assist us in viewing identity through the lens of switching, moving educators, readers, and activists beyond our familiar gender and sex-identity polarities: Who do narrators, and by extension readers, *not get to be* when their identities are fixed? What constraints can be identified? What might it cost a character, narrative, or reader when the focus is on a fixed identity, rather than on a shifting desire or shifting identity? What is made visible, or invisible, when naming a character based on something they like to do? Which doors open and which close?

Feminist and queer theory and activism rely on stretching into new and uncomfortable territory in order to birth new possibilities: switching, and the uncertainty with gender and sexuality that live there, is a theory we could use to activate our layered, interdisciplinary conversations and theories. Switching—and the expanding spaces of gender and sexual variancy that it allows—serves to reignite our understanding and connecting with complex variances of identities, over our differences, and make a real difference in our feminist, queer, and progressive theory and practices thriving.

Considering this expansive possibility, what might switching as both a theory and an action make possible? Especially in climates where there can be either a mistrusting of new gender and sexuality identity descriptors *or* challenges to fixed identities. Switching is an important and valuable location and identity to incorporate and use.

The personal praxis of the switch: "You can say almost anything you please, can't you?"

(Alice B. Toklas's note to Stein, *Baby Precious Always Shines*, 161)

Gender and Sexual Fluidity in 20th Century Women Writers: Switching Desire and Identity has been located in prose, poetry, memoir, lettered narratives, and in the theoretical model of the switch and theory. The chapters and authors were chosen to present a new, exciting, bold, and subversive methodology and theory: the switch is the interconnection between each chapter, author, and life. My writers write variations of a switching self: rivers of variant identities wind through narratives into oceans, seeking a freedom to know and experience their expansive identities newly. They write with an urgency that means their aliveness, and ours. Rather than living a life of survival, making it and making do, these authors weave streams of intoxicating, lyrical turns that explore both the murky depths of these seas and the clear, expansive sky.

With a watchful eye on the socially constructed waves of constraint and clouds of conformity, these five writers cross barriers of time as they persist in writing gender and sexual desire newly. These are high stakes of uncertainty here. The switch need not be an identity that limits, fixes, or constrains. It need not be an identity that is juxtaposed or compared. It can be an identity that exists in a realm where there is "no true or false, real or distorted acts of gender [or sexuality] … the postulation of a true gender [and/or sexual] identity would [thus] be revealed as a regulatory *fiction*" (italics mine, Judith Butler, 180). In exploring gender and sexuality through the action of switching, my writers lead the way in experiencing greater freedom in gender, sexuality, and identity. Literature, like academic discourse and theory, represents a life: the imagination and worlds of their creation reflect what is ours to dive into.

Many years ago, Eve Kosofsky-Sedgwick and I had long conversations on my theory of switching: what it could contribute to literary, feminist, and queer theory, the various liberation and activist movements, and, most importantly for me, to people's lives. How could the visibility and theory of switching honour multiple, queer, variant identities and allow the experience of affinity, authenticity, and tribe, while at the same time create freedom and play with signifiers and social and cultural identities?

As I wrestled with my quest to both experientially live and intellectually develop my theory, I remember Eve being adamant that age-of-consent laws were counter-intuitive and damaging. As a lesbian mother to a young son at that time, I found myself wondering how that could be, how safe was the argument and rationale, and what the connection was to my work. With the gift of time and experience, and the wisdom both bring, the answer would be revealed when my son was almost twenty: trusting oneself and others to make the best and right choices for their own lives proves a better tool than any rule, law, or social norm.

The long process of dwelling on and developing my theory of switching was often informed by that, and similar, conversations. I kept asking myself to see the connections and to ask how gender, sexual, and identity freedom are given *and* taken? And then, later: How and when is freedom most *experienced* and expressed? Are our youth, or any of us, empowered *or* disempowered by being told that something is off limits? Are LGBTQ people empowered in their agency for self-defined sexual pleasure and partnership when anti-sodomy or heterosexist marriage laws restrict their choice of partnership? How, and for whom, do sexually related and/or gender-informed laws, serve? Regardless of one's personal values and beliefs, do we as a society think that people are empowered when laws control our right to choose what's best for our life or body? How do laws governing gendered and sexual choices and activities contribute to or diminish the ability of people to learn and experience self-directed agency and responsibility: for example, the power to say "yes" or "no" and to express consent and/or choice. For Sedgwick, the progressive possibilities of radical acceptance and freedom existed in a relaxing of laws and restrictions, as well as in considering the dismissal of categories.

The resistance *or advocacy* of ideas, theories, policies, and laws that concern our choices and freedom being constrained and policed (arguably, as one New York City police officer told me, "to avoid anarchy") continues to open up sites for personal, community, and collective discussion, research, and (re)examination. Judith Butler drew attention to the "internal paradox" of foundationalist frames that can fix or constrain "the very 'subjects' that it hopes to represent and liberate" (*Gender Trouble* 189–190). Butler cautioned to "be careful not to idealize certain expressions of gender that, in turn, produce new forms of hierarchy and exclusion" (viii). Certainly, we have many examples of this wrestling with both the internal and external paradoxes of identity theory occurring in both academia and culture (including subcultures). The invisibility of gender, sexual, variant, and switch folks can be a subtle and deep form of exclusion.

Someone who switches and/or is variant in any way with their sex practices, desires, gender experiences, body, and/or identity does not fit in to the fixed, singular categories of gender and sexual practices and identities that define our heteronormative society. Many years of study have shown that there is continued need for subversive practices and intersecting identities to be given the space to be heard, seen, respected, and known. Intellectual and activist dialogues have been confronting and bridging interlocking oppressions for decades; however, we need to further include and make visible variant LGBTQ genders, desires, and sex practices, especially in a climate of fear around feminism and social justice.

As Chapter 1 illustrated, writers who navigate the more subversive and s/witchy elements of sexuality, desire, and identity can have those elements ignored in their work. Non-normative, variant locations make up the fringes of literary discourse and critical theory; this applies as well to scholars who study and ruminate in the fields. The more "perverse," or "radical," the more likely they are to be relegated to the sidelines of what is considered "Literature" or "teachable." Yet many of us would agree that higher education has the primary purpose of introducing students to new, challenging ideas and areas of study so that they might expand their knowledge, intelligence, and skills. Staying safe, and out of the realm of the uncomfortable, does not contribute to this mandate; in fact, it stifles and curtails it.

The sexual- and gender-variant spaces of writing—especially for women, and LGBTQ women in particular—continue to remain peripheral and underground/subcultural.[1] The discursive cultural and visual norms of sex and sexuality, and the secrecy, the hiddenness, and silence that lie in the participatory relationships between literary narratives, pornography, BDSM, performance, Internet, and visual locations of desire illustrate a world of dichotomies, pluralities, and absence. Women's variant/transgressive identity spaces are relatively invisible compared to heterosexual and gay men. LGBTQ women have far less social space to explore, either voyeuristically or exhibitionistically, with their sex and their desires.[2] Works of literature and writing thus constitute very important, if liminal, public spaces by which to understand and make visible this location.

In *Art Objects: Essays on Ecstasy and Effrontery*, Winterson herself would write of risk-taking, art, and writing: "[T]he riskiness of Art, the reason why it affects us, is not the riskiness of its subject matter, it is the risk of creating a new way of seeing, a new way of thinking" (*Art Objects*, 52). Truly, this is the call my authors have answered: each of them taking great risks with publishing their writing, inventing and creating new ways of thinking, seeing, and experiencing the world by "overturning the habits and conventions of previous generations" (52).

Certainly, risk-taking and visionary newness are at the heart of the readings and authors I have chosen. I see these writers as having both a creative genius and great courage. Looking at how switching with identity, desire, sexual, and gender practices are delineated, explored, and complicated in my authors, this book asks the reader to consider to what extent we resist or accept the unfamiliar. My narrators play with switching in the most unconventional ways, and so it has been for the author of this book, who could not possibly deconstruct the layers of these switches without having herself undergone both soft and hard switches of gender, sexuality, identity, and roles, from before the conception of this theory and idea to the writing and completing of this particular "book of hours" (*The Powerbook*, 289) in your hand. The experimental, vanguard writing of all of my authors is a contribution to what Winterson calls "the rebellion of art ... a daily rebellion against the state of living death routinely called real life" (*Art Objects*, 52).

All of us girls have been dead so long.

(Kathy Acker, *Pussy, King of the Pirates*, 109)

Choosing to walk the world as gender or sexual variant requires *extreme social agility*. It is a very risky act, to switch. The need for visible, safe and celebratory queer and sexually variant spaces that "support forms of affective, erotic, and personal living that are public in the sense of accessible, available to memory, and sustained through collective activity" (Berlant and Warner, 562) is incredibly important to counter heteronormative hegemonies. Supporting that which empowers a person, in *all aspects of their life*, cannot be underestimated as a foundation for a society and culture committed to personal freedom, agency, and choice. Because, while sex and sexuality are all around us every day, our culture, texts, bodies, and experiences have been desexualized at the same time as hyper-sexualized; sex and desire have been constrained while also being fetishized; gender has been compartmentalized and boxed up while also abandoned with a fundamentalist zeal.

We all need the empowerment that an expanding feminist praxis offers us. Further, we need intersectional feminist practice *and* theory that supports and inspires reading and teaching complex, difficult and/or uncomfortable writing and conversations around variant sexuality, desire, and identity. I, for one, do not want scholarship, writing, classrooms, narratives, theory, ideas, or art that conform or don't challenge me to expand what I already know—most especially in the realm of desire.

It is up to all the teachers, students, and activists who stand for sexual, gender, and identity variancy and freedom to create the conversations we wish to further. How can we be as bold as my writers in telling the stories we need to tell? In reading and teaching the stories we need to read? The ones that enliven us the most? How can we fuel conversations and create space for narratives that allow for gender and sexual switching? How can we become more allied with a complex, variant, and fluid world of switching that favours present-based, lively, and transformational identity locations? Where in the dusty corners of our own cultural, social, and familial upbringing and privilege might familiarity, certainty, scarcity, and/or fear, need to be cleaned up?

We are well beyond being interdisciplinary in our academic theories and pursuits: we are multi-disciplinary thinkers who can advocate, read, write, and teach for a body (and canon) of literature that embraces complex notions of gender, sexuality, and desire *while at the same time* holding the space for *all* chosen identities to be respected. Once aware of the water we swim in, a space to re-read, theorize, and create newly can help direct our spawning migration. In her ten-year anniversary "Preface" to *Gender Trouble*, in 1999, Judith Butler would write:

> I opposed those regimes of truth that stipulated that certain kinds of gendered expressions were found to be false or derivative, and others, true and original. The point was not to prescribe a new gendered way of life that might then serve as a model for readers of the text. Rather, *the aim of the text was to open up the field of possibility for gender without dictating which kinds of possibilities ought to be realized.* One might wonder what use "opening up possibilities" finally is, but no one who has understood what it is to live in the social world as what is "impossible," illegible, unrealizable, unreal, and illegitimate is likely to pose that question.
>
> (Italics mine, viii)

We have the privilege—and responsibility—of co-creating the world we want, and teachers and educators are especially called to do this. Through our literature choices and language use, especially within the Humanities and Social Sciences (yet irrespective of discipline), we can either advocate for and celebrate switching and variant gender and sexual identities, inspiring educated and empowered free-thinking generated from a *field of possibilities, or* we can be canonical gatekeepers. The student/teacher commitment is to educate and empower, to stretch the knowing and knowledge, and to mentor the process of discovery and the process of acquiring of new skills. The commitment many of us who are in the teaching and serving professions have is to explore, venture into, and experience new-found freedoms through expanding our knowledge. We are truth seekers; and this space exists and manifests most fully when our practices and methods are infused with both the intellectual *and* experiential.

Bridging the personal and the political has historically paved the way for exciting new thought and research. In the case of this books mission, identifying the pattern of the switch and deconstructing and examining where switching occurs in language, agency, and locations of queer and/or variant desires in the writings of Stein, Winterson, Acker, Myles, Carson, and Carson's translation of Sappho, as well as looking at some of the historical and current conversations, provides an opportunity to galvanize the study and conversations of women's writing, literature, gender, sexuality, and identity studies to the extent that the continued process of transformation in these fields is possible.

Without question, the addition of the switch and switching will be a marked revolutionary step in identity politics, sexuality studies, and queer theory. It is *critically important* for feminist and queer theory to continue to thrive on the equality foundations they were built upon while also moving into new, groundbreaking arenas. One area is where literature, theory, the personal and the political live and collide: in mapping the many crossroads where narratives seek to share, experience, and celebrate variantly gendered and sexed lives. *Switching* is an action-based idea and concept (used as both a noun and a verb), which "coexists synchronically" with "multiple temporalities." *Switching* is a term that can be used outside of a BDSM or sexual context yet still be infused with the notion of play and consent.

This book, and the texts within it, have sought to mindfully consider some of these questions: How do these locations, perspectives, boundaries, and autonomy-seeking switching actions provide spaces for us, as adult readers, to look at the inauthenticites of conformity in own lives? How can we begin to take ownership over mapping onto others our fear, unfamiliarity, and/or inexperience of gender and sexual identities and practices? What new ways of navigating and respecting variant/non-normative identities, spaces, and locations are now open to us? How can we, through literature (as well as other creative forms), create the space and awareness to experience gender and sexual switching and identity? Newly and with curiosity?

Once we begin to engage in the process of considering switching in gender, desires, sexuality, and identity, where are we free to allow—and even invite and embrace—the unfamiliar and uncomfortable language and aspects of switching identities? A bold and fearless writing of sexual and gender switching has emerged, one that complicates the preconceived notions and patterns of what these authors are exploring. Additional language to accompany the theory and visibility of the switch in reading variancies could be added: code-switching might use descriptors like *gendershift* and *sexualshift* as adjectives, nouns, and adverbs: *switchshifter, genderswitcher, gendershifter, sexualswitcher, sexualshifting*, and so forth.[3]

The switch as a celebrated, fluid identity has the capacity to have real, tangible, and positive impacts on all people—not just women, queer folk, gender variants, or sexual variants—to bridge narratives of empowered lives and create a new context. The reality is that the concept of the switch is much bigger than any discipline, department, or theory: actual lives—as well as the work of many intellectual, artistic, and cultural contributors—are waiting to be newly read, (re)discovered, created, and made visible by employing the pattern and action of the switch.

If the multiple locations and axis of switching are invited into our classrooms and writing, what might be made available to our educational aims and practices? What could the theory of switching involve and mean for us as educators committed to an inclusive, diverse, robust, and expansive education? How might switch identities and narratives newly inform progressive curriculums? Literary as well as gender, queer, and sexuality studies and theory—and the activism that such progressive disciplines are founded on. How could new, expanded, and accessible readings of complex literature and writing that engages both gender *and* sexual switching work in tandem to facilitate this?

While *Gender and Sexual Fluidity in 20th Century Women Writers: Switching Desire and Identity* has a specific focus to demonstrate my theory, I also hope that this book will mean something quite significant in the direction that English Literature, Literary scholarship, Gender, Sexuality, Queer, and Identity Studies are taking: a more inclusive, liberating, and sexy theory and practice. Further questions to direct this expansion might ask: How can intersectional, accessible readings and deconstructions that incorporate layers of switching and variancy widen the pathways we currently use to deconstruct and teach literature, language, gender, sexuality, and identity? How could we use the theory of switching in our seeking to understand, respect, and celebrate self-defined genders, self-defined sexualities and desires, and/or self-defined identities—especially ones we may not relate to? In complicated and contentious areas and conversations of identity studies, where and how can we both listen for and offer connections that bridge, rather than looking for that which divides and separates?

My readings and theory advocate for new readings and activism that are outside any one discipline: switching is a theory unconfined by any one theoretical or scholarly rubric. Where could switching serve inter-disciplinary collaborations? How might *various disciplines* engage in new, scholarly, and accessible conversations that are informed by the complexities, possibilities, and freedom that can be found in switching narratives and identities? And where could switching further research in other disciplines such as ethnicity and race studies, disability studies, and cultural studies? As well as more specific audiences of sexuality and gender, such as gay men, trans folk, and teens who could utilize the theory of switching to expand both scholarship and activism?

Invitations (and examples) of alternative, future focus

One intention of this book is that my theory of the switch and switching will enter into our academic, theoretical vocabulary and thereby extend into the larger society in profound and revolutionary ways. In the fields of gender, sexuality, ethnicity, and identity I look forward to other scholars and writers applying and using my theory of switching. For example, I see my theory as important on the evolutionary pathway for men and the study of masculinity: a deeper awareness, understanding, appreciation, and visibility of the variancies of male and masculine gender and sexual identity and expression are still needed in many disciplines.

At the level of self as authentically created and experienced, versus socially constructed and generationally inherited, men have been robbed of options as much as women have. Like women, men are culturally encouraged to keep to given and chosen roles, and are severely penalized when they deviate. For most men in North America, any movement along the gender and sex continuums comes with consequences that are difficult to live with and can be so severe that the "don't ask, don't tell" policy of closeting and silence continues to be reinforced. Consider that, while the media has recently done an important job of focusing on the preventable horror of teen suicide rates, the highest rates of suicide in the United States are amongst middle-aged white and Native-American men. In the youth category, consisting of ages 15–24, boys and young men previously accounted for three quarters of all suicides in Canada. In the last decade this number has changed, with girls' and young women's suicides increasing by 38 percent. Non-fatal suicide attempts peak in young adults, and it is girls and young women who account for the majority of these numbers (in part, perhaps, because girls and young women are more willing to disclose emotional issues and seek help).

Seriously revised and expanded education and awareness around understanding, accepting, and celebrating variancy (in all its forms) could be part of the solution to these preventable tragedies. We must continue to teach, advocate, and support safe, inclusive, nurturing spaces for our youth—and all who are questioning and/or reforming their identities—as they embark on the complicated journey of self-discovery. Our educational and activist aims need to expand where and how we allow for empowering gender and sexual discoveries and choices to be made—rather than support structures that fuel fear, disempowerment, hopelessness, or shame. An empowered and supportive context is something everyone can experience in a world where fluid gender and sexual identities, and switching specifically, is understood, accepted, and part of our knowledge and practice base.

In the areas of race and ethnic studies, the theory of switching could be used to allow for a much fuller embracing of the multiple narratives of diverse ethnicities. In many parts of the world, multi-ethnic distinctions are celebrated. In America, however, the 1892 Supreme Court ruling of Homer Plessy, which became known as the "one drop rule," while no longer enforced, is still used to classify as black people of mixed heritage who have "one drop" of African ancestry (see the 1982 Louisiana ruling against Susie Phipps, who was denied changing her vital statistics record to white based on state law that cites one-thirty-second percentage of African ancestry equates to black ethnicity). A hegemonic, systemic, societal structure that supports such legal rulings does not value the visible and/or invisible simultaneous coexistence of variant, multi-ethnic or multi-racial identities. The negative impacts and implications manifest in many segments of US society; accepted states of privilege are both obvious and subtle in private and public as racist political, economic, social, verbal, and written codes are reinforced.

Most of us would acknowledge that "identities overlap with ancestries, but they are also shaped by knowledge, socialization, physical appearance, and culture, among other factors." In their comprehensive study on *The Changing Racial and Ethnic Composition of the US Population: Emerging*

American Identities, Anthony Daniel Perez and Charles Hirschman assert that

> although ancestry can be defined as an objective attribute based on geographic descent or genetic markers, reported racial and ethnic identities are subjective articulations of group attachment and affinity. Ancestry influences identity, but its impact is mediated by ethnic admixture across generations, knowledge of ancestral origins, and the number of generations removed from the arrival of immigrant ancestors. Second, while family and community socialization are the primary mechanisms through which identities are reinforced, racial and ethnic categories are shaped by institutional and political forces through 1) laws and sanctions that regulate group rights and opportunities; 2) customs that affirm group claims for recognition and entitlements; and 3) systems of measurement and classification used in administrative records of race and ethnicity at the individual level or in aggregate counts of populations by race and ethnicity (censuses).
>
> (8)

Their studies demonstrate what many of us ethnically hybrids know: that while intermarriage (and migration patterns) has produced a population that is multi-ethnic, and North Americans have increasingly moved towards pan-ethnic categories (such as Asian American and African American, Italian Canadian, and Chinese Canadian) and our world has become more inclusive of multi-ethnic diversity, hybrid, mixed-race folks are still not celebrated for the *full* diversity that we embody. A mixed-race person who is in the media, from artistic performers to athletes, can be "encouraged" to choose and represent one culture or ethnicity over the other and thus downplay their mixed ethnic ancestry or "otherness." People of mixed ethnicity and colour can also be encouraged to downplay ethnic or racial group affinity; they are told they are "coming off" "too Afrocentric," or "too Indian." Critical writers and thinkers, who are most often in the alternative media and news rather than on NBC or ABC, continue to report that white hegemonic assumptions that dictate and reinforce assimilation are still a major factor in being accepted and successful in North American society. The US census encourages this: as late as 2000, while offering more ethnic choices than ever, the census was fraught with wording and categories that break ethnicity down to "race," and thus the census does not deliver a true or real picture of the diverse multi-ethnic ancestry or identity in the United States. The Canadian census does: 41 percent of Canadians report "multi-ethnic origins."

While racial identity and ethnic grouping may be something many people are committed to—and not something that people may try on like a coat or can choose to change every day like a pair of socks—people with mixed ancestral and cultural ethnicity may often emphasize, *and de-emphasize,* variant aspects depending on both need (safety, economics, inclusion, etc.) and the circumstances. For some, code switching with one's language use, style, and speaking is a common practice dictated by the setting and custom. Different environments and audiences—public and private gatherings, familial and work settings, diverse social circles and working environments—will elicit switch moments in speech, behaviour, and action. It is not uncommon to code switch when moving from speaking with a peer to speaking with a parent or elder. While most people can accept this as normal and appropriate, we don't offer the same space for switching in identity: it is rare to have the various expressive cultures of a hybrid, mixed race, mixed ethnicity artist or author regarded and represented *equally and with equal respect.*

The notion of self-policing ethnic and racial embodiments and performances, holding ourselves and others accountable, continues to be a familiar theme in North American discourse, thought, and action. The policing of divergence is enforced, and sometimes very strictly. When one does not adhere to the proscribed identity category or role, be it one's perceived racial, gendered, class, or sex role, violence and punishment of some degree will often result. Omi and Winant coined the term *racial state* to "describe the way in which the government has made a person's fundamental rights and entitlements depend on the race to which he or she is assigned" (as cited in Brodkin, 196). We can add the terms, *ethnic state, gendered state, sexual state,* and *class state,* all of which are rigorously policed. Racial, class, and economic states most certainly would influence switching. Systemic systems of power and oppression do not allow people to switch at will. The violence of systemic racism, classism, and sexism rigorously polices any and all variant expressions. When faced with socioeconomic disenfranchisement and oppression, gender and sexual switching would not be regarded as a choice or a needed or wise survival strategy. What is important to note is that gender and sexual switching occur very differently in public versus private worlds. Private worlds are closeted and safe compared to exposed and potentially dangerous public ones. The policing of variancy is met at the intersections of race, class, gender, and sexuality deviations: identifying and radically accepting switching and switch moments in both private and public would allow for an expansion and freedom of identity.

The more visible the telling of diverse and variant identity experiences (including heterosexual, lesbian, bi-sexual, genderqueer, non-binary, and non-conforming) through writing as well as other cultural mediums that explore variant narratives and ideas, the more empowered we are *no matter where we are on the spectrum* of sexuality, gender, and identity. Switching in the uncomfortable territory of borders, where outsiders gather, is a powerful place of both unity *and* contradiction: "living on the borders and in the margins, keeping intact one's shifting and multiple identity and integrity, is like trying to swim in a new element, an 'alien' element" Gloria Anzaldúa would write in *Borderlands/La Frontera*.

> To live in the Borderlands means you ...
> To survive the Borderlands
> you must live *sin fronteras* (without borders)
> be a crossroads.
>
> (Anzaldúa, 195)

If we spend some time located at the various switch moments that occur at the crossroads, in "the limen,"[4] a gap location, a place between and betwixt, where "one becomes most fully aware of one's multiplicity," we can form and create "liberatory syllogisms." This would be highly effective when considering the intersubjectivity and placement of the switch within multiple linguistic, cultural, ethnic, and racial-identity locations. Now, more than ever, in the current climate of both renewed racial violence and awareness of the injustices of racism in the United States and elsewhere, these narratives and stories are ripe for a new form of deconstruction and inclusion: my theory of "the switch" can be utilized as both a bridge and a pathway for an evolved and inclusive understanding of identity in the areas of communal associations, ethnicity, and race.

I'll meet you on the bridge

Where might we continue to bridge language and literature with people's experiences, making visible a much-needed diversity where the axis of theory and activism can be expand—and so chart a new direction for our institutes of higher learning *and by extension* our society? Can we envision what this might elicit and make possible? And are we willing to take the risks to get there? From non-government organizations to social work, environmental protectionism to progressive spiritual theology, intercultural communication to political policy, evolving and expansive theories of fluid and switching gender, and sexual identities put into practice—these can be slow to permeate North American society. What would be required for the theory and concept of switching to have an articulable, established "intelligible cultural life"? A discourse that would influence and permeate mainstream culture and society with some ease and grace, rather than force and compliance? Where might writers, teachers, counsellors, therapists, policy makers, lawyers, journalists, researchers, and activists help form a more inclusive language of gender variancy and sexual difference through our work and daily life? I offer these questions to expand how and where we can create and live in locations and spaces that serve to open new possibilities of gender, sexuality, roles, desires, and identity. They are raised for the reader to be inquiring, to take on as possibilities and potential practices, not necessarily to answer.

Consider what could evolve if the typology of the switch and switching was seen and adopted? And in an easy way rather than a forceful one. More sites and demonstrations of self-expression and variancy would present themselves (which would not be limited to literature, writing, and the classroom); further, they would be *welcome* additions to our intellectual culture(s). Quite possibly, a freer, creation-based society would emerge. Conformity could become a thing of the past and authentically generated and created ways of being valued in its place. We would experience a greater recognition and affiliation in and with the complex variancies of the other, even as experiencing difference. We would experience more connection and less isolation through sharing and seeing the variant parts of ourselves and others, no matter how slight, and a greater curiosity, rather than confusion, around notions of difference. Reflecting a variant, yet common, humanity with authenticity, creativity, and integrity taking the place of silence and invisibility. The strategies of identity survival and separation based on gender and sex differences would fade.

It's time. It's time to remove the significance and attachment to singular forms and expressions of gender, sexuality, desire, roles, and identity. It's time to stand for an expansion of new possibilities and a playful existence with the impermanent and changeable categories of sexual and gender identity. It's time to say good-bye to self-imposed, family, group, community, society and/or culture-adopted gender and sexual constraints that do not serve us. It's time to take responsibility for the writing, directing, performing, witnessing, and celebrating of the gender and sexual narrative scripts and plays of our personal and collective lives. Coming from a "yes" to freedom and what's possible, rather than a "no" of protection and survival, *switching* becomes a sharp tool we can use: its purpose to facilitate both *power and play*.

Fuel for freedom

My intention is that, by reading any of my chapters the idea and theoretical model of the switch is made visible in a more universal way, and that new vocabulary and theory might emerge. Further, that the theory of "the switch," and the practice of "switching," will radiate from the academic world and, dare I say it, into the mainstream as a rich identity with currency and value. Switching would have a profoundly positive and freeing influence when adopted and given currency. As we continue to courageously deepen our understanding of the complex issues of gender, sexuality, and identity, especially gender and sexual variancy, may the timeless words of Emily Dickinson inspire us: "I found / that hunger—was a way / of persons outside windows / the entering—takes away" (*The Poems of Emily Dickinson*, #439, 203).

What I have explored with these authors and their texts is the new-found freedom that arises when characters have the courage to walk unfamiliar passageways towards windows and doors that open into something utterly new: it is through these experimental and transformative gateways that a fundamental shift is possible in how gender, sexuality, and identity occurs. The narrator's, characters, and texts become privately and publicly bound: weaving chapters that cross boundaries as they craft *books* of *power*. *Powerful* ideas, open *skies*, and *pirateous* ways of being and thinking about gender, sexuality, identity, roles, desires, and the self transform through each narrative and identity quest. Transgressive practices and language fuel these transformations.

At the heart of this book is the freedom that is elicited and can be experienced when gender and sexual identity are locations of exploration and play rather than something static, confined, or to be fixed. Identity, like feminism, is and can be a living, breathing experience: deeply personal, confrontingly political, culturally impactful, and tenderly profound. It is time that switches had their identities named, seen, and cherished through the telling and witnessing of both narratives and lived experiences; the switch can then become an empowering and affirming identity of value and freedom.

Notes

1 A genderqueer may or may not see themselves as gender switching, of course, and may or may not engage in the act of sexual switching.
2 From bathroom stalls and bath houses to parks and rest stops; from nightclubs and bars to community organizations and online networks, gay and bisexual men especially, and heterosexual men as well, have mastered the art of cruising and public sex. Gay men have a large range of acceptance, expression, and deviancy within their subculture; further, they have a host of locations and spaces within which perverse and subversive sexual practices and identities can be explored and honored. Straight men have gentlemen's clubs, strip bars, escort services, massage parlors, online options, and, in some cases, access to powerful, economic positions that allow for sex and desire to be "acceptable" forms of masculine sexual expression.
3 In contrast, women, regardless of their sexual preference or gender identity—who are similarly transgressive in their identity and/or sexual desires—have fewer communities and networks and far less visibility and acceptance. The virgin, mother, or whore: good versus loose or easy stereotypes pervade and run deep, especially for heterosexual women. Of course, women's transgressive, alternative sexualities and desires do exist, and they find expression, especially in many of the larger cities in North America like New York and San Francisco (and online). These spaces are fairly underground and exist within subcultures. Most LGBTQ and by-women-for-women spaces and events pop up and then disappear; those that last often morph or change in some way with either their name or location.
Community connection, visibility, safety, consent, socializing, and a space of acceptance, fun, and play with variant demonstrations of sexuality, gender,

pleasure, desire, and self-expression are the cornerstones of such spaces and events. These small communities and subcultures often give gender and sexual variants a supportive and safe community that values acceptance and, sometimes, intersectional awareness. However, even within the safety of LGBTQ subculture, switching can be risky and not always seen or valued.

4 A term invented by Maria C. Lugones.

References

Acker, Kathy. *The Adult Life of Toulouse Lautrec, by Henri Toulouse Lautrec*, illustrated by William Wegman. New York: TVRT Press, 1977.

———. *Blood and Guts in High School*. New York: Grove Press, 1978.

———. *Great Expectations*, New York: Grove Press, 1983.

———. *My Death My Life by Piero Paolo Pasolini*. London: Pan Books, 1984.

———. *The Childlike Life of the Black Tarantula by the Black Tarantula*. Originally published in 1975 by TVRT Press and Viper's Tongue Books, New York. Reprinted in *Portrait of an Eye: Three Novels*. New York: Pantheon, 1992.

———. *Pussy, King of the Pirates*. New York: Grove, 1996.

———. *Essential Acker: The Selected Writings of Kathy Acker*. Amy Scholder and Dennis Cooper, Eds. New York: Grove, 2002.

Anderson, Sherwood. "Introduction: The Work of Gertrude Stein," *Geography and Plays* by Gertrude Stein, Boston: The Four Seas Company, 1922.

Anzaldúa, Gloria. *Borderlands/La Frontera: The New Mestiza*. San Francisco: Aunt Lute Books, 1987.

Bataille, Georges. *Story of the Eye*. San Francisco: City Lights, 1987.

Beasley, Chris, Ed. *Gender and Sexuality: Critical Theories, Critical Thinkers*. Thousand Oaks: Sage, 2005.

Berlant, Lauren. "Starved." *After Sex? On Writing Since Queer Theory*. Janet E. Halley and Andrew Parker, Eds. Durham: Duke UP, 2011 (79–90).

Berlant, Lauren and Michael Warner. "Sex in Public," *Critical Inquiry* Vol. 24, No. (2), Intimacy (Winter, 1998), pp. 547–566. University of Chicago Press.

Birken, Lawrence. *Consuming Desire: Sexual Science and the Emergence of a Culture of Abundance, 1871–1914*. Ithaca, NY: Cornell UP, 1988.

"Blind," Hercules and Love Affair and Antony Hegarty. DFA Records, March 03, 2008.

Bornstein, Kate. *My Gender Workbook*. New York: Routledge, 1998.

Bridgman, Richard. *Gertrude Stein in Pieces*. New York: Oxford UP, 1970.

Brockes, Emma. "Magical Thinking," *The Guardian*, December 30, 2006.

Brodkin, Karen. *How Jews Became White Folks & What That Says About Race in America*. New Brunswick, NJ: Rutgers UP, 2002.

Butler, Judith. *Gender Trouble: Feminism and the Subversion of Identity*. New York: Routledge, 1990.

Califia, Pat. *Public Sex: The Culture of Radical Sex*. Pittsburgh: Cleis Press, 1994.

Carson, Anne. *Autobiography of Red: A Novel in Verse*. New York: Knopf, 1998.

————. *IF NOT, WINTER: Fragments of Sappho*. New York: Knopf, 2002.

Clark, Danae. "Commodity Lesbianism," *The Lesbian and Gay Studies Reader*. Henry Abelove, Michele Aina Barale, David M. Halperin, Eds. New York: Routledge, 1993 (186–201).

Cope, Karen. *Passionate Collaborations: Learning to Live with Gertrude Stein*. Victoria: ELS Editions, 2005.

Cossman, Brenda, Shannon Bell, Lise Gotell, and Becki L. Ross, Eds. *Bad Attitudes on Trial: Pornography, Feminism, and the Butler Decision*. Toronto: University of Toronto, 1997.

Crane, Diana. *The Transformation of the Avant-Garde*. Chicago: University of Chicago, 1987.

Davidson, Arnold I. "Closing up the Corpses: Diseases of Sexuality and the Emergence of the Psychiatric Style of Reasoning." *Meaning and Method: Essays in Honor of Hilary Putnam*. George Boolos, Ed. Cambridge: Cambridge UP, 1990 (307–309).

Davis, Murray S. *Smut: Erotic Reality/Obscene Ideology*. Chicago: University of Chicago Press, 1983.

Dickinson, Emily. *The Poems of Emily Dickinson*, Reading Edition. R.W. Franklin, Ed. Cambridge, MA: Belknap Press of Harvard UP, 1999.

Doan, Laura. *Fashioning Sapphism: The Origins of a Modern English Lesbian Culture*. New York: Columbia UP, 2001.

Duggan, Lisa. "Queering the State," in *Sex Wars: Sexual Dissent and Political Culture*. Lisa Duggan and Nan D. Hunter, Eds. New York: Routledge, 2006.

Dworkin, Andrea. *Intercourse*. New York: Free Press, 1987.

Dydo, Ulla E., Ed. *A Stein Reader: Gertrude Stein*. Evanston: Northwestern UP, 1993.

————. *Gertrude Stein: The Language That Rises: 1923–1934*, with William Rice. Evanston: Northwestern UP, 2003.

Ellis, Havelock. *Studies in the Psychology of Sex, Vol. 1: The Evolution of Modesty: The Phenomena of Sexual Periodicity, Auto-Eroticism*. Philadelphia: F. A. Davis, 1919.

Evans, Mari. *Black Women Writers (1950–1980): A Critical Evaluation*. Garden City, NY: Anchor Press/Doubleday, 1984.

Fausto-Sterling, Anne, "The Five Sexes: Why Male and Female are not Enough," from *The Sciences* March/April 1993, reprinted in *Sexualities: Identities, Behaviors, and Society*. Michael Kimmel and Rebecca F. Plante, Eds. New York: Oxford UP, 2004 (39–44).

Foisy, Ferron, "It Won't Take Long," Nemesis Publishing (BMI), 1983. Reissued on *Boulder*. Short Story Records, 2012.

Foucault, Michel. *The History of Sexuality, Vol. I: An Introduction*. New York: Vintage, 1978.

————. *The Use of Pleasure, Vol. II: The History of Sexuality*. Trans. R. Hurley. New York: Vintage, 1985.

————. "Critical Theory, Intellectual History." *Michel Foucault: Politics, Philosophy, Culture: Interviews and Other Writings*. Lawrence Kritzman, Ed. New York: Routledge, 1988.

Frecero, Carla. "Queer Times," in *After Sex? On Writing Since Queer Theory*. Janet E. Halley and Andrew Parker, Eds. Durham: Duke UP, 2011 (17–26).

Gagne, Patricia, Richard Tenksbury, and Deanna McGangley. "Coming Out and Crossing Over: Identity Formation and Proclamation in a Transgendered Community." *Gender & Society 11*(4): 478–508, Sage, 1997.

Goldman, Jane. *Modernism 1910–1945: Image to Apocalypse.* New York: Palgrave, 2004.

Grahn, Judy. *Really Reading Gertrude Stein: A Selected Anthology with Essays.* Freedom: Crossing Press, 1990.

Hacking, Ian. "Making up People," in *Forms of Desire,* as cited in *Sexuality,* Robert Nye, Ed. New York: Oxford UP, 1999.

Halley, Janet E. and Andrew Parker, Eds. "Introduction." *After Sex? On Writing Since Queer Theory.* Durham: Duke UP, 2011, (1–16).

Hausman, Bernice. *Changing Sex: Transsexualism, Technology, and the Idea of Gender.* Durham, NC: Duke UP, 1995.

Heilbrun, Carolyn G. *Towards Androgyny: Aspects of Male and Female Literature.* London: Victor Gollancz, 1973.

Hekma, Gert, "How Libertine is The Netherlands? Exploring Contemporary Dutch Sexual Cultures," in *Regulating Sex: The Politics of Intimacy and Identity.* Elizabeth Bernstein and Laurie Schaffner, Eds. New York: Routledge, 2005 (209–223).

Herzog, Dagmar. *Sex in Crisis: The New Sexual Revolution and the Future of American Politics.* New York: Basic Books, 2008.

Hollibaugh, Amber. *My Dangerous Desires: A Queer Girl Dreaming Her Way Home.* Durham: Duke UP, 2000.

Imhof, Robin. *The Queer Encyclopedia of the Visual Arts.* Claude J. Summers, Ed. San Francisco: Cleis, 2004 (277–279).

Katz, Jonathan Ned. "Homosexual and Heterosexual: Questioning the Terms," in *A Queer World: The Center for Lesbian and Gay Studies Reader.* Martin Duberman, Ed. 1997 (177–180).

Kimmel, Michael S., and Rebecca F. Plante, Eds. *Sexualities: Identities, Behaviors, and Society.* New York: Oxford UP, 2004.

———. "Becoming Sexual, Introduction," in *Sexualities: Identities, Behaviors, and Society.* Michael Kimmel and Rebecca F. Plante, Eds. New York: Oxford UP, 2004.

Kinsey, Alfred C. *Sexual Behavior in the Human Male.* Philadelphia: W. B. Saunders. 1948.

Krafft-Ebbing, Richard von. *Psychopathia Sexualis, With Especial Reference to the Antipathic Sexual Instinct.* Trans. Franklin S. Klaf. New York: Stein & Day, 1965, as cited in *Sexuality,* Ed. Robert A. Nye. New York: Oxford UP, 1999.

Kraus, Chris. "'Cancer Became my Whole Brain': Kathy Acker's Final Year." *The New Yorker,* August 11, 2017.

Lammer, Christina, Ed. *Digital Anatomy.* Vienna: Turin and Kant, 2001.

Langdridge, Darren. "The Time of the Sadomasochist: Hunting With(in) the 'Tribus,'" in *Introducing the New Sexuality Studies.* 2nd Ed. Steven Seidman, Nancy Fischer, and Chet Meeks, Eds. New York: Routledge, 2011.

Lerner, Gerda. *The Creation of Patriarchy.* New York: Oxford UP, 1986.

Lord, James. "Where the Pictures Were," as cited in *Six Exceptional Women: Further Memoirs.* New York: Farrar Strauss Giroux, 1994.

Lorde, Audre. *Sister Outsider: Essays and Speeches.* Freedom, CA: Crossing Press, 1996.

Madeline, Laurence, Ed. *Correspondence: Pablo Picasso Gertrude Stein*. Trans. Lorna Scott Fox. New York: Seagull, 2008.

Malcolm, Janet. *Two Lives: Gertrude and Alice*. New Haven: Yale UP, 2007.

Maracle, Lee. *I am Woman: Native Perspectives on Sociology and Feminism*. Vancouver: Press Gang, 1996.

Martin, Douglas. "Barney Rosset Dies at 89; Defied Censors, Making Racy a Literary Staple," *New York Times*. February 22, 2012.

McCaffery, Larry. *Some Other Frequency: Interviews with Innovative American Authors*. Philadelphia: University of Pennsylvania Press, 1996.

McFadden, Patricia. "Why Women's Spaces are Critical to Feminist Autonomy." Isis International, Women in Action, Volume 1, 2001, Special issue: Men's Involvement in Women's Empowerment, May 28 2007.

Meese, Elizabeth. *Crossing the Double Cross: The Practice of Feminist Criticism*. Chapel Hill: University of North Carolina Press, 1986.

Myles, Eileen. *Not Me*. New York: Semiotext(e), 1991.

———. *Skies*. Santa Rosa: Black Sparrow, 2001.

Nye, Robert A., Ed. *Sexuality*. New York: Oxford UP, 1999.

O'Conner, Daniel and Neil Ortenberg, Directors. *Obscene: A Portrait of Barney Rosset and Grove Press*. Documentary. USA: 2007.

Perez, Anthony Daniel and Charles Hirschman. "The Changing Racial and Ethnic Composition of the US Population: Emerging American Identities." *Population and Development Review* 35(1): 1–51, 2009.

Puri, Jyoti, "Sexuality, State, and Nation," in *Introducing the New Sexuality Studies*. Steven Seidman, Nancy L. Fischer, and Chet Meeks, Eds. London: Routledge, 2006.

Quartermain, Peter. *Disjunctive Poetics: From Gertrude Stein and Louis Zukofsky to Susan Howe*. Cambridge: Cambridge UP, 1982.

Radicallesbians. "The Woman-Identified Woman," first published in May 1970, as cited in *We Are Everywhere: A Historical Sourcebook of Gay and Lesbian Politics*. Mark Blasius and Shane Phelan, Eds. New York: Routledge, 1997 (396–399).

Réage, Pauline. *The Story of O*. New York: Grove Press, 1965.

Roof, Judith. *A Lure of Knowledge: Lesbian Sexuality and Theory*. New York: Columbia UP, 1991.

———. *What Gender Is, What Gender Does*. Minneapolis: University of Minnesota Press, 2016.

Rosset, Barney. *The Subject Was Left Handed: An Autobiography of Barney Rosset Jr*. New York: OR Books, 2016.

———. *My Life in Publishing and How I Fought Censorship*. New York: OR Books, 2017.

Rubin, Gayle. "Thinking Sex," *The Lesbian and Gay Studies Reader*. Henry Abelove, Michele Aina Barale, and David Halperin, Eds. New York: Routledge, 1993 (13–44).

Sawyer, Julian. *Gertrude Stein, A Bibliography*. New York: Arrow Editions, 1941.

Scharf, Michael. "Skies: New Poems/On My Way," *Publishers Weekly* 249(3) (January 21): 85–86, 2002.

Seidman, Steven. "From Outsider to Citizen" *Regulating Sex: The Politics of Intimacy and Identity*. Elizabeth Bernstein and Laurie Schaffner, Eds. New York: Routledge, 2005 (225–245).

Simon, William. *Postmodern Sexualities*. New York: Routledge, 1996.

Sitwell, Edith. *Poetry and Criticism*. London: Hogarth Press, 1925.

Starr, Daniel. *The Queer Encyclopedia of the Visual Arts.* Claude J. Summers, Ed. San Francisco: Cleis, 2004 (329–330).

Stein, Gertrude. *Three Lives.* New York: Grafton Press, 1909.

———. *Tender Buttons.* New York: Claire Marie, 1914.

———. *A Valentine to Sherwood Anderson. The Little Review* 9 (Spring 1923).

———. *A Book Concluding with A Wife Has A Cow: A Love Story.* (September 1923) Editions de la Galerie Simon: Paris, 1926.

———. *An Elucidation.* Printed in *Transition,* April 1927.

———. *Before the Flowers of Friendship Faded Friendship Faded.* Paris: Plain Edition, 1931.

———. *The Autobiography of Alice B. Toklas.* New York: The Literary Guild/ Harcourt, Brace and Company, 1933.

———. *Selected Writings of Gertrude Stein.* Carl Van Vechten, Ed. New York: Modern Library, 1962 edition.

———. *Geography and Plays.* Madison: University of Wisconsin Press, 1993.

———. *Stanzas in Meditation.* Los Angeles: Sun & Moon Press, 1994.

———. *Lifting Belly.* Rebecca Mark, Ed. Tallahassee: Naiad, 1995.

———. *Baby Precious Always Shines: Selected Love Notes Between Gertrude Stein and Alice B. Toklas.* New York: St. Martin's Press, 1999.

Stimpson, Catharine. "The Somograms of Gertrude Stein," *Poetics Today* 6, No. 1–2 (1985).

Toklas, Alice. *Aromas and Flavors of Past and Present.* Harper & Brothers: New York, 1958.

Traub, Valerie. "The Present Future of Lesbian Historiography," *A Companion to Lesbian, Gay, Bisexual, Transgender, and Queer Studies.* George E. Haggerty and Molly McGarry, Eds. Oxford: Blackwell, 2007 (124–145).

Van de Velde, T. H. *Ideal Marriage: Its Physiology and Techniques.* New York: Random House, 1930.

Vaid, Urvashi, *Virtual Equality: The Mainstreaming of Gay and Lesbian Liberation.* New York: Doubleday, 1995.

Weeks, Jeffrey. *Sexuality.* London: Routledge, 1986.

Winterson, Jeanette. *Oranges Are Not the Only Fruit.* London: Pandora, 1985.

———. *The Passion.* New York: Grove, 1987.

———. *Written on the Body.* New York: Vintage, 1992.

———. *Art Objects: Essays on Ecstasy and Effrontery.* New York: Vintage, 1995.

———. Interview: "Jeanette Winterson: The Art of Fiction," *The Paris Review,* No. 150, Spring, 1999. www.theparisreview.org/interviews/1188/ the-art-of-fiction-no-150-jeanette-winterson.

———. *The Powerbook.* New York: Knopf, 2000.

———. "Introduction," *Essential Acker: The Selected Writings of Kathy Acker.* New York: Grove Press, 2002.

———. "All I Know About Gertrude Stein," *Granta* 115; Summer, 2011.

Index